A Lawyer's Basic Guide
to Secured Transactions

American Law Institute American Bar Association Committee on Continuing Professional Education

ALI ABA

STUDENT EDITION

A Lawyer's Basic Guide to Secured Transactions

Donald W. Baker
of The University of Alabama School of Law

ALI ABA

AMERICAN LAW INSTITUTE-AMERICAN BAR ASSOCIATION
COMMITTEE ON CONTINUING PROFESSIONAL EDUCATION
4025 CHESTNUT STREET • PHILADELPHIA • PENNSYLVANIA 19104

Library of Congress Catalog Number: 83-71296

Printed in the United States of America

ISBN: 0-8318-0435-1

Foreword

Of all the Articles in the Uniform Commercial Code, Article 9 has generated the greatest volume of literature, and for good reason. Its innovative approach to the treatment of security interests in personal property was a conceptual revolution. It spawned a new terminology and reoriented practices, commercial and legal. The analytical attention focused on the Article also led to its being the first to be revised, and after a decade, as revised, it has been enacted in 42 jurisdictions.

ALI-ABA early published two Article 9 paperbacks, now out of print, and more recently, an extensive treatise, *Secured Transactions* by Davenport and Murray. The purpose of Professor Baker's new text, *A Lawyer's Basic Guide to Secured Transactions,* is to afford practitioners and students a means for quick access to this complex but commercially vital subject. The volume treats the original and revised versions of Article 9 and should serve as a useful and ready reference for dealing with matters within its province.

PAUL A. WOLKIN
Executive Director,
The American Law Institute-
American Bar Association Committee
on Continuing Professional Education

May 27, 1983

Preface

This book was written primarily for the busy practitioner who wishes to educate himself or herself on the fundamentals of secured financing under Article 9 of the Uniform Commercial Code without having to spend the time required to wade through larger works on the subject. One of the author's major objectives is to discuss some of the very basic principles of secured transactions that tend to get "lost in the forest" in lengthier works. The book is also designed to provide lawyers who are already knowledgeable in the field with a succinct guide to such developments as the 1972 Code and the Bankruptcy Reform Act of 1978. Since a number of states have not yet enacted the 1972 Code, the 1962 version is also discussed. The book has a couple of unusual features, one being the listing in Chapter 1 of reference works in the field—a reflection of the author's own experience in practice that one of the most difficult questions facing the practitioner (particularly the novice) is, quite simply, where to look. The other is the use of diagrams, which the author's teaching experience has shown to be a valuable aid to conceptualization of the complex fact situations arising in this area.

Roughly speaking, the book is designed to be read on two levels: The text alone supplies one of the shortest coverages of the law of secured transactions in print; the text together with the footnotes affords a relatively comprehensive treatment of the fundamentals of the subject.

The author wishes to thank his wife for her patience and understanding, Dean Thomas Christopher and other friends at the University of Alabama School of Law for their support, Robert McCurley (Director of the Alabama Law Institute) and the lawyers on the Alabama Revised Article 9 Review Committee for the invaluable learning experience derived from serving as Reporter for the Committee, and Morton S. Freeman, Director of Publications for ALI-ABA, for his awesome patience.

Donald W. Baker

Contents

Chapter 2

Creation of the Security Interest 67

Chapter 4

Priorities   147

Chapter 5

Chapter 6

Chapter 7

Default   297

1

Introduction

§ 1–1. HISTORICAL BACKGROUND

A. Origin of the UCC

Prior to the advent of the Uniform Commercial Code, various types of commercial transactions were governed by a number of separate, so-called uniform state acts, including the Uniform Negotiable Instruments Law, Uniform Sales Act, Uniform Warehouse Receipts Act, Uniform Bills of Lading Act, Uniform Stock Transfer Act, Uniform Conditional Sales Act, and the Uniform Trust Receipts Act. By the late 1930s the need for reform in the commercial law area had become apparent. Several of the "uniform" acts had been enacted by only a handful of states, varying interpretations had been placed on them by the courts of different states, and changing patterns of doing business had rendered many of their provisions obsolete. Moreover, a number of important types of transactions, such as bulk sales and bank collections, were subject to highly variable state statutes that never even purported to be uniform.

In 1944, the National Conference of Commissioners on Uniform State Laws and The American Law Institute agreed to jointly sponsor the drafting of a single, comprehensive code that would subsume and modernize the subject matter of the old acts. After several years of drafting and consultation with practitioners, judges, and academicians, the sponsors published the first version of the Uniform Commercial Code—the 1952 Official Text. Although adopted by Pennsylvania, the 1952 Text met with considerable skepticism in New York, which instructed its Law Revision Commission to examine the Code with a view to making improvements. After a three-year study, the Commission recommended numerous changes, many of which were accepted by the sponsors and incorporated into the 1957 Official Text. Subsequent changes of a minor nature resulted in the issuance of 1958 and 1962 Official Texts. By 1968, the Code had been enacted, essentially in the form of the 1962 Official Text, in 49 of the 50 states.[1]

In 1961, the joint sponsors of the UCC established a continuously functioning body—the Permanent Editorial Board for the Uniform Commercial Code—to discourage nonuniform amendments by the states and to recommend changes in the Code language when it became apparent that particular provisions were unworkable or had been rendered obsolete by new commercial practices. The Board issued reports in 1962, 1964, and 1966 containing proposed changes in Code language, amendments to Code comments, and criticisms of changes made in the Official Text by the enacting states.

B. Article 9—The "1962 Code" and the "1972 Code"

As noted, by the late 1960s, the Code, including Article 9, was in force essentially in the form of the 1962 Official Text in virtually every state. Overall, Article 9 performed reasonably well and was generally regarded as a substantial improvement over pre-Code law.[2] Nevertheless, flaws existed, some sufficiently serious to elicit criticism from practitioners and law professors across the country. More than 30 states attempted, with indifferent success, to remedy actual or perceived defects on a piecemeal basis by enacting nonuniform amendments. Finally, in 1966, rising demands for uniform change on a national basis prompted the Permanent Editorial Board to appoint a Review Committee to undertake a comprehensive reexamination of Article 9. In 1971, the Review Committee

---

[1] Louisiana eventually adopted some portions of the Code, but not Article 9. Most states made at least a few nonuniform modifications in the Official Text.

[2] See § 1-1 C infra.

submitted its final report containing recommendations for change in numerous provisions of Article 9 and in a few related sections in other articles of the Code. These suggestions were substantially adopted by The American Law Institute and National Conference of Commissioners and were embodied in the 1972 Official Text of the UCC.[3] To date, 36 states have adopted the 1972 Official Text (often referred to as "Revised Article 9"),[4] although 13 states still retain the older version.

In this book the pre-1972 version of Article 9 (and relevant provisions in other articles of the Code) will be referred to as the "1962 Code," the "1962 version," or, in the context of a particular section, "1962 Section. . . ." The version of Article 9 (and relevant provisions in other articles of the Code) found in the 1972 Official Text will be referred to as the "1972 Code," the "1972 version," or in the context of a particular section, "1972 Section. . . ." A reference to a Code section without either the "1962" or "1972" designation means that, with respect to the particular topic under discussion, the 1962 and 1972 versions of that section are substantively identical, no change having been made in the 1972 Code.

C. Article 9—Impact on Pre-Code Chattel Security Law

Despite the fact that all chattel security arrangements have the same basic purpose—to give certain creditors special, exclu-

---

[3] A later Official Text, published in 1978, contains changes made in Article 8 to accommodate uncertificated ("book entry") securities. A few conforming changes were made in Sections 9–103, 9–105, 9–203, 9–302, 9–304, 9–309, and 9–312. The essential impact on Article 9 is to shift rules governing attachment and perfection of security interests in securities to Article 8, leaving Article 9 to govern other matters, including priority and default.

[4] Alabama, Arizona, Arkansas, California, Colorado, Connecticut, Florida, Georgia, Hawaii, Idaho, Illinois, Iowa, Kansas, Maine, Maryland, Massachusetts, Michigan, Minnesota, Mississippi, Nebraska, Nevada, New Hampshire, New Jersey, New York, North Carolina, North Dakota, Ohio, Oklahoma, Oregon, Rhode Island, Texas, Utah, Virginia, Washington, West Virginia, and Wisconsin.

sive rights in particular property of the debtor as an assurance of payment of the debt—under pre-Code law the practitioner had to deal with a variety of different security devices, each distinguished from the others on the basis of artificial differences in form, each having its own set of terminology and its own system for public recordation, and each governed by a separate body of law that varied from state to state. These devices included the pledge, the chattel mortgage, the conditional sale, the trust receipt, and the factor's lien. Suppose, for example, that a borrower in a pre-Code state applied to his bank for a secured loan to enable him (1) to purchase a new delivery truck for his business, (2) to install a new piece of equipment in his plant, (3) to purchase raw materials abroad for processing into finished goods at his plant, and (4) to meet payroll and operating costs during the manufacturing season when income from sales was low. The bank might view the situations as calling for four separate transactions:

1. The purchase of the vehicle might be accomplished by the bank's discount or purchase of a conditional sale contract between the borrower and the seller of the truck.

2. The equipment might be purchased by the borrower with funds advanced by the bank in exchange for a chattel mortgage on the equipment.

3. The raw material acquisition might require the use of a letter of credit and trust receipt transaction in which the bank paid the foreign seller and permitted the borrower use of the raw materials for the process of manufacture in exchange for trust receipts.

4. The payroll and operating expenses might be met with funds advanced under a factor's lien, involving a general security interest in the borrower's inventory and an assignment by the borrower of his accounts receivable created upon open credit sales of finished goods.

The degree of flexibility with which the bank could accommodate its borrower in the foregoing illustration depended on the availability in the particular state of the appropriate security device statutes. Moreover, each transaction required a separate set of forms employing different terminology; and given the artificial distinctions often drawn on the basis of formalities in execution,[5] the parties could never be sure whether a transaction they had set up as one security arrangement, for example, as a conditional sale,[6] might later be determined by a court to be something else, such as a chattel mortgage. Since many states required different types of public recordation for the two devices,[7] the typical result of such a determination was to deprive the lender of his security interest as against competing creditors.

The foregoing discussion gives some indication of the complexity and confusion that existed in the field of personal property financing prior to adoption of the Code. Article 9 radically simplified chattel security law by replacing the multiplicity of pre-Code security devices and terms [8] with a single security device (the "Article 9 security interest")[9] governed by a single,

---

[5] For example, many chattel mortgages were held invalid for lack of proper acknowledgement, although conditional sale agreements required no acknowledgement.

[6] A conditional sale essentially involved a situation in which a seller sold goods on credit and reserved title to them until the purchase price was paid. By contrast, the chattel mortgage was often taken to secure a loan against goods already owned by the debtor (although the device could also be used in installment sales), with the creditor not purporting to reserve title.

[7] Some states required recordation of chattel mortgages but not recordation of conditional sales.

[8] *E.g.*, "pledge", "pledgor", "pledgee"; "chattel mortgage", "chattel mortgagor", "chattel mortgagee"; "conditional sale", "conditional vendor", "conditional vendee"; "trust receipt", "entruster", "entrustee."

[9] Section 9–102(2) provides that "[t]his Article applies to security interests created by contract, including pledge, assignment, chattel mortgage, chattel trust, trust deed, factor's lien, equipment trust, conditional sale, trust receipt, other lien or title retention contract. . . ." As stated in the Comment to Section 9–101, "this does not mean that the old forms may not be used, and Section 9–102(2) makes it clear that they may be." In other words, a seller who is still using old conditional-sale agreement forms purporting to retain title until the purchase price is paid *will* be deemed

uniform body of law, with a single filing system and a single set of terminology: "security interest," "collateral," "debtor," and "secured party." [10] Artificial distinctions based on form have been abolished.[11] This does not mean that the rules laid down by Article 9 are the same regardless of the circumstances; some distinctions, based on the type of collateral involved [12] or the type of arrangement between the parties,[13] remain, but the distinctions are drawn along functional rather than formal lines.

---

to have a security interest, but it will be governed by the rules of Article 9, rather than pre-Code conditional sales law. It should also be noted that there *are* different *types* of Article 9 security interests—for example, possessory versus non-possessory and purchase money versus non-purchase-money—some of which have characteristics similar to the pre-Code devices.

[10] For a further discussion of the terminology of Article 9, see § 1–3 C *infra*. It should be noted that a few pre-Code terms, although not found in the statutory language of Article 9 (other than in Section 9–102(2)), are still commonly used today by practitioners and commentators. For instance, the word "pledge" is often used to refer to what Article 9 technically labels a "possessory security interest," meaning a situation in which the creditor retains possession of the collateral. The terms "conditional sale," "conditional seller," and "conditional sales contract" are frequently used in reference to one type of purchase money security interest under Section 9–107, namely, that taken by a seller of goods on credit to secure repayment of the purchase price. Note, however, that these references are to types of *Article 9* security interests, which are governed by *Article 9* rules rather than the pre-Code rules that applied to security devices carrying these labels.

[11] For instance, unlike the situation under pre-Code law, the rules of Article 9 do not vary depending on whether the creditor (as opposed to the debtor) technically has title to the collateral. U.C.C. § 9–202.

[12] *E.g.*, an Article 9 security interest in goods can be perfected by filing, but an Article 9 security interest in an instrument can be perfected only by the secured party's taking possession. *See* U.C.C. § 9–304(1).

[13] *E.g.*, under Section 9–203(1), an Article 9 security interest can be validly created without a written security agreement when the secured party takes possession of the collateral, but a writing is required if the security interest is a non-possessory one; and under Section 9–312, different rules of priority obtain, depending on whether the Article 9 security interest is a purchase money or non-purchase-money one.

§ 1–2. RESEARCHING ARTICLE 9 PROBLEMS

Since no single source will supply all the answers needed in every situation, it is important for the lawyer to know how to research Article 9 problems. The following discussion will provide some assistance in this regard. It should be observed that the lists of references set forth below do not purport to be exhaustive and do not imply an endorsement of publications mentioned over those not mentioned; these are simply the sources the author most often consults in researching Article 9 problems.

A. *The Security Agreement and Other Documents*

If the dispute is between the debtor and the secured party, the security agreement should always be consulted. Since Article 9 allows the parties to a secured transaction considerable freedom of contract,[14] the answer may be found in their agreement,[15] without the need for further research. Moreover, the absence of requisite formalities in the execution of the security agreement or financing statement (if any)[16] or the secured party's failure to file the latter in the proper place [17] may render the secured party's interest vulnerable to the claims of competing creditors or other third parties. Finally, irrespective of the rights the secured party might otherwise have under Article 9, if he has entered into an agreement to subordinate his

---

[14] U.C.C. § 9–101, Comment. Certain rules concerning procedures on default, as prescribed by Part 5 of Article 9, cannot be contractually varied. Also the debtor and secured party have little ability, as between themselves, to contractually affect the rights of third-party claimants, such as other creditors with a claim to the same collateral.

[15] The various clauses that may be included in the security agreement are discussed in Chapter 2 *infra.*

[16] The requirements for execution of the security agreement, set forth in Section 9–203, are discussed in Chapter 2, *infra.* The requirements for execution of the financing statement, set forth in Section 9–402, are discussed in Chapter 3 *infra.*

[17] The proper place for filing, as prescribed by Section 9–401, is discussed in Chapter 3 *infra.*

interest to that of another party, or vice versa, the agreement will be enforced.[18]

B. The Statutory Language of Article 9

(1) Where To Find Article 9

It is important to remember that an Official Text of the UCC,[19] including Article 9 thereof, is nothing more than a *proposed* set of rules recommended to the states for adoption; the Code acquires the force of law only by virtue of its enactment by the legislature of each state. The version of Article 9 with which the lawyer is usually concerned, therefore, is that found in the state code of the relevant jurisdiction.[20] The various Official Texts of the UCC are primarily useful as legislative history,[21] as a means of locating state variations,[22] and, insofar as the 1962 and 1972 Official Texts are concerned, as an aid in studying the changes made by the 1972 Code in states that have adopted it.[23] Copies of all Official Texts of the UCC[24] have been published jointly by The American Law Institute and the National Conference of Commissioners on Uniform State Laws, but pre-1962 versions are difficult to find in all but the largest libraries.[25]

---

[18] U.C.C. § 9–316.

[19] See §§ 1–1 A and 1–1 B *supra.*

[20] For a discussion of how to determine which state's Article 9 will apply in a multi-state situation, see Chapter 5 *infra.*

The UCC is usually found in state codes under the heading "commercial law" or "commercial code." Virtually all states have retained the basic section numbering system of the Official Texts, but some have added one or more numbers as a prefix; for instance, Section 9–101 in the Official Text is Section 7–9–101 in the Alabama Code.

[21] See § 1–2 C (1) *infra.*

[22] See § 1–2 B (3) *infra.*

[23] See § 1–1 B *supra.*

[24] The various Official Texts are listed in §§ 1–1 A and 1–1 B *supra.*

[25] Copies of the 1962 Official Text can be found in the following publications: 4 Anderson on the Uniform Commercial Code (The Lawyers Co-operative Publishing Company); 6A Bender's Uniform Commercial

(2) Finding Relevant Provisions Within Article 9

The literature and caselaw to be discussed will, of course, cite Article 9 sections that may be relevant to one's problem. In addition, it is often helpful to scan the table of contents listing section numbers and their headings at the beginning of Article 9. When one finds a particular section that bears on the problem at hand, the cross references at the end of the Comment following that section should be consulted for other sections of possible relevance. Also, a handy listing of sections under the various types of collateral [26] to which they apply is found in Comment 5 to Section 9–102.

(3) State Variations

It is important to be aware that virtually every state, upon enactment of the UCC, made at least some modifications in the language of the Official Texts,[27] with the result that the rules

CODE SERVICE (Matthew Bender & Company); UNIFORM COMMERCIAL CODE REPORTING SERVICE, One-Star Current Materials Binder (Callaghan & Company); and 3 UNIFORM LAWS ANNOTATED (West Publishing Co. 1968).

Copies of the combined 1962 and 1972 Official Texts, showing changes made by the latter, can be found in the following publications: 5A & 6A BENDER's UNIFORM COMMERCIAL CODE SERVICE (Matthew Bender & Company); V. COUNTRYMAN, A. KAUFMAN & Z. WISEMAN, COMMERCIAL LAW: SELECTED STATUTES 547 (Little, Brown and Company 1980); R. HENSON, HANDBOOK ON SECURED TRANSACTIONS UNDER THE UNIFORM COMMERCIAL CODE, Appendix (2d ed., West Publishing Co. 1979); QUINN, UNIFORM COMMERCIAL CODE COMMENTARY AND LAW DIGEST (Warren, Gorham & Lamont 1978); SELECTED COMMERCIAL STATUTES, Appendix I (West Publishing Co. 1981); and UNIFORM COMMERCIAL CODE REPORTING SERVICE, One-Star Current Materials Binder (Callaghan & Company).

Copies of the 1972 Official Text alone can be found in the following publications: V. COUNTRYMAN, A. KAUFMAN & Z. WISEMAN, COMMERCIAL LAW: SELECTED STATUTES 1 (Little, Brown and Company 1980); SELECTED COMMERCIAL STATUTES 1 (West Publishing Co. 1981); 3 UNIFORM LAWS ANNOTATED (1980 Pamphlet) (West Publishing Co.).

[26] Classifications of collateral are discussed in § 1–5 *infra*.

[27] Modifications are not restricted to the time of initial enactment of the Code, of course; from time to time a state legislature may make further nonuniform amendments.

in a particular Article 9 section in one's own state may differ from those found in the same section in a neighboring state.[28] In addition, the Official Texts themselves set forth alternative versions of some sections of Article 9, allowing each state to choose among them.[29]

A comprehensive, frequently supplemented list of variations made by each state can be found in the "State Correlation Tables" volume of the Uniform Commercial Code Reporting Service (Callaghan & Company). Other sources showing state variations include:

4 Anderson on the Uniform Commercial Code (The Lawyers Co-operative Publishing Company)

6A Bender's Uniform Commercial Code Service (Matthew Bender & Company)

1 CCH Secured Transactions Guide (Commerce Clearing House)

3 Uniform Laws Annotated (West Publishing Company)

(4) Interaction Between Article 9 and Other Articles of the UCC

As will be noted in appropriate places in this book, the provisions of Article 9 interrelate, at least to a small degree, with every other article of the UCC. This is particularly true with respect to Article 1, which sets forth general rules applicable to all the other articles and, among other things, defines a number of terms used in Article 9.[30] Various Article 9 sections also

---

[28] A discussion of the rules for determining which state's version of Article 9 applies in a multi-state situation is found in Chapter 5 *infra*.

[29] The most prominent example is Section 9–401(1) concerning the proper place for filing, which is presented in both the 1962 and 1972 Official Texts in three alternative versions. Also a few sections contain "optional language" that some states have included in their Code and others have not. For example, Section 9–402(5) of the 1972 Official Text contains optional language concerning the extent to which a financing statement covering fixtures must describe the real estate involved.

[30] U.C.C. § 1–201.

interact with the rules in Article 2 (Sales), Article 3 (Commercial Paper), Article 4 (Bank Deposits and Collections), Article 5 (Letters of Credit), Article 6 (Bulk Transfers), Article 7 (Documents of Title), and Article 8 (Investment Securities). In addition, Article 10 establishes the effective date of the original UCC in the state, lists pre-Code statutes repealed upon enactment of the Code, and lays down rules for transition from pre-Code law to the UCC. The 1972 Official Text contains a new Article 11, which establishes the effective date of the 1972 Code in the state and lays down rules for transition from the 1962 Code to the 1972 Code.

(5) Interaction Between Article 9 and Non-UCC Law

Even though a particular secured transaction problem falls within the ambit of Article 9,[31] various aspects of the dispute may be governed by non-UCC law. For instance, a debtor in conflict with his secured creditor can assert common law contract defenses, such as lack of capacity, unconscionability, fraud, mistake, or duress, even though Article 9 makes no mention of these principles.[32] Moreover, state and federal statutory and regulatory law can have a bearing. Various provisions of Article 9 may be overridden by state small loan acts, retail installment sales acts, consumer protection acts and usury laws,[33] and by federal consumer credit and bankruptcy acts.[34]

C. Legislative History

The UCC has an extensive legislative history, which can be extremely helpful in interpreting Code language.

---

[31] The applicability of Article 9 is discussed in § 1–4 *infra*.

[32] The "gateway" for importation of common-law rules into UCC cases is Section 1–103.

[33] *See* U.C.C. § 9–201, 1962 U.C.C. § 9–203(2), and 1972 U.C.C. § 9–203(4). The impact of these acts is relatively minor, however, since they are largely concerned with protecting the debtor, whereas the bulk of Article 9 rules (aside from those in Part 5 pertaining to default) are aimed at conflicts between the secured creditor and some other creditor.

[34] For a discussion of the interaction between Article 9 and the federal Bankruptcy Act, see Chapter 6 *infra*.

(1) The Comments and Other General Sources

The following are sources of legislative history for both the 1962 and 1972 versions of the Code.

The Comments: The "Official Comments" following each section of the Code are the most accessible and widely cited sources of legislative history. They are an invaluable aid to interpretation because they discuss at length the meaning of, and rationale behind, Code provisions. It must be remembered, however, that although the comments are usually published in state codes alongside the statutory language of the UCC,[35] they have not been enacted by state legislatures and therefore do not have the force of the law.[36]

Pre-Code Law: Since some of the language of Article 9 was derived from pre-Code chattel security statutes like the Uniform Conditional Sales Act and the Uniform Trust Receipts Act,[37] these old acts are sometimes helpful in interpreting present-day Code language.[38]

Prior Official Texts: Changes in Code language from one Official Text to the next sometimes shed light on the meaning of the language in the present version.[39]

New York Law Revision Commission Reports: Since these

---

[35] If the comments are not printed in one's state code, they can be found in any of the publications listed in the footnotes in § 1–2 B (1) *supra.*

[36] The lawyer usually brings up this point when his argument as to the meaning of particular Code language appears to run contrary to a statement in the relevant comment. It is also worth noting that although in theory legislators enacted the UCC with an awareness of the statements in the comments, in reality few legislators read the comments at all, and few of those who did understood them.

[37] The texts of these statutes can be found in 3 Uniform Laws Annotated, Appendix (West Publishing Company 1968).

[38] The origins of each Article 9 section are shown under the heading "Prior Uniform Statutory Provision" at the beginning of the comment following the section.

[39] The Official Texts are discussed in §§ 1–1 A and 1–1 B *supra.* Copies of the Official Texts can be found in the publications listed in the footnotes in § 1–2 B (1) *supra.*

reports, issued in 1954, 1955, and 1956, had a considerable impact on the 1958 Official Text,[40] much of which was retained in later Official Texts, they can be helpful in interpreting Code language.

State Legislative Reports: At the time of enactment of the Code, some states published reports, studies, or state annotations, which shed light on the meaning of state variations.[41]

Reports of the Permanent Editorial Board: These reports,[42] issued in 1962, 1964, and 1966, contain proposed changes in Code language, amendments to Code comments, and critical commentary on particular state variations.[43]

(2) The 1972 Code

In addition to the general sources listed above, there are two special sources of legislative history for the 1972 Code:

(1) *Reasons for 1972 Change.* When The American Law Institute and the National Conference of Commissioners on Uniform State Laws issued the 1972 Official Text,[44] they appended to each Code section, under the heading "Reasons for 1972 Change," an explanation of the changes made in the

---

[40] See § 1–1 A *supra.*

[41] These publications are listed by state in M. EZER, UNIFORM COMMERCIAL CODE BIBLIOGRAPHY (American Law Institute-American Bar Association Committee on Continuing Professional Education 1972) and are also cited, together with law review articles in the same vein, under the heading "Background Material" in the "State Correlation Tables" Volume of the UNIFORM COMMERCIAL CODE REPORTING SERVICE (Callaghan & Company).

[42] See § 1–1 A *supra.*

[43] The three reports, with commentary on state variations deleted, are reproduced in 1 UNIFORM LAWS ANNOTATED xxv–xxxvi (West Publishing Company 1976). The Board's comments concerning state variations can be found at the end of the coverage of each Article 9 section in 6A BENDER'S UNIFORM COMMERCIAL CODE SERVICE (Matthew Bender & Company).

[44] See § 1–1 B *supra.*

1962 version. These explanations are very helpful in understanding the language of the new Code.[45]

(2) *Final Report of the Review Committee for Article 9.* The changes embodied in the 1972 Code are also explained, sometimes in more detail than in the Reasons for 1972 Change, in the final report issued by the committee that drafted the 1972 Official Text.[46]

D. The Case Law

There is a rapidly growing body of case law interpreting and applying virtually every section of Article 9. Access to the case law can, of course, be had through the National Reporter system. In addition, there is a multi-volume service—the Uniform Commercial Code Reporting Service (Callaghan & Company)—devoted exclusively to reporting the full text of UCC decisions from state and federal courts across the country.

Digests of Article 9 cases can be found in the following publications:

6E and 6F Bender's Uniform Commercial Code Service (Matthew Bender & Company; supplemented).

---

[45] In states that have enacted the 1972 Code, the Reasons for 1972 Change may be published in the state code along with the comments; if not, they can be found in the following publications: 5A and 6A Bender's Uniform Commercial Code Service (Matthew Bender & Company); V. Countryman, A. Kaufman & Z. Wiseman, Commercial Law: Selected Statutes 421–545 (Little, Brown and Company 1980); R. Henson, Handbook on Secured Transactions Under the Uniform Commercial Code, Appendix (2d ed., West Publishing Co. 1979); Selected Commercial Statutes, Appendix I (West Publishing Co. 1981); Uniform Commercial Code Reporting Service, One-Star Current Materials Binder (Callaghan & Company). It should be noted that some of the changes are explained in the Official Comment following each section of the 1972 Code.

[46] See § 1–1 B *supra.* The full title of this report is as follows: Permanent Editorial Board for the Uniform Commercial Code Review Committee for Article 9 of the Uniform Commercial Code, Final Report (April 25, 1971). The report is reproduced in Selected Commercial Statutes 679–726 (West Publishing Company 1979).

QUINN, UNIFORM COMMERCIAL CODE COMMENTARY AND LAW
  DIGEST (Warren, Gorham & Lamont 1978; supplemented).

6, 7 & 8 UNIFORM COMMERCIAL CODE CASE DIGEST (Callaghan
  & Company; supplemented).

The AMERICAN LAW REPORTS (The Lawyers Co-operative
Publishing Co., Bancroft-Whitney Co.) periodically publishes
extensive annotations citing numerous cases dealing with various topics under Article 9.

E. The Literature on Article 9 [47]

(1) The UNIFORM COMMERCIAL CODE BIBLIOGRAPHY

Any list of reference sources on the UCC must include mention of the UNIFORM COMMERCIAL CODE BIBLIOGRAPHY by
Mitchel Ezer (American Law Institute-American Bar Association Committee on Continuing Professional Education 1972)[48]
—a full-length book listing books, pamphlets, reports, studies,
and law review articles on the UCC by author, topic, and state.

(2) Treatises and Other Books on Article 9

It should be noted that in the Commercial Code field there
are two major methods of entrance into reference works: (1) by
topical index, and (2) by UCC Section number. Under the latter method, when a UCC section relevant (or potentially relevant) to one's problem is known, discussions of that section in
a particular work (including this book) can be found by consult-
ing the table of statutory citations in the front or back of the
work.

---

[47] As is true in other parts of § 1–2, only an abbreviated list of publications is given; for a full listing, see M. EZER, UNIFORM COMMERCIAL CODE
BIBLIOGRAPHY, described in this section.

[48] There are two supplements: 1971–72 and 1973–77, the latter by
Alphonse Squillante.

The following is a selected list of works on Article 9:

Shorter Work

H. Bailey, Secured Transactions in a Nutshell (West Publishing Co., 2d. ed. 1981).

Intermediate-Length Works

B. Clark, The Law of Secured Transactions Under the Uniform Commercial Code (Warren, Gorham & Lamont 1980).

W. Davenport & D. Murray, Secured Transactions (American Law Institute-American Bar Association Committee on Continuing Professional Education 1978).

R. Henson, Handbook on Secured Transactions Under the Uniform Commercial Code (West Publishing Co., 2d ed. 1979).

J. White & R. Summers, Handbook of the Law Under the Uniform Commercial Code 873–1135 (West Publishing Co., 2d ed. 1980).

Lengthy Works and Looseleaf Services

4 R. Anderson, Anderson on the Uniform Commercial Code (The Lawyers Co-operative Publishing Co., Bancroft-Whitney Co.; supplemented).

CCH Secured Transactions Guide (Commerce Clearing House; supplemented).

P. Coogan, W. Hogan & D. Vagts, 1, 1A & 1B Bender's Uniform Commercial Code Service (Matthew Bender & Company; supplemented).

G. Gilmore, Security Interests in Personal Property (Little, Brown and Company, 2 vols. 1965).

(3) Forms for Drafting

Forms for drafting can be found in the following sources:

2 R. ANDERSON, ANDERSON ON THE UNIFORM COMMERCIAL CODE LEGAL FORMS (The Lawyers Co-operative Publishing Company, Bancroft-Whitney Co.; supplemented).

F. HART & W. WILLIER, 5A BENDER'S UNIFORM COMMERCIAL CODE SERVICE, FORMS AND PROCEDURES (Matthew Bender & Company; supplemented).

2B J. RABKIN & M. JOHNSON, CURRENT LEGAL FORMS WITH TAX ANALYSIS (Matthew Bender & Company; supplemented).

5 UNIFORM LAWS ANNOTATED (West Publishing Company; supplemented).

(4) Periodicals; Keeping Current

Law review articles dealing with various aspects of secured transactions are listed in the INDEX TO LEGAL PERIODICALS under the headings "Commercial Law" and "Secured Transactions," and in the UNIFORM COMMERCIAL CODE BIBLIOGRAPHY.[49]

Three journals devoted heavily to UCC matters are the BANKING LAW JOURNAL (Warren, Gorham & Lamont), COMMERCIAL LAW JOURNAL (Commercial Law League of America), and the UNIFORM COMMERCIAL CODE LAW JOURNAL (Warren, Gorham & Lamont).

The Practising Law Institute of New York publishes several paperback books each year dealing with recent developments in the secured transactions area.

Recent Article 9 decisions in one's state can be found quickly by checking the Cumulative Statutes Construed table in the front of the National Reporter System advance sheets. Also, monthly supplements to the UNIFORM COMMERCIAL CODE REPORTING SERVICE (Callaghan & Company) contain the full text of decisions from across the country.

---

[49] See § 1–2 E (1) *supra.*

Discussions of recent cases are found in the monthly Uniform Commercial Code Law Letter (Management Reports, Incorporated, a research affiliate of The Bankers Magazine and The Banking Law Journal) and in the annual Uniform Commercial Code survey published in the Business Lawyer (Section of Corporation, Banking and Business Law of the American Bar Association).

§ 1–3. AN OVERVIEW OF SECURED TRANSACTIONS UNDER ARTICLE 9

A. *A Word of Advice for Novices*

The subject of secured transactions might be described as the archetypal "seamless web." It is impossible to separate topics under Article 9 into discrete, watertight compartments; rather the rules in any given section often interact with the rules stated in numerous other sections, with the result that the beginner in the field will have difficulty fully understanding concepts discussed in earlier portions of this book until he has obtained a grasp of concepts covered further on, and vice versa. Thus a thorough understanding of the subject may require multiple readings of all, or at least some parts of, the book.

B. *Significance of a Security Interest; Unsecured Creditors and the Process of Obtaining a Judicial Lien*

Assume that Debtor Corporation purchases business equipment from Supply Company on "open account," that is, "on its signature" alone, that is, on unsecured credit. When Debtor fails to repay Supply Company at the appropriate time, may Supply Company simply repossess the equipment? No; as an *unsecured* creditor, Supply Company cannot retake the equipment until it has first gone through the sometimes lengthy, expensive process of obtaining a "judicial lien." In many states this process, sometimes called the "collection process," requires that the unsecured creditor file suit on the debt, obtain a judgment, and—if the defendant debtor does not voluntarily pay the

judgment—obtain from the court a writ of execution ordering
the sheriff to seize whatever property of the debtor is available.
After seizing the property—called levying—the sheriff sells it at
a public sale, whereupon the proceeds are paid to the creditor
to satisfy the debt.[50] By contrast, had Supply Company taken
a valid Article 9 security interest, it would generally be entitled
to repossess and sell the collateral itself, without resort to
judicial proceedings.[51]

A second major advantage to having a security interest arises
when a third party, such as a competing creditor, lays claim to
the property covered by the security interest. When the rules
of Article 9 give the secured creditor priority, he has sole claim
to the collateral, meaning he can use it to fully satisfy his loan
before the competing party has any rights.[52] This advantage is
apparent, for instance, when the debtor has gone into bankruptcy. Assume the bankrupt's sole asset is a machine having
a resale value of $10,000, against which X, who took an Article 9
security interest, loaned $9,000. The bankrupt debtor has two
unsecured creditors, Y and Z, each of whom he owes $10,000. If
X satisfies the appropriate requirements of Article 9 (and the
Bankruptcy Act), he will be entitled to $9,000, leaving Y and Z
to share in the remaining $1,000. On the other hand, if X were
an unsecured creditor, he would share pro rata with Y and Z,
in this case receiving less ($3,103) than the latter two parties
($3,448 each).[53]

---

[50] Since numerous illustrations in the early portions of this book involve
conflicts between an Article 9 secured creditor and a judicial lienor, it
will be pointed out here that for purposes of the basic provision governing
these conflicts—Section 9–301(1)(b)—the holder of a judgment lien is
deemed to "become a lien creditor" (that is, the lien is deemed to arise)
at the time of levy in most states.

[51] U.C.C. § 9–503.

[52] If the collateral resells for more than the unpaid balance of the
secured creditor's loan, the competing creditor may have a claim to the
surplus.

[53] In reality, the three creditors would have considerably less than
$10,000 to divide in these two situations, since a number of items, such as

C. Basic Concepts and Terminology of Article 9

The parties to a secured transaction are the "debtor" and the "secured party." The "debtor" is the person who owes performance of the obligation secured—usually payment of a debt.[54] The "secured party"[55] (also commonly referred to in the literature as the secured creditor) is the party in whose favor the security interest exists.[56] A "security interest" is an interest in personal property or fixtures that secures payment or performance of an obligation.[57] The "collateral" is the property covered by the security interest.[58] The debtor usually grants the security interest to the secured party in a written contract called a "security agreement."[59]

A security interest is not enforceable by the secured party against anyone—either the debtor or third parties—unless and until it "attaches," which generally requires that the debtor have executed a written security agreement, that the secured party have given value, and that the debtor have acquired rights in the collateral.[60] Upon execution of the security agreement and satisfaction of the other requirements for attachment, the security interest becomes enforceable against the debtor, meaning that should the debtor "default"—as by failure to pay the debt owed the secured party at the appropriate time and in the

---

the expenses of administering the bankrupt's estate, would be taken "off the top."

[54] As defined in Section 9–105(1)(d), the term "debtor" also includes the seller of accounts or chattel paper.

[55] Defined in 1962 Section 9–105(1)(i) and 1972 Section 9–105(1)(m).

[56] The term "secured party" also applies to a buyer of accounts or chattel paper and to a party who has taken an assignment of a security interest from the initial secured party.

[57] U.C.C. § 1–201(37).

[58] U.C.C. § 9–105(1)(c).

[59] The requisites for execution of a valid security agreement are discussed in Chapter 2. In one situation—namely, when the secured party takes possession of the collateral—a written security agreement is not required. U.C.C. § 9–203(1)(a).

[60] The requirements for attachment, set forth in 1962 Section 9–204(1) and 1972 Section 9–203(1), are discussed in Chapter 2 infra.

appropriate manner—the secured party can exercise the rights given him in Part 5 of Article 9, including the right to repossess the collateral and either retain it or sell it to satisfy the debt.

In many instances the secured party will be in conflict with a third party asserting a claim to the collateral, rather than with the debtor. The third party may be an unsecured creditor of the debtor with a judicial lien on the collateral,[61] a buyer who has purchased the collateral from the debtor,[62] another Article 9 creditor with a security interest in the collateral,[63] or a bankruptcy trustee representing the debtor's unsecured creditors.[64] When the debtor has sold the original collateral covered by the security interest, the conflict with the third party may concern the cash or other items received by the debtor upon the sale— called proceeds [65]—rather than the original collateral. In conflicts of the foregoing types, the Article 9 "rules of priority" dictate whether the secured party or the third party prevails.[66] These rules, which vary depending on the type of third party, the type of secured transaction, and the type of collateral involved,[67] generally provide (with important exceptions) that the secured party has priority only if he "perfects" his security interest before the third party's interest arises [68] or (in the case of a competing secured creditor) is perfected. Unless the security interest falls within one of the special categories affording "automatic" perfection upon attachment,[69] perfection usually entails either taking possession of the collateral or filing a public notice

---

[61] Discussed in § 4–1 *infra*.

[62] Discussed in § 4–3 A *infra*.

[63] Discussed in § 4–2 *infra*.

[64] Discussed in Chapter 6 *infra*.

[65] Defined in Section 9–306(1).

[66] The rules of priority are discussed in Chapters 4 and 6 *infra*.

[67] The various classifications of collateral under Article 9, such as "goods," "accounts," "chattel paper," and so forth are discussed in § 1–5 *infra*.

[68] For example, perfection is usually required before the unsecured creditor's judicial lien arises, before the buyer purchases the collateral from the debtor, or before the petition in bankruptcy is filed.

[69] U.C.C. § 9–302.

of the security interest—called a financing statement—in the appropriate state office (the latter method being the most common).[70]

Various Article 9 rules, including the priority rules, hinge on the type of secured transaction involved. For instance, a "possessory" security interest (often called a "pledge") involves the secured party's taking possession of the collateral, whereas under a "nonpossessory" arrangement possession is in the debtor. Another important distinction is that drawn between a "purchase money" security interest and a "non-purchase-money" one.[71] In the "purchase-money" situation the credit advanced by the secured party enables the debtor to purchase the item covered by the security interest. The purchase money creditor may be either the seller himself, who sells the item (for example, an automobile) on credit to the debtor, or some other party, like a bank, that advances funds to the debtor to be paid to the seller.[72] The security interest is a "non-purchase-money" one if the loan is not made to enable the debtor to purchase the collateral, for example, a finance company's advancing funds against an automobile already owned by the debtor.

§ 1–4. APPLICABILITY OF ARTICLE 9

The first question one must always ask is whether the problem at hand is governed by Article 9. The answer will usually be found in the rules set forth in Sections 9–102, 1–201(37), and 9–104, as discussed *infra*.

A. Basic Aspects of Coverage

The basic scope provision of Article 9 is found in Section 9–102, several aspects of which deserve close attention.

---

[70] The requirements for perfection are discussed in Chapter 3 *infra*. Which type of perfection is required or permitted depends on the type of collateral involved.

[71] The difference between the two is discussed in detail in § 4–2 B (4) *infra*.

[72] U.C.C. § 9–107.

Section 9–102(1)(a) provides that, except for certain types of transactions explicitly excluded from its scope,[73] Article 9 applies "to any transaction (regardless of its form) which is intended to create a security interest in personal property or fixtures." This language makes it clear that the determinative factor is the *intent* of the parties to create a security interest, rather than the particular form in which they cast their transaction. Taken together with the broad definition of "security interest" in Section 1–201(37),[74] it also indicates that Article 9 is sufficiently flexible to encompass not only traditional forms of secured transactions (including the various pre-Code devices)[75] but also new arrangements that may be invented by innovative lawyers and businessmen in the future.[76]

Sections 9–102(1) and 1–201(37) also indicate that Article 9 applies only to security interests in *personal property*, as opposed to realty, with one exception: security interest in fixtures, which lie somewhere between the two categories, are covered.[77]

As indicated by the statement in Section 9–102(2) that "[t]his Article applies to security interests created by contract," Article 9 governs encumbrances voluntarily created by the debtor but generally not those imposed by law, such as statutory liens.[78]

Section 9–102(3) indicates that even though certain types of secured transactions are themselves excluded from Article 9, subsequent security transfers relating to them may be covered. Assume, for instance, that *A*, the owner of Blackacre, gives a note and real estate mortgage to *B* as security for a loan from *B*.

---

[73] The exclusions are discussed in § 1–4 F *infra*.

[74] Section 1–201(37) defines a "security interest" as "an interest in personal property or fixtures which secures payment or performance of an obligation."

[75] See § 1–1 C *supra*. Section 9–102(2) lists pre-Code devices now covered by Article 9.

[76] U.C.C. § 9–101, Comment.

[77] Fixtures are discussed in § 4–4 *infra*.

[78] See §§ 1–4 F (2) and 4–1 A *infra*. One exception is found in Section 9–310.

This transaction, involving a security interest in real estate, is outside the scope of Article 9.[79] If *B* then pledges *A*'s note to *C* as security for a loan from *C* to *B*, however, this pledge, involving the creation of a security interest in an instrument, is governed by Article 9.[80]

The major *advantage* in having an Article 9 security interest has previously been discussed,[81] namely that the secured party who has previously perfected his interest will usually prevail against an adverse party, such as a competing creditor or judicial lienor, who lays claim to the collateral. On the other side of the coin, being deemed to have a security interest within the scope of Article 9 can be *disadvantageous* when failure to comply with the perfection requirements results in subordination to the competing claimant under the Article 9 priority rules. In these cases the alleged secured party may well try to argue that his transaction falls outside the coverage of Article 9, in the hope of receiving better treatment under other law—an allegation sometimes made, for instance, by ostensible lessors or consignors of goods, as discussed *infra*.[82]

B. Leases of Goods

It sometimes occurs that the parties to what is, in essence, a conditional sale of goods cast their transaction in the form of a lease,[83] whereupon the ostensible lessor, thinking he does not

---

[79] U.C.C. § 9-104(j).

[80] If *B* assigned the real estate mortgage, the applicability of Article 9 would be questionable because of an arguable conflict between Sections 9-102(3) and 9-104(j).

[81] §§ 1-3 B and 1-3 C *supra*.

[82] §§ 1-4 A (2) and 1-4 A (3) *infra*.

[83] Tax advantages provide one major reason for doing this. For instance, a bank that has no need for airline equipment but has a large enough profit margin to use tax benefits may purchase an airplane to "lease" to an airline that has need of such equipment but whose profits are too low to take full advantage of tax benefits. By purchasing and retaining title, the bank may benefit from investment tax credits and accelerated depreciation, allowing it to lease the item to the airline for a lower rental. Equipment

have a security interest, fails to file an Article 9 financing statement. When the debtor defaults on his debts, his creditors (or perhaps a trustee in bankruptcy representing them) may attempt to seize the item along with the debtor's other property, thereby coming into conflict with the ostensible lessor, who demands return of the item by virtue of ownership. If the transaction is deemed to be a "true" lease, Article 9 does not apply,[84] and the lessor will usually prevail under non-UCC property law. If, on the other hand, a court concludes that the arrangement is, in substance, a conditional sale, in which the lessor has retained title not because he expects return of the goods but rather as security for payment of the purchase price and in which the payments labeled as "rent" are really installment payments against the purchase price, then Article 9 applies, and the ostensible lessor will lose to competing claimants who take priority over an unperfected security interest.

Section 1–201(37) establishes a test for determining whether an alleged lease is an Article 9 secured transaction based on whether, and under what terms, the ostensible lessor has an option to purchase the goods during, or at the end of, the lease term. Although the mere existence of an option to purchase does not, of itself, make the transaction one "intended as security,"[85] a determination that the lessee has the option to acquire ownership for a "nominal consideration" will bring the transaction within the scope of Article 9. Essentially, the "nominal consideration" test means that if the payments labeled

---

leases can also provide tax benefits for a lessee, who may realize more by deducting rental payments as business expense than purchasing outright on credit and writing off depreciation and interest.

[84] U.C.C. §§ 9–102(2), 1–201(37).

[85] The absence of such an option makes it likely, but not inevitable, that the transaction will be deemed a "true" lease. Arguably, a contrary rule would subject all leases to the filing requirements of Article 9. On the other hand, it can be argued that even in the absence of a purchase option, a lease for the entire useful life of the goods, with rental payments approximating the purchase price a buyer would have paid, is the functional equivalent of an installment sale.

as "rent", are, in reality, being applied to reduce the purchase price to a substantial degree, the transaction is a conditional sale in lease's clothing; whereas if the lessee must pay a significant amount for the goods over and above any rental payments made, the transaction is a "true" lease.[86] To illustrate, assume that the leased item is worth $1,000. At one extreme, an arrangement whereunder the lessee can exercise his purchase option by paying only $1 in addition to previous rental payments is likely to be deemed an Article 9 secured transaction. At the other extreme, a requirement that the lessee pay $900 is likely to be regarded as indicative of a "true" lease. Between the two extremes, whether the consideration will be deemed "nominal" is a matter of case-by-case determination.[87]

Under the 1962 Code, a lessor who takes the precaution of filing a financing statement against the possibility of his transaction being brought within Article 9 runs the risk that a court will view the very fact of filing as indicative of a security arrangement. Section 9-408 of the 1972 Code removes this risk by providing that filing, of itself, shall not be a factor in determining whether the lease is intended as security.[88]

---

[86] Some courts determine whether this amount is substantial or "nominal" by comparing it with the market value of the goods at the time the option is exercised (thereby taking into account depreciation), while others compare it with the value of the goods at the outset of the lease term. The "nominal consideration" criterion is sometimes couched in terms of the "building equity" test or the "only sensible alternative" test. If the leasee can acquire ownership by paying no more than a nominal sum over and above rental payments made, the rental payments appear to have gone toward "building equity" in the sense of reducing the purchase price. Likewise, if only a nominal sum need be paid, as compared with the price the lessee would have to pay to purchase a similar item on the market, the "only sensible alternative" for the lessee would be to exercise the option.

[87] Some courts and commentators have suggested that an acquisition price of 25 per cent of what would normally be paid is the cutoff point below which the transaction will be deemed to fall within Article 9.

[88] Section 9-408 also permits use of the terms "lessor" and "lessee" in the financing statement, in lieu of the usual terms "secured party" and "debtor."

C. Consignments

A consignment is basically an arrangement in which the owner of goods—the "consignor"—delivers them to another party—the "consignee"—for sale by the consignee to third persons, with the proceeds of the sale (minus a commission) being remitted to the consignor.[89] If a court finds that the transaction, although labeled a "consignment" by the parties, was, in reality, intended as a conditional sale, with reservation of title in the ostensible consignor serving to secure deferred payment of the purchase price by the consignee, then the arrangement is a secured transaction subject to all the rules of Article 9.[90] In such a case a consignor who has failed to file or otherwise perfect his interest will lose to competing claimants (including creditors of the consignee or a bankruptcy trustee) who take priority over an unperfected security interest. If, on the other hand, the transaction is deemed a "true" consignment not "intended as security," Section 2–326 applies.[91] Under subsection (1) of Section 2–326, a consignment is termed a "sale or return." Under subsection (2), the consignor's interest in the

---

[89] For example, a department store may, rather than purchasing outright, take merchandise from a manufacturer or wholesaler on consignment, under an agreement permitting the consignee to return the goods without liability for the price if they do not sell. Such an arrangement relieves the retailer of the risk of nonsale and frees capital that would be locked in inventory pending sale for other uses. As discussed later, consignments are also sometimes used as a price-fixing device.

[90] U.C.C. §§ 1–201(37) and 9–102(2).

[91] U.C.C. § 1–201(37). One criterion pointing toward the existence of a "true" consignment is the unqualified right in the consignee to return the goods to the consignor without liability for the price. Another is that the parties primarily intended to use the consignment as a price-fixing device (rather than a security device), as manifested by the consignee's agreeing to sell goods at a price set by the consignor. The theory behind such an arrangement is that although the antitrust prohibition of resale price maintenance prevents a *seller's* using his market power to coerce a buyer to resell at a fixed price (title to the goods having passed to the buyer), it does not prevent a *consignor's* setting the price of his *own* goods (the consignor having retained title) in the hands of a consignee.

goods is subordinated to the claims of the consignee's creditors unless the consignor satisfies subsection (3)(a) by complying with a state law providing for his interest in the goods to be evidenced by a sign posted on the consignee's business premises; (b) by establishing that the consignee is generally known by his creditors to be substantially engaged in selling the goods of others; or (c) by complying with the filing provisions of Article 9.[92] Since alternatives (a) and (b) are rarely available,[93] as a practical matter, the consignor must file an Article 9 financing statement to protect his interest against creditors of the consignee even when a "true" consignment exists.

The upshot of the foregoing analysis is that when the sole consideration is the consignor's failure to file a financing statement, an inquiry concerning whether the transaction is a "true" consignment or a "false" consignment/Article 9 security interest is irrelevant;[94] in either case the consignor will lose to competing claimants. There may be considerations that make the distinction relevant, however. For instance, given the brevity of the Section 2–326(2) priority rule, it is uncertain to what extent a court may "tack on" aspects of Article 9 priority rules other than the requirement of filing in resolving a conflict involving a "true" consignment. One illustration involves the

---

[92] The purpose for the Section 2–326(3) requirements is essentially the same as that underlying the Article 9 requirement of filing; namely, by allowing the consignee to retain possession of the goods, the consignor clothes the consignee with the appearance of unencumbered ownership, on which a subsequent creditor may rely in extending credit. The filing of a financing statement (or compliance with the other requirements of Section 2–326(3)) counteracts this misleading appearance by alerting the prospective creditor that someone else (the consignor) has a prior claim to the goods.

[93] Few states have enacted a sign law of the sort referred to in (a), and (b) presents difficult problems of proof.

[94] This would be true, for instance, when Section 2–326(3)(c) (together with Section 2–326(2)) would apply if the arrangement were deemed a "true" lease, although Section 9–312(5)(a) (§4–2 A (1)(a) infra) would apply if the arrangement were called a "false" lease/ Article 9 security interest—filing being the only relevant consideration under either section.

question under the 1962 Code whether a "true" consignor, in order to prevail over an Article 9 secured party who has previously taken a "floating lien" security interest [95] in the consignee's inventory, must not only file, as required by Section 2–326, but also comply with the requirement of Section 9–312(3) that notification be given to the prior creditor.[96] On the rationale that the initial inventory financer needs the same sort of notice from a subsequent "true" consignor as from a subsequent Article 9 purchase-money creditor,[97] the drafters of the 1972 Code have inserted new Section 9–114 to that effect.[98]

Under the 1962 Code, a consignor who files a financing statement as prescribed by Section 2–326(3)(c) runs the risk that a court will regard the very fact of filing as indicative of an Article 9 security interest. Section 9–408 of the 1972 Code removes this risk by providing that filing, of itself, is not to be considered a factor in determining whether the consignment is intended as security.[99]

---

[95] "Floating liens" are discussed in § 2–2 D (2) *infra*.

[96] Another example involves the question under the 1962 Code whether a "true" consignor will, even in the absence of filing, prevail over a judgment lienor who acquired his lien with knowledge of the consignor's interest. The answer would be negative if Section 2–326(2) were applied standing alone, since no mention of knowledge on the competitor's part is made therein, although an affirmative answer would result from application of 1962 Section 9–301(1)(b). (This issue does not arise under the 1972 Code, which omits the knowledge element from Section 9–301(1)(b)). It is possible that some lawyers clothe a conditional sale with the appearance of a consignment not with a view to taking advantage of possible distinctions of this sort but rather simply on the erroneous assumption that non-UCC law will give the consignor priority by virtue of retention of title, without being aware that even a "true" consignment is usually subject to the requirement of filing under Article 9 via Section 2–326.

[97] The rationale for the notification requirement of Section 9–312(3) is discussed in § 4–2 B (2)(d)(i) *infra*.

[98] For a discussion of the ambiguity in 1972 Section 9–114(1)(b) concerning when and to whom the notification must be given, see § 4–2 B (2)(d)(v) *infra*. In states where the 1962 Code is still in effect, the safest course for the consignor is to comply with the requirements of Section 9–312(3).

[99] Section 9–408 also provides that use of the terms "consignor" and

D. Sales of Accounts and Chattel Paper

Article 9 applies not only to assignments of accounts and chattel paper as security [100] but also to outright sales thereof.[101] The latter are included because they are usually as much a form of commercial financing as the former and because "financing on the basis of accounts and chattel paper is often so conducted that the distinction between a security transfer and a sale is blurred." [102]

E. Security Interests Arising Under Article 2 on Sales

Several provisions of Article 2 establish a security interest in favor of a buyer or seller of goods in the context of a sales transaction.[103] Despite the fact that these interests arise by operation of law rather than by agreement, the use of the term "security interest" in Article 2 brings them within Article 9.[104] The *extent* to which Article 9 rules apply, however, depends on

---

"consignee" (instead of "secured party" and "debtor," as prescribed in Section 9–402) on the financing statement will not invalidate it.

[100] U.C.C. § 9–102(1)(a).

[101] Sections 9–102(1)(b) and 1–201(37). The reference to sales of contract rights in 1962 Section 9–102(1)(b) has been omitted in the 1972 version, consistent with the deletion of that term from Section 9–106. Certain sales of accounts and chattel paper that have nothing to do with commercial financing are excluded by Section 9–104(f), as discussed in § 1–4 F (6) *infra*.

[102] U.C.C. § 9–102, Comment 2. For example, sales of accounts are often phrased in terms of "assignment" and vice versa. What is, in essence, a loan against an assignment may be intentionally phrased in terms of a sale to avoid usury laws, which, while imposing a ceiling on *interest* rates charged for loans, do not purport to regulate the *price* for sales. For further discussion of accounts and chattel paper, see §§ 1–5 C (1) and 1–5 B (3), respectively, *infra*.

[103] For example, Section 2–505(1) provides that a seller who procures a negotiable bill of lading has a security interest in the goods covered thereby (as further discussed in § 1–5 B (2)(a) *infra*); and Section 2–711(3) creates a security interest in favor of a buyer for payments made against nonconforming goods he has rightfully rejected. For other examples, see Comment 1 to Section 9–113.

[104] U.C.C. § 9–113, Comment 1.

whether the debtor [105] has possession of the goods, as provided in Section 9–113. If the debtor has possession, the creditor must comply fully with all the provisions of Article 9. So long as the debtor does not have possession, however, Section 9–113 provides that no security agreement is necessary,[106] no filing is required,[107] and rights on default are governed by Article 2, rather than Part 5 of Article 9.[108]

F. Excluded Transactions

A number of transactions, including some that might be characterized as creating a security interest in personalty, are excluded from the coverage of Article 9. These exclusions are largely found in Sections 9–102 and 9–104.

(1) Security Interests Governed by Federal Law

At least some aspects of security transactions involving certain types of collateral are regulated by federal statute.[109] Sec-

---

[105] In this context, "debtor" refers to the seller when the security interest is in favor of a buyer and vice versa.

[106] U.C.C. § 9–113(a). Since Article 2 defines the circumstances under which security interests referred to therein arise, no need exists for a security agreement of the sort required by Section 9–203(1).

[107] U.C.C. § 9–113(b). So long as the debtor does not have possession of the goods, he is not clothed with the misleading appearance of unencumbered ownership, and prospective creditors do not need the warning supplied by a filing.

[108] U.C.C. § 9–113(c). Article 2 contains its own detailed provisions with respect to rights against a breaching party. For instance, compare Sections 2–706 and 9–504.

[109] Ship Mortgage Act of 1920, 46 U.S.C. § 911 *et seq.* (1976), providing for recordation of ship mortgages with the Collector of Customs of the port of documentation and governing priority conflicts with third-party claimants; Federal Motor Vehicle Lien Act, 49 U.S.C. § 313 (1976), under which security interests in trucks and busses operated interstate by carriers under a certificate of public convenience and necessity issued pursuant to the Interstate Commerce Act can be perfected in all states by notation on a certificate of title in a particular state; Section 20(c) of the Interstate Commerce Act, 49 U.S.C. § 20(c) (1976), under which perfection of a secu-

tion 9–104(a) provides, in essence, that *to the extent* such a statute addresses an Article 9 matter, the federal law controls; otherwise, a court is free to apply Article 9 rules.[110]

(2) Nonconsensual Liens

Section 9–102(2) states that "[t]his Article applies to security interests created by *contract*. . . ." [111] This language reflects the idea that, with a few exceptions, Article 9 applies only to *consensual "liens"* (more properly termed "Article 9 security interests")[112] on personalty, which are voluntarily, contractually given to the creditor by the debtor; it does not apply to *nonconsensual* liens, which arise by operation of law. Nonconsensual liens can be divided into two categories: First, there are *"judicial" liens* of the sort obtained by unsecured creditors by judicial process, as previously described.[113] Second, there are *statutory or common-law liens* given by law to suppliers of services or materials and the like. For instance, by state statute

---

rity interest in railroad rolling stock is permitted, alternatively, either by filing under a federal filing system or by filing under Article 9; Federal Aviation Act of 1958, 49 U.S.C. § 1403 (1976), which requires recordation of security interests in aircraft and parts with the Federal Aviation Agency in Oklahoma City (see regulations at 14 C.F.R. Part 49 (1976)); Copyright Act of 1976, 17 U.S.C. § 205 (1976), which provides for recordation of assignments of copyrights in the federal copyright office (see regulations at 37 C.F.R. § 201.4 (1979)); 35 U.S.C. § 261 (1976), which provides for recordation of transfers of interests in patents with the United States Patent and Trademark Office; 15 U.S.C. § 1060 (1976), which provides for federal recordation of assignments of trademarks.

[110] Some federal statutes, for instance, speak to recordation of security interests, thereby preempting the Article 9 filing rules (*see* U.C.C. § 9–302 (3)(a)), but make no mention of matters such as requirements for creation of the security interest, priorities, or rights upon default. With respect to the latter subjects, a court may apply Article 9 rules.

[111] Emphasis added.

[112] In older terminology, consensual security interests in personalty were often called "liens." This usage is now diminishing in the face of the Code's consistent use of the term "lien" in contradistinction to "security interest." See, for instance, U.C.C. §§ 9–301(1)(b), 9–310.

[113] See § 1–3 B *supra*.

a landlord may be given a lien for unpaid rent on personal property brought on the leased premises by the tenant; [114] the warehouseman may have a lien for storage charges on goods deposited with him; the innkeeper may have a lien for hotel charges on the guest's baggage; the carrier may have a lien for transportation charges on goods shipped by him; and so on.[115] The extent to which Article 9 applies to nonconsensual liens can be analyzed as follows.

Article 9 in no way applies to a dispute between two nonconsensual lien holders [116]—for example, when two unsecured creditors have each obtained a judgment lien against the debtor's property, or a landlord with a statutory lien for rent comes into conflict with a judgment lienor. The outcome in these cases will be determined by non-Article 9 statutory rules, common law rules, or both.[117]

No nonconsensual lien is itself an Article 9 security interest.[118] Consequently, no nonconsensual lien is subject to the creation, perfection, or default rules of Article 9. For instance, Article 9 does not purport to govern the circumstances under which a judicial lien of the type referred to in Section 9–301 (1)(b) or an artisan's lien of the type referred to in Section 9–310 arises, the time when it attaches, or the rights enjoyed by the lienor against the debtor.[119]

---

[114] Section 9–104(b) expressly excludes these liens from the operation of Article 9.

[115] Both Section 9–104(c) and the last sentence of Section 9–102 indicate that Article 9 does not apply to these liens, except to the limited extent provided in Section 9–310.

[116] Nor does Article 9 apply to a conflict between a nonconsensual lien holder and a buyer from the debtor.

[117] For example, in some states, the statute providing for judgment liens will give priority to the first of two judgment lienors to levy. See § 1–3 B *supra.*

[118] Security interests arising by operation of law under UCC Article 2, discussed *supra* § 1–4 E, are an exception.

[119] Such things will usually be determined by the state statute providing for the lien in question.

With two exceptions, Article 9 does not apply to non-consensual liens under any circumstances. This means that even disputes involving an Article 9 secured party—for instance, a conflict between a secured party and a landlord with a statutory lien for rent—will be resolved under non-Article 9 rules of law.[120] The two exceptions are judicial liens and artisan's liens, which, although not subject to Article 9 rules relating to creation, perfection, or default, are governed by Article 9 priority rules (Sections 9–301 and 9–310, respectively) when they come into conflict with an Article 9 security interest, as discussed in later sections.[121]

(3) Assignments of Employees' Compensation Claims

Section 9–104(d) excludes from the coverage of Article 9 "transfer[s] of a claim for wages, salary, or other compensation of an employee." Assignments of employee wage claims and the like as security for debts are regulated in many states by non-UCC statutes and involve delicate social issues whose solution was deemed best left to local regulation.[122]

(4) Equipment Trusts Covering Railway Rolling Stock

Section 9–104(e) of the 1962 Code excludes equipment trusts covering railway rolling stock from the coverage of Article 9. This exclusion has been omitted from the 1972 Code on the ground that these interests are essentially purchase money forms of financing.[123]

---

[120] A minority of courts have held that a conflict between a security interest and a statutory landlord's lien is governed by Article 9. A *contractually* created landlord's lien is itself an Article 9 security interest; consequently, a conflict between such a lien and another security interest is clearly governed by Article 9.

[121] §§ 4–1 A and 4–1 B *infra.*

[122] U.C.C. § 9–104, Comment 4.

[123] However, since recordation of such interests is governed by the Interstate Commerce Act, 49 U.S.C. § 20(c) (1970), they are exempted from the Article 9 filing rules by Section 9–302(3)(a).

(5) Security Interests Created by Governmental Debtors

Because governmental borrowings against assignments of water, electricity, or sewer charges, rents on dormitories or industrial buildings, tools, and the like are usually governed by non-UCC law, language has been added in the 1972 Code excluding from the coverage of Article 9 "a transfer by a government or governmental subdivision or agency." [124]

(6) Certain Transfers of Accounts or Chattel Paper

Although Article 9 generally applies to sales of accounts and chattel paper and assignments thereof as security,[125] Section 9–104(f) excludes a sale of accounts or chattel paper as part of a sale of the business out of which they arose, an assignment of accounts or chattel paper that is made for the purpose of collection only, a transfer of a right to payment under a contract to an assignee who is also to do the performance under the contract,[126] and a transfer of a single account to an assignee in satisfaction of a preexisting indebtedness,[127] on the ground that these transfers have nothing to do with commercial financing.[128]

(7) Transfers of Insurance Policies or Claims

Rights under insurance policies are frequently assigned as collateral for loans. Under Section 9–104(g), these transfers are excluded from the scope of Article 9 because they "are often quite special, do not fit easily under a general commercial statute and are adequately covered by existing law." [129]   Uncer-

---

[124] 1972 U.C.C. § 9–104(e). *See* 1972 U.C.C. § 9–104, Comment 5.

[125] U.C.C. § 9–102(1). See § 1–4 D *supra.*

[126] In contracts law terminology, this refers to an assignment of rights coupled with a delegation of duties.

[127] The references to contract rights in 1962 Section 9–104(f) have been removed in the 1972 Code, consistent with the similar change in Section 9–106. The reference to transfer of a single account in satisfaction of a preexisting indebtedness was added in the 1972 Code.

[128] *See* U.C.C. § 9–104, Comment 6.

[129] U.C.C. § 9–104, Comment 7. This exclusion was apparently included

tainty has existed under the 1962 version of Section 9–104(g) concerning the applicability of Article 9 rules to insurance proceeds payable by reason of loss of, or damage to, goods covered by a security interest. Language has been added in the 1972 Code making it clear that these proceeds are covered by Article 9.[130]

(8) Transfers of Deposit Accounts

Section 9–104(k) of the 1962 Code excludes from the coverage of Article 9 "any deposit, savings, passbook or like account maintained with a bank, savings and loan association, credit union or like organization." [131] Although this language clearly excludes deposit or like accounts put up as *original collateral*,[132] it has caused uncertainty concerning whether a creditor's security interest in *proceeds* from a debtor's sale of original collateral, such as goods, is cut off when the debtor deposits the proceeds in a bank account. Section 9–104(*l*) of the 1972 Code makes it clear that the security interest is not cut off by providing that these proceeds are within the coverage of Article 9.[133]

Uncertainty has also existed under the 1962 Code concerning whether the Section 9–104(k) exclusion encompasses certificates

---

at least partly to accommodate the insurance industry, which, having grown accustomed to common law rules, was reluctant to have a new, untried body of law (Article 9) applied to assignments of policies.

[130] The words "except as provided with respect to proceeds (Section 9–306)" have been added in 1972 Section 9–104(g), and a reference to insurance proceeds has been inserted in 1972 Section 9–306(1). For further discussion see § 4–3 B (2)(a) *infra*.

[131] The reason given for this exclusion is the same as for the exclusion of transfers of rights under insurance policies. *See* U.C.C. § 9–104, Comment 7.

[132] For instance, savings accounts in banks often serve as collateral for "passbook" loans.

[133] The language "except as provided with respect to proceeds (Section 9–306)" has been added in 1972 Section 9–104(2), and a reference to deposit accounts has been inserted in 1972 Section 9–306(1). For further discussion see § 4–3 B (2)(b) *infra*.

of deposit. The 1972 Code makes it clear that transfers of certificates of deposit as security are covered by Article 9 by defining "deposit account" in Section 9–105(1)(e) as an account *other than* one evidenced by a certificate of deposit.

(9) Judgments, Set-Offs, and Tort Claims

Section 9–104 excludes from the coverage of Article 9 a transfer of a tort claim,[134] a right of set-off,[135] or a right represented by a judgment [136] on the rationale that these rights "do not customarily serve as commercial collateral." [137] The 1972 Code modifies the exclusion with respect to judgments by stating that "a judgment taken on a right to payment which was collateral" is included within the scope of Article 9.[138]

(10) Real Estate Interests

Section 9–104(j) provides that Article 9 does not apply to "the creation or transfer of an interest in or lien on real estate, including a lease or rents thereunder" except to the extent that provision is made for fixtures in Section 9–313. This language reinforces the notion reflected in Sections 9–102(1)(a) and 1–201(37) that the coverage of Article 9 is, in general, limited to security interests in personal property.[139]

---

[134] U.C.C. § 9–104(k).

[135] U.C.C. § 9–104(i). For a discussion of one type of set-off, see § 4–3 B (3) *infra*.

[136] U.C.C. § 9–104(h).

[137] U.C.C. § 9–104, Comment 8. Transfers of these rights (particularly tort claims for personal injury) are restricted in some states by common law or statute.

[138] 1972 U.C.C. § 9–104(h). This addition removes uncertainty under the 1962 Code whether Article 9 applies to judgments obtained by the secured party or debtor against account debtors on chattel paper or accounts collateral. Since Article 9 applies to rights to payment on such collateral in the absence of a judgment, it would be inappropriate to apply non-Article 9 rules just because a judgment has been taken. The exclusion is aimed at rights under a judgment put up as original collateral.

[139] Even though the initial transaction (for example, creation of a real

G. Surety's Subrogation Rights

When a contractor agrees with an owner to construct a building on the latter's premises, it is common practice for the contractor to obtain a bond from a surety company guaranteeing that the construction will be completed and that materialmen and laborers engaged by the contractor will be paid.[140] When the contractor defaults and the surety steps in and completes the construction and pays off the materialmen and laborers, it will, by virtue of its common law right of subrogation, demand the money the owner originally agreed to pay the contractor. If some other party, such as the contractor's bankruptcy trustee or a bank that has financed the construction, also claims the money, the question arises whether the conflict will be governed by Article 9. If so, and if the surety has not filed a financing statement, the competing party will win. If not, the surety will generally prevail. Although the issue is not explicitly addressed in Article 9, recent decisions have made it clear that the surety's right of subrogation is not an Article 9 security interest, that the conflict is not governed by Article 9, and that the surety can prevail without having filed.[141]

H. Creation of a Security Interest Is Not a Bulk Transfer

When the owner of a business principally engaged in the sale of merchandise from stock *sells* a major part of his inventory, Article 6 imposes on the buyer rather onerous requirements concerning notification of prior creditors of the business in order to protect the latter from having the owner abscond with

---

estate mortgage or lease) is excluded by Section 9–104(j), however, a subsequent security transfer relating to that initial transaction may be covered by Article 9, as discussed in § 1–4 A *supra*.

[140] The owner will demand such a bond to protect himself against so-called "materialmen's liens," which, by state statute, will attach to the property for the benefit of materialmen and laborers who are not paid.

[141] This is not unfair, since a creditor that finances construction should be aware of the likelihood of a surety's involvement.

the sale proceeds without paying his debts.[142] But when the transfer by the owner consists merely in giving a *security interest* in the major part of his inventory, Section 9–111 provides that Article 9, rather than Article 6, applies, thereby relieving the secured creditor of the Article 6 requirements.[143]

§ 1–5. TYPES OF COLLATERAL

Because the applicability of, requirements imposed by, and outcome under, a number of Article 9 rules hinge on the type of collateral involved,[144] counsel's ability to classify collateral properly can be vital. The various types of collateral within Article 9 can generally be grouped into three major categories: (1) tangible personalty—termed "goods" in Article 9—encompassing consumer goods, equipment, farm products, and inventory; (2) semi-intangibles, encompassing instruments, documents, and chattel paper; and (3) pure intangibles, encompassing accounts, contract rights, and general intangibles.[145] These types of collateral, and a few other miscellaneous types, are discussed next.

A. Tangible Personalty—Goods

(1) Definition; Distinguishing Between Subtypes

Tangible personal property is referred to in Article 9 as "goods." Section 9–105 defines "goods" as "all things movable at the time the security interest attaches"[146] and also includes within the definition fixtures, the unborn young of animals,

---

[142] U.C.C. §§ 6–102(1), 6–102(3), 6–104 and 6–105. *See* U.C.C. § 6–101, Comment 2.

[143] Section 6–103(1) is in accord. One justification for the exemption is that imposition of the Article 6 requirements would tend to discourage secured financing.

[144] A convenient listing of the Article 9 sections applicable to the various types of collateral is found in Comment 5 to Section 9–102.

[145] The terms "tangible," "semi-intangible," and "pure intangible" are not mentioned in Article 9 but are widely recognized.

[146] 1962 U.C.C. § 9–105(1)(f); 1972 U.C.C. § 9–105(1)(h).

growing crops, and, under the 1972 Code, standing timber to be cut.[147] Expressly excluded from the definition are money, documents, instruments, accounts, chattel paper, general intangibles, and, under the 1972 Code, minerals or the like (including oil and gas) before extraction.[148]

Section 9-109 subclassifies goods as "consumer goods," "equipment," "farm products," and "inventory." Special rules applicable to each of the four categories are discussed later. It is appropriate at this point to mention that one major reason for distinguishing between these categories is to ascertain the proper place of filing or method of perfection. For instance, under the second and third alternative versions of Section 9-401(1), consumer goods and farm products require local filing, whereas equipment and inventory require central filing. And a purchase money security interest in consumer goods—as opposed to equipment or inventory—is perfected automatically without any need for filing.[149] Thus from the standpoint of place of filing or method of perfection, the distinction between consumer goods and equipment or between farm products and

---

[147] The 1962 Code treats timber as real estate until cut. The change was made to accommodate the timber-cutting states, many of whom had already enacted nonuniform amendments making timber to be cut under conveyances or contracts for sale "goods." The purpose was to facilitate financing by banks of timber to be cut by eliminating the necessity of complying with restrictions relating to real estate mortgages. In a related change the reference to timber was deleted from Section 2-107(1) (in which the "goods" label applies only if the seller is to sever) and added to Section 2-107(2) (in which the "goods" label applies regardless of whether the buyer or seller is to sever).

[148] The exclusion of minerals before extraction was added to clear up an ambiguity in this regard under the 1962 Code and has no significance in states that regard these minerals as realty. In states that regard them as personal property, the appropriate classification under the 1972 Code will be "general intangibles"—the residual category in Section 9-106. *See* 1972 U.C.C. § 9-105, Comment 3. Minerals that have already been extracted (for example, oil standing in a storage tank) are, or course, "goods."

[149] U.C.C. § 9-302(1)(d).

inventory can be crucial; [150] whereas the distinction between equipment and inventory may not be. But the difference between the latter two categories can be significant for other reasons; for instance, Section 9–312(3) imposes more stringent requirements on a purchase money financer of inventory as prerequisites for priority than those imposed by Section 9–312(4) on purchase money financers of equipment.[151] Distinctions among the various categories are also highly relevant in drafting proper collateral descriptions for the security agreement and financing statement.[152]

The four categories listed in Section 9–109 are mutually exclusive, meaning that at any given point in time an item of collateral can occupy only one category.[153] But at different times and under different circumstances, a particular item may fall into different categories. For instance, an automobile held for sale by a debtor-dealer is "inventory"; [154] in the hands of a debtor who uses it as business transportation, it is "equipment"; [155] and in the hands of a debtor who uses it as a family car, it is "consumer goods." [156] These examples point up the fact that, in general, the proper classification hinges not on the nature of the item (for example, cost, size, shape, mechanical function) but rather on its use or intended use by the debtor. Thus a large, expensive "business-model" typewriter, despite

---

[150] In cases of doubt, the safest course is to satisfy the requirements for both categories.

[151] The purchase money financer of inventory is not allowed a ten-day grace period in which to perfect after the debtor receives possession of the collateral and must notify prior financers of his interest. For further discussion, see §§ 4–2 B (2) and 4–2 B (3) *infra*.

[152] See §§ 2–2 C and 3–3 B (5) *infra*.

[153] For instance, the same item cannot be both "equipment" and "consumer goods" at the same time.

[154] U.C.C. § 9–109(4) (goods held for sale by the debtor). See § 1–5 A (5) *infra*.

[155] U.C.C. § 9–109(2) (goods used primarily in business). See § 1–5 A (3) *infra*.

[156] U.C.C. § 9–109(1) (goods used primarily for personal, family or household purposes).

having the appearance of "equipment," is, in fact, "consumer goods" if used by the debtor to type family correspondence. When a dual use is involved, as when an executive jet is used largely for business purposes, but occasionally for family trips, the *principal use controls.*[157] If the initial use is later changed, the use at the time the security interest attaches is generally determinative.[158] When the debtor's intended use (or at least the use indicated to the secured party) conflicts with his actual use—as when the debtor purchases a washing machine on secured credit, warrants in the security agreement that it will be used as consumer goods, and then immediately installs it in a washeteria [159]—the outcome is uncertain,[160] but a strong argument can be made for giving effect to the stated use in order to relieve secured parties of the need for policing the debtor.[161]

(2) Consumer Goods

"Consumer goods" are defined in Section 9–109(1) as goods "used or bought for use primarily for personal, family or household purposes." Common examples include furniture, refrigerators, washing machines, and television sets bought by consumers for home use and automobiles bought for personal, nonbusiness use. The principles to be applied in determining whether an item of collateral falls into this category rather than one of the others listed in Section 9–109 have previously been

---

[157] U.C.C. § 9–109, Comment 2; and see the word "primarily" in Sections 9–109(1) and (2).

[158] See, *e.g.,* Section 9–401(3), to the effect that a filing made in the proper place remains effective, even though the use of the collateral is thereafter changed.

[159] Typically, the secured party in this type of situation will have relied on automatic perfection without filing (Section 9–302(1)(d)), so that if the item is determined to be "equipment" the security interest will be deemed unperfected and thereby subordinate to the rights of a competing claimant, such as another secured party or the debtor's bankruptcy trustee.

[160] Nevertheless, prudence dictates obtaining from the debtor a statement of intended use.

[161] The secured creditor's *knowledge* of a discrepancy between the debtor's stated and actual intent, however, would probably be fatal.

discussed.[162] Special rules applicable to consumer goods under Article 9 are listed in Comment 5 to Section 9–102.[163]

(3) Equipment

Section 9–109(3) classifies goods as equipment "if they are used or bought for use primarily in business (including farming or a profession)." [164] Examples include a delivery truck used by a merchant, tools used by a carpenter, an air compressor used by a painter, and machinery used in a plant. The question sometimes arises whether the proper label is "equipment" or "consumer goods" when a debtor uses an item partly for personal purposes and partly for business purposes.[165] The principles to be applied in making such a distinction have previously been discussed.[166] Special rules applicable to equipment under Article 9 are listed in Comment 5 to Section 9–102.[167]

Article 9 applies a few special rules to "farm equipment" and "equipment used in farming operations." These terms are essentially synonymous and refer to equipment utilized by a person engaged in farming-type operations, though not necessarily a farmer.[168]

---

[162] § 1–5 A (1) *supra*. See also § 1–5 A (3) *infra*.

[163] See the Table of Statutes for the location of discussions of these provisions in this book.

[164] The definition also includes goods used or bought for use by a debtor who is a non-profit organization or a governmental subdivision or agency and goods not included in the definitions of inventory, farm products, or consumer goods. The latter reference makes Section 9–109(3) the residual category for goods not properly classifiable under the other three categories in Section 9–109.

[165] The distinction could be significant, for instance, under the second or third alternative version of Section 9–401(1)(a), which requires local filing on consumer goods, but central filing on equipment.

[166] § 1–5 A (1) *supra*.

[167] See the Table of Statutes for the location of discussions of these provisions in this book.

[168] Neither term is expressly defined in Article 9. Assume, for instance, that a debtor who owns no land and is not a "farmer" in the sense suggested by Section 9–109(3)—that is, is not engaged in growing crops or raising, fattening, or grazing livestock—creates a security interest in a

(4) Farm Products

Section 9–109(3) imposes three requirements for classifying goods as "farm products": (1) The goods must be of a described type; (2) they must be in the possession of a debtor who is a farmer; and (3) they must not have been subjected to a manufacturing process.

With respect to the first requirement, the goods must be "crops or livestock or supplies used or produced in farming operations or . . . products of crops or livestock." "Crops" would include fruit trees as well as corn, wheat, and so forth; "livestock" would include fowl as well as cattle, sheep, and so on; and "supplies" would include hay and other feed, fertilizer, seed, and the like.

The second requirement is that the goods be in the possession of "a debtor engaged in raising, fattening, grazing or other farming operations," that is, a farmer. This means that when the farmer gathers his eggs or harvests his crop, as long as he retains possession the proper category is "farm products"; [169] but upon shipment to a selling agent, cooperative, cannery, and so

---

combine which he uses in his business of harvesting grain for farmers. The secured party files a financing statement centrally in the Secretary of State's office under the second or third alternative version of Section 9–401, which provides that although filings on ordinary equipment are to be made centrally (Section 9–401(1)(c)), filings on "equipment used in farming operations" must be made locally in the county of the debtor's residence (Section 9–401(1)(a)). An adverse party claiming the combine (such as a judicial lien holder invoking Section 9–301(1)(b)) will prevail over the secured party on the argument that the filing was invalid because made in the wrong place.

Other special rules applicable to "farm equipment" are 1962 Section 9–302(1)(c) (exempting from filing certain purchase money security interests in farm equipment, omitted in the 1972 Code, as discussed in § 3–2 A *infra*) and 1962 Section 9–307(2) (pertaining to buyers of farm equipment, omitted in the 1972 Code, as discussed in § 4-3 A (2)(b) *infra*).

[169] Note that livestock or produce held by a farmer for sale could also be classified as "inventory" under Section 9–109(4), were it not for the last sentence of Section 9–109(3): "If goods are farm products they are neither equipment nor inventory."

forth, even though the farmer still has ownership, the classification changes to "inventory." [170]

The third requirement is that the goods remain in an "unmanufactured state," which means that the goods must not have been subjected to anything more than the relatively simple processing traditionally associated with farming operations, such as pasteurizing milk or boiling sap to produce maple syrup.[171] Upon being subjected to a more sophisticated manufacturing process, like commercial canning or processing wheat into flour, the goods become "inventory."

Comment 5 to Section 9–102 lists the special Article 9 rules applicable to farm products.[172] It will be noted that a number of special rules are applied to "crops," a subcategory of farm products.[173]

(5) Inventory

(a) Criteria for Classifying Goods as Inventory

Section 9–109(4) describes five types of goods that fall within the definition of "inventory": (1) goods held for sale, (2) goods held for lease, (3) goods to be furnished under contracts of

---

[170] U.C.C. § 9–109, Comment 4. The distinction becomes important, for instance, under the second and third alternative versions of Section 9–104 (1), in which local filing is required for "farm products" (Section 9–401 (1)(a)), whereas central filing is required for "inventory" (Section 9–401 (1)(c)). Prudence may dictate filing in both places.

[171] See U.C.C. § 9–109, Comment 4.

[172] See the Table of Statutes for the location of discussions of these provisions in this book.

[173] U.C.C. § 9–203(1) (requiring a description of the real estate in the security agreement); 1962 U.C.C. § 9–204(2)(a) (pertaining to when a debtor has rights in crops for purposes of attachment of the security interest, omitted in the 1972 Code); 1962 U.C.C. § 9–204(4)(a) (pertaining to when a security interest in crops attaches under an after-acquired property clause, omitted in the 1972 Code); U.C.C. § 9–312(2) (establishing priorities in certain conflicts pertaining to crops); U.C.C. § 9–401(1)(a) (prescribing a special place of filing); and U.C.C. § 9–402(1) (requiring a description of the real estate in the financing statement).

service, (4) goods that are raw materials or work in process, and (5) materials used or consumed in a business.

The first category—goods held for sale—is the most common form of inventory, encompassing the stock in trade of the manufacturer, wholesaler, and retailer. Suppose the debtor has given a security interest in plant machinery that he sells from time to time as it becomes obsolete. Does the policy of occasionally selling make the proper classification "inventory," rather than "equipment"?[174] Comment 3 to Section 9-109 indicates that it does not, stating that implicit in the "held for sale" test is the notion that the prospective sale is "in the ordinary course of business."

Goods held for lease (or for sale *or* lease, at the customer's option) constitute the second type of "inventory," a prime example being the fleet of cars owned by a car rental agency.

The third type of "inventory" consists of goods "to be furnished under contracts of service." This language removes the necessity of making technical distinctions between sale and service contracts with respect to the painter's stock of paint, prosthetics to be implanted by the surgeon, and the like.

The fourth category—"raw materials" and "work in process" —means that the term *inventory* encompasses goods at all stages of production, not just finished products held for sale.

The last type of inventory described in Section 9-109(4) is "materials used or consumed in a business"—a description that might seem, at first glance, to be encompassed within the definition of "equipment." Comment 3 to Section 9-109 draws the

---

[174] The distinction between "equipment" and "inventory" is unimportant insofar as the proper place for filing is concerned; the "in all other cases" clause in all three alternative versions of Section 9-401(1) calls for central filing for both categories. But the distinction becomes important under Section 9-312, which imposes more stringent requirements for priority over a competing Article 9 creditor on purchase money financers of inventory (Section 9-312(3)) than on purchase money financers of noninventory collateral (Section 9-312(4)), as discussed in §§ 4-2 B (2) and 4-2 B (3) *infra*.

distinction on the basis of whether the item is a fixed asset with a relatively long useful life (like industrial equipment), in which case it is "equipment," or is used up in a relatively short period of time (like fuel for generators, containers used in packaging, and supplies used by secretaries), in which case it is "inventory."

Comment 5 to Section 9–102 lists the special Article 9 rules that are applicable to inventory.[175]

(6) Fixtures, Accessions, Commingled or Processed Goods

The basic categories of goods that serve as collateral for most Article 9 security interests are set forth in Section 9–109, as previously discussed.[176] In a few special situations Article 9 deals with other categories, namely, "fixtures," "accessions," and "commingled or processed goods." These classifications are discussed elsewhere.[177]

B. Semi-Intangibles

A second major class of Article 9 collateral can be called "semi-intangibles" or "specialties"—property rights embodied in "indispensable paper" such that enforcement of the right depends on possession of the paper evidencing it.[178] The three types of semi-intangibles are instruments, documents, and chattel paper, as discussed next.

---

[175] See the Table of Statutes for the location of discussions of these provisions in this book.

[176] §§ 1–5 A (2) through 1–5 A (5) *supra*.

[177] Fixtures are discussed in § 4–4 *infra;* accessions in § 4–5 *infra;* and commingled or processed goods in § 4–6 *infra*.

[178] For instance, under Article 3 a promissory note (one form of "instrument" under Article 9) can be enforced against the maker only by the person who holds possession of the note. U.C.C. §§ 3–307(2) and 1–201 (20). Similarly, a buyer can obtain goods covered by a bill of lading (a form of "document" under Article 9) from a carrier holding the goods only upon surrender of the document. See § 1–5 B (2)(a) *infra*.

(1) Instruments

As defined in Section 9–105,[179] the term "instrument" embraces not only negotiable instruments of the sort governed by Article 3 (drafts, checks, certificates of deposit, and notes)[180] but also investment securities under Article 8 [181] (for example, corporate share certificates and bonds).[182] Assume, for instance, that A borrows money from B on an unsecured basis, giving B his note (that is, his promise in writing to repay the debt). B, in turn, delivers the note into the possession of C, a bank, as security for a loan. The transaction between B and C is an Article 9 secured transaction involving an "instrument" pledged as collateral.[183] The same would be true if B had used as collateral a share certificate issued to him by A, a corporation.

Comment 5 to Section 9–102 lists the special Article 9 rules applicable to instruments.[184]

A few changes in the Article 9 rules governing security interests in investment securities were made in the 1978 Official Text of the Code (adopted by only three states to date),[185] consisting

---

[179] 1962 U.C.C. § 9–105(1)(g); 1972 U.C.C. § 9–105(1)(i).

[180] *See* U.C.C. § 3–104.

[181] *See* U.C.C. § 8–102.

[182] The definition of "instrument" also encompasses "any other writing which evidences a right to the payment of money and is not itself a security agreement or lease and is of a type which is in ordinary course of business transferred by delivery with any necessary indorsement or assignment."

[183] Assume, in the alternative, that the loan transaction between A and B is a *secured* one, in which A not only gives B his note but also executes a security agreement giving B an Article 9 security interest, say, in A's automobile. The combination of the note and security agreement, when put up by B as security for a loan from C, would fall within another category of collateral under Article 9, namely, "chattel paper" (discussed in § 1–5 B (3) *infra*). In cases of this sort, in which an instrument is part of chattel paper, the Article 9 rules pertaining to chattel paper, rather than those pertaining to instruments, apply. U.C.C. § 9–105, Comment 4.

[184] See the Table of Statutes for the location of discussions of these provisions in this book.

[185] Connecticut, Minnesota, and West Virginia.

primarily in transfer of the rules for perfection of these interests from Article 9 to Article 8.[186]

(2) Documents

Section 9–105 provides that the term "documents" means "documents of title," as defined in Section 1–201(15).[187] For practical purposes, the only "documents" encountered in security transactions are bills of lading and warehouse receipts. Situations involving both types of documents will be discussed briefly; for more extensive discussion, see R. Riegert & R. Braucher, Documents of Title (3d ed., 1978, American Law Institute-American Bar Association Committee on Continuing Professional Education).

(a) Bills of Lading

A bill of lading is essentially a document issued by a carrier, such as a railroad, evidencing the receipt of goods for shipment.[188] Bills of lading play a role in the procurement of credit by both buyers and sellers of goods. Sellers often use bills of lading to obtain the purchase price of goods more quickly than

---

[186] The perfection rules were shifted primarily to Section 8–321. For a discussion of the changes in the 1978 Text, see *Coogan, Security Interests in Investment Securities Under Revised Article 8 of the Uniform Commercial Code,* 92 Harv. L. Rev. 1013 (1979).

[187] 1962 U.C.C. § 9–105(1)(e); 1972 U.C.C. § 9–105(1)(f). The 1972 Code adds to the definition of "document" "a receipt of the kind described in subsection (2) of Section 7–201" to cover the type of situation in which a large dealer of grain or liquor stores his own products and then issues a "warehouse receipt" to *himself,* which he uses as security for a loan. Since the definition in the 1962 Code refers only to Section 1–201(15), which speaks only in terms of a document issued by a "bailee," it might be argued that such a transaction is not within Article 9 (even though it is commonly assumed to be). The new reference to Section 7–201(2), which speaks to "a warehouse receipt . . . issued by a person who is the owner of the goods," makes it clear that Article 9 does apply.

[188] *See* U.C.C. § 1–201(6).

would otherwise be true,[189] as in the following sequence (on which there are a number of variations). After entering into a contract of sale with the buyer providing for payment against documents of title, the seller delivers the goods to a carrier, which issues a bill of lading to the seller. The bill, commonly negotiable in form,[190] runs to the order of the seller and authorizes the carrier to release the goods only to the person who surrenders the bill, properly indorsed by the seller . The seller then draws a draft against the buyer ordering the latter to pay the purchase price of the goods, indorses the draft and bill of lading, and turns both over to his bank. Since procurement of the bill gives the seller a security interest in the goods [191] and since the seller's bank succeeds to this interest,[192] the bank has sufficient security to advance the amount of the purchase price (or at least a portion thereof) to the seller. Thus, in effect, the seller obtains his money at the time of shipment without having to wait for later payment from the buyer. The bank forwards the draft and bill of lading to a bank or other agent in the buyer's city with instructions to present the draft and demand payment from the buyer upon arrival of the goods. If the buyer pays, he is given the indorsed bill of lading, which he can then surrender to the carrier to obtain possession of the goods. If the buyer does not pay, the seller's bank retains the bill of lading and thereby has a security interest that enables it to seize the goods, resell them, and apply the proceeds to satisfy the seller's debt.

---

[189] If the parties are located at a distance from one another, shipping will be required, so that a cash-on-delivery arrangement will not yield funds for days or weeks; the buyer's questionable or untried creditworthiness may make a sale on open credit (that is, a sale on unsecured credit, with payment to be made in 30 or 60 days) undesirable; and the buyer may be unwilling to make payment in advance of delivery.

[190] The bill will be negotiable not within Section 3–104, as is true of negotiable instruments, but rather within Section 7–104.

[191] U.C.C. § 2–505(1). Since this is a security interest arising under Article 2, various Article 9 requirements need not be complied with. See Section 9–113 and the discussion thereof in § 1–4 E *supra*.

[192] U.C.C. §§ 2–506(1), 2–104(2).

A buyer may obtain an advance for the purchase price of goods through the use of a bill of lading as follows. The buyer persuades his bank to issue a letter of credit to the seller authorizing the latter to draw drafts on the bank. When the bank, in effect, pays the seller for the goods by honoring the drafts, it obtains the negotiable bill of lading issued by the carrier with whom the goods are shipped. If the buyer fails to repay the advance, the bank has, by virtue of the bill of lading, a security interest [193] that enables it to seize the goods in satisfaction of the debt.

(b) Warehouse Receipts—Terminal and Field Warehousing

Warehouse receipts are receipts "issued by a person engaged in the business of storing goods for hire." [194] They appear in two different types of arrangements—terminal warehousing and field warehousing. A "terminal" warehouse is a facility for the storage of goods off the owner's premises (the sort of facility the general public associates with the term "warehouse"). Upon storing goods, the depositor is commonly issued a negotiable receipt [195] that can be negotiated to a lender as security for a loan. "Field" warehouses, on the other hand, exist for financing purposes rather than storage. A creditor who lends against a merchant's inventory may wish to exercise close supervision over the debtor's disposition of the collateral to guard against any impairment of security. Since needs such as processing, proper storage, and accessibility for marketing often preclude moving the goods off the debtor's premises, the creditor, in effect, takes possession *in situ* by setting up a field warehouse. This is accomplished by hiring a warehousing company, which

---

[193] Because of the involvement of Article 5, this is not a security interest arising "solely" under Article 2 within the meaning of Section 9–113 (discussed in § 1–4 E *supra*) and is therefore subject to all the provisions of Article 9. *See, e.g.,* U.C.C. § 9–303, Comment 2.

[194] U.C.C. § 1–201(45).

[195] Article 7 (Section 7–104), rather than Article 3, determines the negotiability or nonnegotiability of documents of title.

leases a portion of the debtor's premises for a nominal sum, sequesters the goods within the leased area by fencing, partitioning, or the like, and appoints a custodian (usually an employee of the debtor) who monitors access to the goods.[196] Warehouse receipts, commonly non-negotiable in form, are then issued to the lender against goods deposited, and the custodian allows goods to be removed only upon instructions from the lender. The arrangement may require the debtor to maintain a certain minimum level of inventory in storage, with goods being released only when goods of an equivalent value are substituted or when a proportionate amount of the loan is repaid.

(3) Chattel Paper

Section 9–105(1)(b) defines "chattel paper" as "a writing or writings which evidence both a monetary obligation and a security interest in or a lease of specific goods." [197] The most familiar example is the conditional sale contract [198] signed by the consumer who purchases a relatively expensive item like an

---

[196] Sequestering may take the form of a fence around lumber, a locked door on a grain silo, a lock on the spigot of a beer vat, or a room or floor partitioned off from the rest of the debtor's plant, with the custodian having the only key.

[197] The 1972 Code adds "but a charter or other contract involving the use or hire of a vessel is not chattel paper." This language was inserted to resolve uncertainty under the 1962 Code as to whether these contracts should be classified as "accounts," in which case filing is the only permissible means of perfection (Section 9–302 and Comment 1 to Section 9–305), or "chattel paper," in which case the creditor can perfect by taking possession of the paper (Section 9–305). The difficulty with the "chattel paper" characterization is that in international transactions there may be numerous executed copies of the charter, so that the secured party's possession of the paper does not necessarily prevent the debtor from having a copy and thus does not necessarily warn prospective lenders of the existing encumbrance. The 1972 Code resolves the question by explicitly excluding charters and similar contracts from the definition of "chattel paper" in Section 9–105(1)(b) and including them within the definition of "accounts" in Section 9–106.

[198] This term, inherited from pre-Code law, is still commonly used in reference to a sale on credit governed by Article 9.

automobile, boat, or refrigerator on credit from a dealer.[199] The buyer will give the dealer two things: (1) a security agreement granting the dealer a security interest in the item to secure payment of the price, and (2) a promise to pay, usually in installments. Both may be included in the same document, or the promise to pay may be set forth in a separate note; in either case, the writing or writings taken together constitute "chattel paper." [200] If there is a separate note, the Article 9 rules pertaining to chattel paper, rather than those pertaining to instruments, apply.[201]

It will be noted that the term "chattel paper" enters the picture only in the second of two distinct Article 9 security transacions, each of which involves different labels. In the first transaction, the customer buys from the dealer on credit, giving a security agreement and note, as stated. Here the customer is called the "debtor," the dealer is called the "secured party," and the "collateral" is the auto, refrigerator, and so forth.[202] In the second transaction the dealer either sells the combination of the security agreement and note outright or assigns it as security [203] to a financer (usually a bank or finance company). Insofar as this second transaction is concerned, the customer becomes an "account debtor," [204] the dealer is now the "debtor," the financer is the "secured party," and the collateral, in the form of the security agreement plus note, is "chattel paper."

Chattel paper figures prominently in financing of dealers' inventories of durables, such as automobiles. In the typical "floor plan" financing pattern, the financer lends the dealer the

[199] Purchases on charge accounts with retailers and on bank credit cards like MasterCard and Visa are *un*secured credit transactions, which are not governed by Article 9.

[200] For the sake of convenience, the author will hereafter refer to chattel paper as consisting of a security agreement plus a note.

[201] U.C.C. § 9–105, Comment 4. See § 1–5 B (1) *supra* for a discussion of instruments.

[202] The quoted terms are defined in Section 9–105.

[203] Article 9 governs in either case, as discussed in § 1–4 D *supra*.

[204] U.C.C. § 9–105(1)(a).

funds it needs to purchase its inventory of automobiles from the manufacturer. In return, the dealer gives the financer a security interest in the inventory and, at the same time, agrees to assign or sell to the financer the chattel paper the dealer obtains when his customers purchase automobiles on credit. Although the interest the financer charges the dealer for the inventory-financing portion of the arrangement is too low to be worth the trouble, the financer makes a tidy profit by acquiring the chattel paper and with it most or all of the large finance charge the dealer assesses the customer on the latter's credit transaction. In some instances, as is common in auto dealer financing, a "notification" or "direct collection" arrangement is employed in which the dealer delivers the chattel paper to the financing agency, which notifies the customer of the transfer and itself collects the customer's monthly payments. Under this arrangement the financer typically buys the paper outright on a "non-recourse" basis, meaning that the financer absorbs the loss, if any, when an account debtor defaults on payments. In other instances, as is often the case in financing of furniture dealers, a "non-notification" or "indirect collection" system is used. Here the chattel paper, although assigned, may be left in the hands of the dealer, who collects from the customer and then remits to the financer. Non-notification arrangements often give the financer recourse against the dealer when customers default.[205]

The special Article 9 rules pertaining to chattel paper are listed in Comment 3 to Section 9–102.[206]

C. Pure Intangibles

A third major class of Article 9 collateral can be called "pure intangibles"—property rights that are not embodied in "indispensable paper" whose possession is required for enforce-

---

[205] The dealer may be obligated to repurchase goods repossessed by the financer from defaulting account debtors.

[206] See the Table of Statutes for the location of discussions of these provisions in this book.

ment of the right.[207] The category includes "accounts," "contract rights" (under the 1962 Code), and "general intangibles."

(1) Accounts and Contract Rights

(a) In General; Definitions; Elimination of "Contract Rights" in the 1972 Code

Section 9–106 of the 1962 Code defines an "account" (often referred to in the business vernacular as an "account receivable") as "any right to payment for goods sold or leased or for services rendered which is not evidenced by an instrument or chattel paper." The section defines a "contract right," on the other hand, as "any right to payment under a contract not yet earned by performance and not evidenced by an instrument or chattel paper." This distinction between a right to payment already earned and one not yet earned [208] has caused confusion in several respects under the 1962 Code.[209] Consequently, the

---

[207] For a discussion of the significance of this characteristic in connection with the rules governing perfection by possession, see § 3–4 A *infra*.

[208] For example, at the time a manufacturer obtains a contract entitling it to payment upon future delivery of goods to a buyer, it has a "contract right." But at the later time of delivery, what was formerly a contract right ripens into an "account," the right to payment then having been earned.

[209] Assume, for instance, that on Day 1 Creditor$_1$ files a financing statement listing only "accounts" as collateral. On Day 2, Creditor$_2$ files a financing statement claiming "contract rights and proceeds." The contract in question calls for delivery of goods by the debtor-manufacturer to a buyer. If the priority conflict between Creditor$_1$ and Creditor$_2$ arises on Day 4 (by virtue of the debtor's default at that point) prior to delivery, it is uncertain whether Creditor$_1$, having referred only to "accounts" in his financing statement, has any claim to what is arguably still a "contract right" to future payment.

Or suppose the conflict arises on Day 6, after the debtor has delivered, earned the right to payment, and thereby clearly created an account. On the one hand, it can be argued that Creditor$_1$ should win under 1962 Section 9–312(5)(a) because he *filed* first as to "accounts"—the type of collateral now in controversy. On the other hand, it can be argued that Creditor$_2$ should prevail, on the following reasoning: Section 9–306(1) of the 1962 Code defines "proceeds" to include "the account arising when the

1972 Code abolishes the distinction by eliminating the term "contract right" and incorporating the definition thereof within the definition of "account": "~~Account means any right to payment for goods sold or leased or for services rendered which is not evidenced by an instrument or chattel paper,~~ *whether or not it has been earned* ~~by performance.~~" [210] The remainder of the present discussion will focus solely on accounts, with the understanding that "contract rights" are subsumed under it.

It will be noted that rights to payment other than those for goods sold or leased or services rendered—for instance, for sales of real estate—are excluded from the definition of accounts in Section 9–106. Also excluded are rights to payment evidenced by an instrument or chattel paper, both of which are classifications of collateral unto themselves. [211] Rights to payment earned under a ship charter are, however, expressly included under the 1972 Code. [212]

It will be recalled that under Section 9–104(f) certain transfers of accounts having nothing to do with commercial financing are excluded from the scope of Article 9. [213]

Two prominent examples of situations in which accounts arise are unsecured credit sales of goods by one merchant to

---

right to payment is earned under a contract right." Moreover, under the 1962 Code, the first-to-file rule of Section 9–312(5)(a) (see § 4–2 A (1)(a) *infra*) does not clearly govern priority with respect to proceeds; priority might be based on who *perfected* first. If the latter is true, Creditor$_2$ perfected first by virtue of having a continuously perfected interest in the accounts as proceeds dating back to his filing on the original collateral (contract rights) on Day 2. 1962 U.C.C. § 9–306(3). And under 1962 Section 9–204(2)(d) (see § 2–4 *infra*), Creditor$_1$'s security interest did not attach and thus did not become perfected until the account "came into existence" on Day 5.

[210] 1972 U.C.C. § 9–106 (emphasis added).

[211] On instruments, see § 1–5 B (1) *supra*. For a discussion of chattel paper, see § 1–5 B (3) *supra*.

[212] 1972 U.C.C. § 9–106. On the reason for insertion of this language in the 1972 Code, see § 1–3 B (3) *supra*.

[213] See § 1–4 F (6) *supra*.

another (for example, by a manufacturer to a dealer or whole-saler)[214] and consumer charge accounts with retail stores. Using the latter example to illustrate the appropriate Article 9 termi-nology to be applied to the three parties involved in an accounts financing situation, the customer who charges goods on his ac-count, that is, the debtor on the account, is termed the "account debtor"; [215] the store, which sells the account or assigns it to a financer as security for a loan,[216] is the "debtor"; [217] and the financer is the "secured party." [218] It will be noted that the initial credit transaction in which the account arises (for ex-ample, between customer and store) is an *un*secured one; [219] only the second transaction (for example, between the store and its financer) is secured.

Accounts receivable financing, virtually nonexistent a few decades ago, is today the source of billions of dollars of credit. Although hybrid versions exist, the financing of accounts com-monly takes one of two forms.[220] The first may be called "non-notification" or "indirect collection" financing. Under this arrangement what is sometimes termed a "general" financer does not buy the debtor's accounts outright but rather takes an assignment of them as security for a loan; [221] the account debtor, who is not notified of the assignment, makes payment to the debtor, who then remits to the secured party, who retains a right

---

[214] In these situations, often referred to as sales "on open account," pay-ment is usually required within 30 to 90 days.

[215] U.C.C. § 9–105(1)(a).

[216] It will be recalled that Article 9 applies equally to sales of accounts and to assignments thereof for security. See § 1–4 D *supra.*

[217] U.C.C. § 9–105(1)(d).

[218] 1962 U.C.C. § 9–105(1)(i); 1972 U.C.C. § 9–105(1)(m).

[219] If the initial transaction were a secured one, chattel paper (in the form of an installment sales contract), rather than an account, would be generated. See § 1–5 B (3) *supra.*

[220] On the two arrangements subsequently discussed in the text, see Comment 2 to Section 9–502.

[221] The financer may also take a security interest in the debtor's inven-tory.

of recourse against the debtor in the event that the account proves uncollectible. The second form of accounts financing, often called "factoring" (or "notification" or "direct collection" financing), involves an outright sale of the account [222] to a "factor," which is essentially a financing organization.[223] Under this arrangement the account debtor is notified that the account has been transferred and that payment is to be made directly to the secured party. The secured party assumes the credit risk; that is, he retains no right of recourse against the debtor in the event of the account debtor's inability to pay.[224] The advantages of a merchant-debtor entering into a factoring arrangement can be substantial: In addition to assuming the risk of bad accounts, the factor takes over the costly burdens of keeping records concerning the accounts, of investigating the credit standing of prospective account debtors, and of making collections on delinquent accounts.[225] Most importantly (as is also true of assignments for security), the transfer of accounts for immediate cash releases assets that would otherwise be unproductively tied up in the business for use for such things as operating expenses and plant expansion.

(b) Relaxation of Pre-Code "Policing" Rules—Section 9–205

Under pre-Code law the status of non-notification accounts

---

[222] Incidental to the purchase of accounts, the factor may also lend against the security of the debtor's inventory in anticipation of the accounts that will be generated upon the sale thereof.

[223] At one time, "factors" were selling agents for manufacturers. Gradually, they began to take over the function of lending funds to their principals, and the selling function dropped off, so that today the "factor" is, in everything but name, a banker.

[224] The risk of nonpayment because of a defect in goods sold or services rendered to the account debtor remains with the debtor, however. The factor often requires the right to maintain a reserve against which chargebacks for return of defective goods or the like are to be made.

[225] The merchant of course pays for these benefits via the discount at which the accounts are purchased. But, particularly for smaller business concerns, the alternative of maintaining credit and collection departments can be even costlier.

financing arrangements was placed in doubt by the Supreme
Court decision of *Benedict v. Ratner*,[226] which was thought to
render these transfers invalid as a fraud on creditors and therefore voidable in bankruptcy by reason of the debtor's having
unfettered dominion over the collateral. This dominion might
be deemed to reside, for instance, in the debtor's freedom to
collect, commingle, and use the proceeds of the assigned accounts as it saw fit, to grant discounts or allowances, or to accept
return of the goods involved, commingle, and resell them, without strict accountability to the secured party. Consequently,
costly, inconvenient policing devices were deemed necessary to
prevent invalidation, such as strict segregation of collections,
daily reports by the debtor to the creditor, and prompt remit-
tance to the lender of all collections received (even though the
amounts remitted were immediately returned to the debtor in
order to keep the loan from falling below the agreed level).[227]
Section 9–205 of the Code overruled *Benedict v. Ratner*, making it clear that these policing devices, although perhaps still
desirable as a matter of sound business practice,[228] are not
mandatory.[229] The section provides:

> A security interest is not invalid or fraudulent against creditors
> by reason of liberty in the debtor to use, commingle or dispose of
> all or part of the collateral (including returned or repossessed
> goods) or to collect or compromise accounts or chattel paper, or to
> accept the return of goods or make repossessions, or to use, com-
> mingle or dispose of proceeds, or by reason of the failure of the
> secured party to require the debtor to account for proceeds or
> replace collateral.

(c) Rights Between the Parties Upon Assignment—Sections 9–318 and 9–206

The subject of rights arising among the three parties in-

---

[226] 268 U.S. 353 (1925).

[227] *See* U.C.C. § 9–205, Comment 1.

[228] § 2–2 D (4) *infra*.

[229] U.C.C. § 9–205, Comments 1–5. This section is one of those in Article
9 frequently cited as upholding the validity of "floating liens," with respect
to which see § 2–2 D (2) *infra*.

volved when an account [230] is assigned is governed by Sections 9–318 and 9–206. It will be noted that although the present discussion is subsumed under a treatment of accounts, the following rules generally apply to an assignment of a security interest via an assignment of chattel paper [231] and to an assignment of a general intangible as well as to an assignment of an account.[232] It will be recalled that Article 9 generally applies the labels "account debtor" to the debtor on the initial obligation, "debtor" to the obligee who assigns the obligation to his financer, and "secured party" to the financer who is the assignee.[233] Consistent with the terminology employed in Section 9–318, however, the present discussion will use the terms "account debtor," "assignor," and "assignee," respectively, for these parties.

Suppose an account debtor wishes to resist the assignee's demands for payment on the assigned contract by asserting defenses or claims he may have against the assignor. The extent to which this is permitted is governed by Section 9–318(1), which provides that unless the account debtor has effectively waived his rights in this regard pursuant to Section 9–206, he may assert claims or defenses to varying degrees in two types of situations. The first situation is that in which the claim or defense arises from the assigned contract. In such a case the assignee is subject to all the terms of the contract between the account debtor and the assignor and to any defense or claim arising therefrom, irrespective of whether the defense or claim accrues before or after the account debtor is notified of the assignment.[234] Assume, for instance, that on May 1, the account

---

[230] In the present discussion the term "account" will be used to include what was termed under the 1962 Code a "contract right." See § 1–5 C (1)(a) *supra.*

[231] For further discussion of assignments of security interests, see § 3–3 I *infra.*

[232] The term "account debtor" used throughout Section 9–318 is defined in Section 9–105(1)(a) to mean "the person who is obligated on an account, chattel paper or general intangible."

[233] U.C.C. § 9–105. See § 1–5 C (1)(a) *supra.*

[234] U.C.C. § 9–318(1)(a). *See* U.C.C. § 9–318, Comment 1.

debtor, a dealer, enters into a contract to purchase machine parts from a manufacturer, with delivery to be made by the latter on September 1. On May 2, the manufacturer assigns its right to payment to a bank and notifies the dealer of the assignment. On September 1, the manufacturer breaches its contract with the dealer by either failing to deliver or delivering defective goods.[235] Insofar as the dealer has not paid the purchase price, he may assert a defense to the bank's efforts to collect; and to the extent that he has paid, he may assert a "claim" against the bank for a refund.[236] The second situation addressed by Section 9–318(1) is that in which the claim or defense arises independently of the assigned contract. Here the account debtor's ability to resist payment is more circumscribed: He may assert against the assignee claims or defenses accruing *before* he receives notification of the assignment, but not those accruing thereafter.[237] Assume for instance, that under the preceding facts the dealer had, on March 1, entered into a separate contract to buy certain equipment from the manufacturer that was delivered on March 15 in a defective state. Under Section 9–318(1)(b), this breach, albeit in an unrelated transaction, could also be asserted against the assignee. But it would not be assertable if the breach had occurred after May 2.[238]

---

[235] It will be assumed that the latter constitutes a breach of warranty under Sections 2–313 through 2–315 and is not covered by an effective disclaimer of warranties under Section 2–316 or limitation-of-damages clause under Section 2–719.

The example given in the text is not meant to suggest that "accounts" are confined to the sale of goods. The term also encompasses the right to payment "for services rendered" (Section 9–106), which would include, for instance, the right to payment under a construction contract.

[236] As indicated in Section 9–317, the assignee cannot be held liable beyond losing its ability to collect the amount owed on the assigned contract—as for damages for breach of warranty by the assignor.

[237] U.C.C. § 9–318(1)(b). *See* U.C.C. § 9–318, Comment 1. The term "claim," although not defined, is widely regarded as including counterclaims and setoffs.

[238] As used in Section 9–318(1)(b), the term "accrues" apparently refers to the time when the cause of action comes into existence.

When the unrelated cause of action accrues after notification, the account debtor still has his remedy against the assignor.

The foregoing rules become academic, however, if the account debtor has made an enforceable agreement not to assert against an assignee claims or defenses he may have against the assignor, as provided in Section 9–206. Under that section such a waiver is enforceable by the assignee: (1) if the assignee takes his assignment for value, in good faith, and without notice of a claim or defense; (2) if the defense in question is not a so-called "real" defense of a type that may be asserted against a holder in due course of a negotiable instrument under Section 3–305(2); [239] and (3) if the waiver is not invalidated by non-Code state or federal statutory or decisional law protecting buyers or lessees of consumer goods.[240] Even if there is no explicit waiver, the account debtor will be deemed to have waived his rights (subject to the foregoing limitations) when, as part of one transaction, he signs both a negotiable instrument and a security agreement.[241] It will be noted that, in Article 9 terminology, these two items together constitute "chattel paper." [242]

The question whether an account debtor and assignor may substitute for, or modify the terms of, their contract without the assignee's consent even after the account debtor has been notified of the assignment has presented a difficult issue in the law of contracts. Section 9–318(2) makes it clear that for Article 9 purposes such a modification or substitution is permissible: (1) insofar as the right to payment or a part thereof under the

---

[239] Such defenses include infancy, incapacity, duress, certain types of illegality and misrepresentation, and discharge in insolvency proceedings. *See* U.C.C. § 3–305, Comments.

[240] A number of states have consumer credit protection laws that restrict or prohibit "waiver of defenses" clauses in credit contracts entered into by consumers. Moreover, these clauses are now generally invalidated under the Federal Trade Commission's "holder in due course" rule, 16 C.F.R. Pt. 433, which requires that consumer installment sales contracts assigned to financers bear a legend stating that any holder of the contract is subject to all claims and defenses which the debtor could assert against the seller of goods or services obtained pursuant thereto or with the proceeds thereof.

[241] U.C.C. § 9–206.

[242] See § 1–5 B (3) *supra*.

assigned contract has not been fully earned by performance (that is, to the extent that the contract is still executory); (2) if the modification is made "in good faith and in accordance with reasonable commercial standards"; and (3) if the account debtor has not agreed otherwise. The assignee, however, acquires corresponding rights under the modified or substituted contract.[243] And although the modification or substitution will not be rendered invalid by a clause proscribing it in the agreement between the assignor and assignee (security agreement), the agreement may provide that a modification or substitution is a breach by the assignor, entitling the assignee to declare a default against the assignor. Such a clause would not, however, be enforceable against the account debtor. The importance of giving the account debtor and assignor the right to modify is particularly apparent in the area of large-scale government procurement contracts, in which the government may have, and may exercise, the right to amend an existing contract, necessitating a similar adjustment between the prime contractor (account debtor) and perhaps hundreds of subcontractors (assignors). Section 9–318(2) gives the prime contractor the right to make the required adjustments directly with the subcontractors, without first having to obtain the consent of the many banks to whom rights under the contracts may have been assigned.[244]

When an assignment is made, the question arises: Whom may the account debtor safely pay without incurring double liability? Section 9–318(3) provides that payment to the assignor is authorized until: (1) the account debtor receives notification that the amount in question has been assigned and that payment is to be made to the assignee; [245] (2) the notification rea-

---

[243] Thus when the modification consists of changing the price to be paid for goods under a long-term supply contract from a set price to one keyed to a fluctuating market, a market shift in one direction would disadvantage the assignee, although a shift in the other direction would accrue to its benefit.

[244] U.C.C. § 9–318, Comment 2.

[245] In the absence of notification, payment to the assignor remains appropriate even though the account debtor knows of the assignment.

sonably identifies the rights assigned; and (3) upon request by the account debtor, the assignee seasonably furnishes reasonable proof that the assignment has been made.[246] Once these conditions are fulfilled, the account debtor must pay the assignee; if he persists in paying the assignor, he can be held liable for a second payment to the assignee.

Section 9–318(4) makes it clear that a term in the contract between the account debtor and the assignor prohibiting assignment of an account [247] or requiring the account debtor's consent thereto is invalid. This rule departs from older principles of contract law but comports with the more recent trend among courts to construe away such prohibitions or to simply ignore them, in light of the modern commercial need to facilitate accounts financing.

It will be noted that a few nonsubstantive changes have been made in the wording of Sections 9–318(2), 9–318(3), and 9–318(4) of the 1972 Code to reflect the elimination of the term "contract rights" in Section 9–106 [248] and to resolve confusion arising from the fact that although the term "account debtor" used in these sections is defined in Section 9–105 to include debtors under general intangibles as well as accounts, the latter item is the only one referred to in the 1962 version.

On what constitutes an effective "notification," without which the account debtor may disregard the assignment and continue to pay the assignor, see Sections 1–201(25) and 1–201(26). The mere sending of a notification will not suffice; it must be received. And notification of the assignment alone is inadequate; there must also be a directive to make payment to the assignee.

[246] These requirements are designed to diminish the risk that the debtor will make the wrong decision: if he pays the assignee and the assignment turns out to be invalid or nonexistent, he will be obligated to pay again to the assignor; but if he continues to pay the assignor and the assignment turns out to be valid, he will be obligated to pay again to the assignee.

[247] The 1972 Code adds a reference to prohibiting creation of a security interest in a general intangible for money due or to become due.

[248] See § 1–5 C (1)(a) *supra*.

(2) General Intangibles

All pure intangibles other than those coming within the definition of "accounts" (or, under the 1962 Code, "contract rights")[249] fall within the catchall category of "general intangibles," defined in 1972 Section 9–106 as "any personal property (including things in action) other than goods, accounts, chattel paper, documents, instruments, and money." [250] Examples include copyrights, patents, trademarks, rights to performance, literary rights, goodwill, income tax refunds, liquor licenses, and interests in partnerships and joint ventures.[251]

---

[249] See § 1–5 C (1)(a) *supra.*

[250] In addition to deletion of the term "contract rights" (*id.*), the 1972 Code adds a reference to "money," for the reason discussed *infra* § 3–4 A.

[251] Article 9 is partially preempted by federal statutes governing interests in copyrights, patents, and trademarks. See § 3–3 A *infra* and the footnotes to § 1–4 F (1) *supra.*

2

Creation of the Security Interest

§ 2-1. INTRODUCTION: SIGNIFICANCE OF ATTACHMENT

In order for a secured party to enjoy the maximum protection afforded by Article 9, he must satisfy two overlapping sets of requirements: (1) the requirements for "attachment" (essentially the Code term for creation) of the security interest and (2) the requirements for "perfection." The subject of attachment is taken up in this chapter; perfection is discussed in the next.

A determination of whether, and when, the requirements for attachment have been satisfied is important in two distinct respects: First, attachment is a condition precedent to enforcement of the secured party's Article 9 rights against the debtor upon default.[1] Second, attachment is a prerequisite to perfection of the security interest,[2] and in most cases the secured party must perfect in order to prevail over third-party claims to the collateral under the Article 9 priority rules.[3]

---

[1] 1972 U.C.C. § 9–203(1). These rights, set out in Part 5 of Article 9, are discussed in Chapter 7 *infra*. It will be noted that the secured party's inability to proceed against the collateral under the rules of Article 9 does not prevent him from enforcing the underlying debt in the same manner as unsecured creditor, that is, by suing the debt to judgment and obtaining execution against the debtor's assets. See § 1–3 B *supra* and § 7–3 *infra*.

[2] U.C.C. § 9–303(1).

[3] See Chapter 4 *infra*. Perfection is relevant only in conflicts with third parties; it has no bearing on rights against the debtor.

The requirements for attachment are set forth in Section 9-204(1) of the 1962 Code and Section 9-203(1) of the 1972 Code. As stated in the latter section, the requirements are (1) that the debtor have executed a written security agreement (unless the secured party has taken possession of the collateral),[4] (2) that the secured party have given "value," and (3) that the debtor have acquired "rights" in the collateral. Each of these requirements will be examined in turn in the sections that follow. It is important to note that the three events may take place in any order and that the time of attachment will be the time when the last of the three, whichever that may be, occurs.[5]

§ 2-2. THE SECURITY AGREEMENT

One of the prerequisites for attachment is that the debtor have executed a security agreement satisfying the requirements

---

[4] Because the 1962 Code contains two separate, differently worded references to "agreement"—the requirement of a written security agreement as a condition to enforceability in Section 9-203(1) and the requirement of an "agreement that it [the security interest] attach" as a condition to attachment in Section 9-204(1)—the possibility exists that the latter requirement might be satisfied by an *oral* agreement and therefore that a security interest might attach and even be perfected but still be unenforceable for lack of a written security agreement. This might be the situation, for instance, on Day 3 in the following sequence: On Day 1 a verbal agreement is made, and a financing statement is filed; on Day 2 "rights" are acquired; on Day 3 "value" is given; but not until Day 4 is a written security agreement executed. To avoid this unintended result, the 1972 Code consolidates the language of 1962 Sections 9-203(1) and 9-204(1) in a single section—Section 9-203(1)—and omits the reference to "agreement that it attach," so that 1972 Section 9-203(1) clearly requires execution of a written security agreement as a prerequisite to both enforceability *and* attachment. Since the problem under the 1962 Code just mentioned rarely arises in practice (because the written security agreement seldom postdates all of the other events for attachment—verbal agreement, "value" and "rights"), the author will, for the sake of convenience, hereafter refer to the written security agreement as if it were a condition to attachment under both the 1962 and 1972 versions of the Code.

[5] The parties may, however, by explicit agreement postpone the time of attachment until a later date. 1962 U.C.C. § 9-204(1); 1972 U.C.C. § 9-203(2).

of Section 9-203(1); [6] namely, the agreement must: (1) be in writing (unless the secured party has possession of the collateral) and contain language indicative of an intent to create a security interest, (2) be signed by the debtor, and (3) adequately describe the collateral and, in some cases, the real estate involved. The secured party's failure to meet these requirements can have dire consequences, the most common one being lack of perfection (because of the absence of attachment) resulting in subordination of the security interest to the claim of a third party.

A. The Writing Requirement: Financing Statement Combined with Other Documents as the Security Agreement

In all cases except one the security agreement must be reduced to writing. The one exception is the situation involving a pledge, wherein the secured party takes possession of the collateral.[7] In that case, an agreement for security is still required,[8] but it may be oral. Nevertheless, it is customary to obtain a writing in the pledge situation as a matter of good business practice.

The writing requirement is in the nature of a statute of frauds,[9] meaning that the contents of the writing, unaided by parol evidence, must convince the trial judge as a matter of law that the parties at least *possibly* intended to create a security

---

[6] Under the opening language of Section 9-203(1), no security agreement is required for the security interest of a collecting bank arising under Section 4-208 (see § 3-2 D *infra*) or, except when Section 9-113 provides to the contrary (see § 1-4 E *supra*), for a security interest arising under Article 2 on Sales.

[7] For a discussion of pledges, see § 3-4 *infra*. From an evidentiary standpoint, there is less need for a writing evidencing an agreement and specifying what collateral stands as security when the collateral has been handed over to the creditor.

[8] The requirement that possession be taken "pursuant to agreement" is made explicit in Section 9-203(1) of the 1972 Code; it was implicit in the 1962 version. The requirement would, for instance, prevent an unsecured creditor from asserting secured status by virtue of having seized the collateral.

[9] U.C.C. § 9-203, Comment 5.

interest. (The definition of "security agreement" in Section 9-105(1) requires only "an agreement which creates *or provides for* a security interest.") If the judge so concludes, the finder of fact will then determine, on the basis of parol evidence, prior course of dealing and the like,[10] whether the parties did indeed intend a security agreement and what the terms of that agreement were. The security agreement need not be labelled as such: As previously discussed, an agreement ostensibly providing for a lease or consignment of goods [11] may well be deemed to create an Article 9 security interest. Likewise, a bill of sale, although purporting to effect an absolute transfer, can be shown to have been, in actuality, an agreement for security.[12] And pre-Code labels such as "chattel mortgage" or "conditional sale" will not prevent a court from finding that the parties have created a security interest within Article 9.[13]

It is often said that an agreement need not contain a "granting" clause ("debtor hereby grants a security interest . . .") or other formalistic terminology. Nonetheless, the inclusion of a granting clause is universal practice among cautious drafters, and courts are far more likely to find that a document qualifies as a security agreement in the presence of standard Article 9 terminology such as "security," "security interest," "secured party," "collateral," and the like. There must, in all events, be *some* language indicating an intent to create a security interest. The need for adequate terminology is manifest in cases in which a creditor who cannot produce the usual document obviously qualifying as a security agreement offers instead a filed financing statement—either alone or in combination with other papers. The courts have uniformly held that a standard-form financing statement (Form UCC-1), by itself, will not satisfy the security agreement requirement,[14] but some (though not

---

[10] See the definition of "agreement" in Section 1-201(3).

[11] §§ 1-4 B and 1-4 C, respectively, *supra.*

[12] U.C.C. § 9-203, Comment 4.

[13] *See* U.C.C. § 9-101, Comment.

[14] The presence of a filed financing statement, even though signed by the debtor, is not indicative of a security agreement, since Section 9-402(1)

all) have been willing to uphold a financing statement coupled with another document such as a letter between the parties, a loan application or a promissory note—particularly when the other paper contains interlocking "security" language. Thus compliance with Section 9–203(1) has been found in the case of a filed financing statement plus a board of directors' resolution authorizing the filing of the financing statement and referring to the "security interest" given by the corporation to a named "secured party," and in the case of a filed financing statement which mentioned that it was "securing a note" plus a note which stated that it was "secured by a financing statement."

It must be kept in mind that the security agreement is a contract; hence unless superseded by particular Code provisions, the general principles of contract law relating to offer and acceptance, consideration, capacity, mistake, misrepresentation, unconscionability, and the like apply.[15]

B. The Signature Requirement

Section 9–203(1) requires that the security agreement be signed by the debtor in order to be valid.[16] A complete, manually inscribed signature is not necessary, however: Section 1–201(39) broadly defines "signed" to include "any symbol executed or adopted by a party with present intention to authenticate a writing," and Comment 39 to the section observes that the signature may be printed or stamped, may consist of initials, may be on any part of the document, and may even be found in a billhead or letterhead—as long as there is "present intention to authenticate."

---

permits filing before a security agreement is made; that is, the parties may well have broken off negotiations after filing without ever concluding an agreement. The insertion of granting language in the financing statement may, however, satisfy Section 9–203(1), and some cautious lawyers routinely add this language as a precaution against the possibility of the security agreement becoming lost.

[15] See U.C.C. § 1–103.

[16] The signature need not be acknowledged before a notary or verified. Nor is there any requirement that the secured party sign, although (the security agreement being a contract) he must be contractually bound.

The signature requirement has given rise to several issues, one of which concerns the effectiveness of a security agreement filled in or changed by the secured party after the debtor has signed—as when one automobile is substituted for another as security and the collateral description in the security agreement is altered accordingly. The better view is that the post-signature insertion or alteration is permissible as long as it is made with the approval of the debtor, but the matter is not free from doubt; hence prudence dictates having the debtor sign or initial the change.

Another issue is whether the security agreement has been signed by the "debtor" when, for instance, a husband purchases an automobile on credit as a gift for his wife, signs the security agreement himself, and then inserts the wife's name on the certificate of title. A competing claimant (such as a trustee in bankruptcy) may prevail on the argument that the wife, being the owner, is the "debtor" and that the husband's signature on the security agreement is therefore invalid. The obvious solution from a planning standpoint is for the secured party to obtain both signatures.

A third issue concerns the validity of a signature made by a person (such as a corporate officer) purporting to act as an agent of the debtor. Here the principles of agency and business organizations law will determine the outcome.[17]

C. The Description Requirement

The security agreement must contain a description of the collateral securing the obligation.[18] The agreement may fail under this requirement because the collateral description is absent, erroneous, or lacking in specificity. The clearest case of invalidity is that in which the creditor neglects to include a description at all. Also usually fatal is a substantial misidentifi-

---

[17] *See* U.C.C. § 1–103.
[18] U.C.C. § 9–203(1).

cation of the collateral ("Ford" versus "Chevrolet")[19] or mis-classification ("consumer goods" versus "equipment"). In the latter regard the principles to be applied in differentiating among the various categories of collateral under Article 9 have previously been discussed.[20]

More difficult questions are presented when the alleged basis of invalidity is that the description is too broad. Here Section 9-110 indicates the approach envisioned by the drafters: "For the purposes of this Article any description of personal property or real estate is sufficient whether or not it is specific if it reasonably identifies what is described." The accompanying Comment observes: "Under this rule courts should refuse to follow the holdings, often found in the older chattel mortgage cases, that descriptions are insufficient unless they are of the most exact and detailed nature, the so-called 'serial number' test." By and large, courts have heeded this admonition, sustaining broadly worded descriptions. Thus a description such as "all accounts" or "all inventory" should suffice. (In a "floating lien" arrangement, of course, no greater specificity can be expected with respect to collateral not yet acquired by the debtor.)[21] There are limits, of course: A reference merely to "the debtor's property" or "all personal property of the debtor" is likely to be deemed fatally vague, as is "one automobile owned by the debtor," when the debtor owns three automobiles, each of a

---

[19] It should be noted that partial errors in serial numbers and the like are not necessarily fatal if enough other information is included to identify the item.

[20] For a discussion of each of the Article 9 classifications, see § 1-5 *supra*. On distinguishing between the subtypes of goods listed in Section 9-109, see § 1-5 A (1) *supra*.

[21] On "floating liens," see § 2-2 D (2) *infra*. Whether the term "accounts" or "inventory" encompasses future collateral without additional language by way of an after-acquired property clause (for example, "all inventory now owned or hereafter acquired") is the subject of dispute. Needless to say, from a drafting standpoint one should always include an after-acquired property clause if the parties intend the security interest to extend to future collateral.

different make. And from a drafting standpoint, the obvious rule is that one should err on the side of specificity.

Note should also be taken of the discussion of the collateral description requirement for the financing statement (Section 9–402(1)) in the next chapter.[22]

When certain collateral related to real estate is involved, Section 9–203(1) requires that the security agreement contain a description of the realty as well as of the chattels themselves. Under the 1962 Code this is true with respect to oil, gas or minerals to be extracted, crops, and timber to be cut.[23] The 1972 Code omits the reference to "oil, gas or minerals to be extracted," since a security interest in this collateral is not recognized until after extraction.[24] It will be noted that the liberal language of Section 9–110, quoted above, applies to real estate descriptions as well as descriptions of personal property. Thus a "legal description" (for example, by metes and bounds) of the sort used in real estate deeds and mortgages is not necessary; a common description such as a street address or a guide to a recorded map or plat will suffice.[25]

---

[22] § 3–3 B (5) *infra*. The rather abstract argument is sometimes made that the description in the security agreement should be more specific than that in the financing statement because the purpose of the former is to "minimize the possibility of future disputes [between the debtor and secured party] . . . as to what property stands as collateral for the obligation" (Comment 3 to Section 9–203), whereas the latter is intended to be only "a simple notice" to third parties calling for "further inquiry" about "the complete state of affairs" (Comment 2 to Section 9–402). A counter-argument is that the permissive language of Section 9–110 applies equally to both description requirements.

[23] Given the fungible nature of this collateral, a description of the real estate is often the best means of identifying the chattels.

[24] *See* 1972 U.C.C. § 9–105(1)(h).

[25] For further discussion and examples, see the treatment of the similar real estate-description requirement for the financing statement in § 3–3 B (6) *infra*.

D. *Other Provisions in the Security Agreement*

(1) Reference to Proceeds

There has been some confusion under the 1962 Code concerning whether the security agreement must contain a reference to proceeds obtained by the debtor upon sale of the original collateral in order for the proceeds to be covered by the security interest. The last sentence of 1962 Section 9–203(1) ("In describing collateral, the word "proceeds" is sufficient . . .") appears to require such a reference, whereas the language of Section 9–306(2) suggests that a security interest in collateral automatically extends to the proceeds thereof. Section 9–203(3) of the 1972 Code clarifies the ambiguity (and reflects what is probably the prevailing view under the 1962 Code) by making clear that no reference to proceeds is necessary—the theory being that the parties to a security agreement virtually always intend proceeds to be covered.[26]

(2) Future Advance and After-Acquired Property Clauses; the "Floating Lien"

If the parties anticipate that the collateral will secure advances made subsequent to the execution of the security agreement, the agreement should contain a "future advance" clause.[27] These clauses are authorized in 1962 Section 9–204(5) and 1972 Section 9–204(3). These sections recognize that the security agreement may either *require* the secured party to make future advances (an "obligatory" or "mandatory" clause)—as when the creditor contractually commits to make a line of credit available

---

[26] The parties may explicitly provide otherwise if they wish.

[27] Example: "As security for the payment of all indebtedness of the Debtor to the Secured Party, now existing or hereafter incurred, including all loans now or in the future made hereunder, the Debtor grants a security interest in. . . ."

to the debtor—or it may simply provide that he *may* do so as he sees fit (a "voluntary" or "optional" clause).[28]

When the parties intend that property to be acquired by the debtor after the execution of the security agreement shall stand as security for the indebtedness in question, an "after-acquired property" clause should be included in the agreement.[29] It appears from the language of 1962 Section 9–204(3) and 1972 Section 9–204(1) (which provisions validate such clauses)[30] that an after-acquired property clause must be present in order for the secured party to claim an interest in subsequently obtained property.[31]

The provisions in Section 9–204 just mentioned make possible one of the more significant forms of security transaction—the "floating lien"—so named because the security interest "floats over" existing and after-acquired property. "Floating lien" security interests are generally taken in inventory, accounts, or both. Unlike, say, a consumer debtor, who may need only a one-time loan to purchase his automobile, a dealer will often need to have loan funds available on a continuing basis to meet operating expenses, to purchase replacement inventory, and so on. In these cases the creditor would not be adequately protected by a security interest limited to the debtor's accounts

---

[28] Whether at least a voluntary future advance clause in the original security agreement *must* be present in order for the secured party to have priority over the intervening interest of a third-party claimant is the subject of debate, despite the language of Comment 8 to 1962 Section 9–204 and Comment 5 to 1972 Section 9–204, both of which appear to require that such a clause be present. It will be noted that there is clearly no need to refer to future advances in the financing statement. 1972 U.C.C. § 9–204, Comment 5.

[29] Example: "The Secured Party shall have a security interest in all inventory of the Debtor, now owned or hereafter acquired" (or "in all accounts receivable of the Debtor, now existing or hereafter arising").

[30] For a discussion of the rationale behind the allowance of after-acquired property clauses, see Comment 3 to 1962 Section 9–204 and Comment 2 to 1972 Section 9–204.

[31] There is no need to refer to after-acquired property in the financing statement, however. 1972 U.C.C. § 9–204, Comment 5.

or inventory existing at the time of the security agreement: When the accounts were paid or the inventory sold, the amount of collateral would diminish, but (by hypothesis) the amount of debt outstanding would not. Adequate protection is afforded by the "floating lien," however, whereunder new accounts acquired by the dealer or new items of inventory purchased by him continually replace security in the form of old accounts that are paid or old items of inventory that are sold. In one version of the "floating lien" arrangement, a single loan is made at the outset against the debtor's existing and after-acquired inventory or accounts or both—say, $50,000—that remains outstanding on an ongoing basis as a "line of credit." The debtor need not remit proceeds (for example, cash received upon the sale of inventory to customers) to the creditor; rather, he may use them for such things as the purchase of new inventory, and so forth. As new items of inventory or new accounts are acquired, they are automatically covered by the after-acquired property clause. In another type of arrangement, the "revolving loan" situation, as inventory is sold or accounts are collected, the proceeds are remitted to the secured party and applied to reduce the outstanding balance of the initial loan. Periodically thereafter, the creditor makes new advances against incoming inventory or new accounts.

Section 9-204 of the 1962 Code imposes two limitations on the effectiveness of after-acquired property clauses. The first is the provision in subsection (4)(a) that no security interest attaches under such a clause to crops that become such more than one year after the security agreement is executed unless the agreement involves certain real estate transactions.[32] This language was intended to protect the necessitous farmer from encumbering his crops far into the future, thereby impairing his

---

[32] The exception to the limitation is that "a security interest in crops which is given in conjunction with a lease or a land purchase or improvement transaction evidenced by a contract, mortgage or deed of trust may if so agreed attach to crops to be grown on the land concerned during the period of such real estate transaction."

ability to obtain credit for raising crops in later years from some other lender. The limitation has proved ineffective, however, because the secured party can simply have the debtor execute a new security agreement each year and can file a single financing statement effective for *five* years [33] that covers subsequent years' crops and that, under the rule of Section 9–312(5), giving priority to the first to file irrespective of the time of attachment,[34] protects the creditor's priority position as effectively as if an after-acquired property clause in the initial security agreement were valid. Knowing this, subsequent prospective creditors are, under the 1962 Code, reluctant to lend, so that the purpose of the limitation is effectively thwarted. Consequently, the restriction has been omitted in the 1972 Code.

The second limitation on the operation of after-acquired property clauses is found in both the 1962 and 1972 versions of Section 9–204: "No security interest attaches under an after-acquired property clause to consumer goods other than accessions (Section 9–314) when given as additional security unless the debtor acquires rights in them within ten days after the secured party gives value." [35] This language would, for instance, invalidate an "add-on" clause whereby a department store attempted to secure a present extension of credit by taking a security interest in all goods purchased by a consumer debtor from the store in the future.

(3) Consumer Legislation Affecting the Security Agreement

When the debtor is a consumer, the terms of the security agreement may be affected by non-Code state or federal consumer credit legislation. For instance, the federal Truth-in-Lending Act [36] may require disclosure of various credit terms; a state consumer finance act may require a statement in boldface type such as "Caution—It is important that you thoroughly

---

[33] U.C.C. § 9–403(2).

[34] See § 4–2 A (1)(a) *infra*.

[35] 1962 U.C.C. § 9–204(4)(b); 1972 U.C.C. § 9–204(2).

[36] 15 U.S.C. § 1601 *et seq.* (1970).

read the contract before you sign it"; and the Uniform Consumer Credit Code, in states that have adopted it, restricts the effectiveness of acceleration clauses.[37] It will be noted that the requirements of Section 9–203 are expressly made subject to legislation such as small loan acts, retail installment sales acts, and the like.[38]

(4) Freedom of Contract; Clauses Commonly Found in the Security Agreement

The parties to the security agreement (debtor and secured party) may not by agreement between themselves adversely affect the priority status afforded third parties by various Article 9 provisions.[39] Nor may they contractually eliminate the obligations of good faith, diligence, reasonableness, and care imposed by the Code.[40] Nor may they vary (at least by agreement *before* default) most of the rights of the debtor and duties of the secured party upon default.[41] Subject to these limitations (and those imposed by non-Code consumer regulatory statutes of the sort discussed above),[42] however, the parties have considerable freedom to contract as they wish. Clauses commonly found in the security agreement in addition to those previously discussed include the following: (1) a statement of the amount of the secured debt (including principal and interest or finance charges) and the terms of repayment; (2) a promise by the debtor not to sell the collateral without prior permission from the secured party;[43] (3) a promise by the debtor to care for the

---

[37] See § 7–2 B *infra.*

[38] 1972 U.C.C. § 9–203(4); 1962 U.C.C. § 9–203(2). *See also* Section 9–201.

[39] Such provisions include, for example, Sections 9–301, 9–307, and 9–312. Under Section 9–316, however, a third party who is entitled to priority may himself agree to subordinate his claim.

[40] U.C.C. § 1–102(3).

[41] *See* U.C.C. § 9–501(3). The rights and duties referred to are set forth in Part 5 of Article 9, as discussed in Chapter 7 *infra.*

[42] § 2–2 D (3) *supra.*

[43] See § 4–3 A (1)(a) *infra.*

collateral and to pay insurance and taxes thereon; (4) a promise by the debtor to remit proceeds from the sale of the collateral to the secured party or to deposit them in a special account and to maintain records with respect thereto which the secured party may inspect; [44] (5) a clause permitting the debtor to use, commingle, or dispose of the collateral; [45] (6) a promise by the debtor to supply additional collateral under certain conditions (for instance, when the market value of the existing collateral has diminished) or upon request by the secured party when he deems himself insecure; [46] (7) a waiver by the debtor of defenses against assignees; [47] (8) a clause listing "events of default"; [48] (9) a clause listing the remedies available to the secured party upon default [49] and requiring that notice of resale after default be sent to the debtor no later than a specified number of days before the sale; [50] (10) an "acceleration" clause providing that upon an event of default (or perhaps when the creditor deems himself insecure) the entire remaining balance of the loan shall become due and payable immediately; [51] (11) a provision for recovery by the secured party of the costs of realization upon default, including attorneys' fees; [52] (12) a clause requiring the debtor to assemble the collateral in one place upon default; [53] and (13) a choice-of-law provision.[54]

§ 2–3. REQUIREMENT THAT THE SECURED PARTY GIVE VALUE

The second requirement for attachment of a security interest

---

[44] See § 4–3 B (3) *infra.*

[45] *See* U.C.C. § 9–205.

[46] *See* U.C.C. § 1–208, discussed *infra* § 7–2 B.

[47] *See* U.C.C. § 9–206, discussed *supra* § 1–5 C (1)(c).

[48] See § 7–2 A *infra.*

[49] Although commonly included, insofar as such a list reiterates the rules in Part 5 of Article 9, it is unnecessary.

[50] See § 7–1 *infra.*

[51] *See* U.C.C. § 1–208 and § 7–2 B *infra.*

[52] *See* U.C.C. § 9–504(2)(a), discussed *infra* § 7–4 C (1).

[53] *See* U.C.C. § 9–503, discussed *infra* § 7–4 A.

[54] *See* U.C.C. § 1–105, discussed *infra* § 5–1.

is that the secured party give "value." [55]   Under the definition
in Section 1-201(44), this means that the secured party must
take the security interest "(a) in return for a binding commitment to extend credit or for the extension of immediately available credit . . . or (b) as security for or in total or partial satisfaction of a pre-existing claim; or . . . (d) generally, in return
for any consideration sufficient to support a simple contract."

The significance of the "value" requirement and of the defining language quoted above can perhaps best be illustrated in
the context of a priority dispute between a secured party and
an unsecured creditor who has obtained a judicial lien against
the collateral. First, however, it is necessary to consider briefly
the priority rules involved in such a conflict and the elements
that determine the timing of perfection. The basic priority rule,
Section 9-301(1)(b), provides that when the secured party perfects his security interest before the lienor obtains his lien, the
secured party is entitled to priority (that is, has first claim on the
collateral subject to the security interest); whereas the lienor
prevails if his lien attaches before the secured party perfects.[56]
Insofar as future advances are concerned, the situation is somewhat complicated by the new language in Section 9-301(4), discussed more fully at a later point.[57] But, setting aside the language in that section dealing with future advances made by a
secured party with knowledge of the lien, the "core" priority
rule is, at least arguably,[58] essentially the same as that in Section
9-301(1)(b); namely, if perfection is not accomplished with
respect to the future advance before the lien arises, the lienor
prevails.[59]

---

[55] 1962 U.C.C. § 9-204(1); 1972 U.C.C. § 9-203(1).

[56] The 1962 version of Section 9-301(1)(b) also requires that the lienor
not have knowledge of the security interest at the time of obtaining his
lien. For present purposes, this aspect of the rule will be ignored; that is,
it will be assumed that the lienor does not have such knowledge. As to the
time when a judicial lien is deemed to attach, that is, come into existence,
see § 1-3 B *supra*.

[57] § 4-1 A (3) *infra*.

[58] See § 4-1 A (3) *infra*.

[59] The words "while a security interest is perfected" in 1972 Section
9-301(4) lead to this conclusion.

As regards the timing of perfection, Section 9–303(1) provides that "[a] security interest is perfected when it has attached and when all of the applicable steps required for perfection have been taken." And it will be recalled that attachment takes place when the last of the three requirements listed in 1962 Section 9–204(1) or 1972 Section 9–203(1) is satisfied: the making of a security agreement, the giving of "value," and the acquisition of "rights" in the collateral by the debtor. Thus assuming that the filing of a financing statement is the "applicable step required for perfection," [60] four events are necessary for perfection: filing, the execution of a security agreement, the giving of "value," and the acquisition of "rights." The four events may occur in any order, and perfection takes place when, and only when, the last of the four occurs.

In light of the foregoing, the operation of paragraph (b) of Section 1–201(44), to the effect that a secured party gives "value" for rights if he acquires them as security for a pre-existing claim, is illustrated in the following situation: Bank lends funds to Debtor "on open account," that is, on an unsecured credit basis. Later, Debtor asks for an extension of time for repayment. Bank agrees, on the condition that it be given a security interest in equipment then owned by Debtor (that is, in which Debtor already has "rights"). Bank takes a security agreement and files a financing statement. Still later, an unsecured creditor obtains a judgment lien against Debtor's assets, consisting solely of the equipment in question. When Debtor defaults, the question arises: Which creditor has first claim on the equipment, assuming the resale value thereof will not satisfy both debts? The lien creditor might attempt to argue that the security interest was not perfected before his lien arose (and therefore that he takes priority under Section 9–301(1)(b)), even though the filing, security agreement, and "rights" requirements were satisfied prior thereto because "value" was not given—past consideration being no consideration under the general law of contracts. Pur-

---

[60] For a discussion of the types of situations in which filing is appropriate, see § 3–3 A *infra*.

suant to Section 1-201(44)(b), however, the bank will prevail, since the taking of a security interest for an antecedent debt suffices as "value."

The language in paragraph (b) of Section 1-201(44), to the effect that a binding commitment to extend credit constitutes "value," comes into play in the following type of situation: On January 1, Secured Party lends $10,000 to the debtor and takes a security interest in a piece of machinery then owned by the debtor. Secured Party contractually commits to make a future advance of an additional $5,000. On the same day, Secured Party files a financing statement. On January 15, an unsecured creditor obtains a lien on the debtor's property in the amount of $15,000. On February 1, Secured Party makes the obligatory advance. Does Secured Party have first claim on the machine for the full $15,000, or only for the initial $10,000 advance? The "rights," security agreement, and filing requirements for perfection having clearly been satisfied before the lien arose, the question is whether the remaining requirement—"value"—was also satisfied prior thereto or not until the $5,000 was actually advanced on February 1. Section 1-201(44)(a) makes it clear that value was given at the earlier time of the binding commitment to lend; thus attachment and perfection with respect to the future advance occurred prior to the time the lien arose, and the secured party has priority for the full $15,000.[61] The same would be true if the secured party had made no advance on January 1 but had loaned the entire $15,000 on February 1 pursuant to a binding commitment to do so entered into on January 1.

A more difficult question is presented when the security agreement provides only for voluntary future advances. Assume that a security agreement containing a clause providing for future advances to be made by the secured party at will is

---

[61] Other examples of a "binding commitment" satisfying the "value" requirement at the time of contracting include a promise to sell goods on credit to the future debtor and a promise to pay a third-party seller for goods the future debtor purchases.

executed on January 1. On the same day the debtor acquires rights in the collateral and the secured party advances $10,000 and files a financing statement. On January 15, an unsecured creditor obtains a lien. On February 1, the secured party makes an optional advance of an additional $5,000. Here the argument might be made that the secured party had two separate security interests—one for the initial $10,000 and another for the later $5,000—and that the latter did not attach and thus was not perfected until after the lien arose, "value" (in the absence of a prior binding commitment) not being given until the money was actually loaned on February 1. The prevailing view, at least among commentators, rejects this argument, however, on the notion that the two advances were secured by a single security interest (which simply increased in amount), with the initial $10,000 advance serving as sufficient "value" for the entire transaction under the "any consideration sufficient to support a simple contract" language of Section 1–201(44)(d).[62] Thus perfection with respect to the $5,000 advance was accomplished on January 1, prior to attachment of the lien, and the secured party takes priority for the full $15,000.[63] If one changes the facts, however, to assume that no initial advance was made on January 1 and that the entire $15,000 was loaned on February 1 under an optional future advance clause, then there would be no basis for finding "value" (and thus no attachment and no perfection) prior to attachment of the lien, and the security interest would be subordinated in its entirety to the lien.[64]

---

[62] This accords with the "peppercorn" theory of consideration under the law of contracts.

[63] The new language in Section 9–301(4) of the 1972 Code may or may not clinch this result. See § 4–1 A (3) *infra*. From a policy standpoint it can be argued that this outcome does not harm the lienor: He has lost the ability to realize upon the item serving as collateral for the security interest, but the addition of the future advance to the debtor's cash assets enhances the lienor's ability to recover therefrom. (It will be recalled that a judicial lien generally attaches to *all* of the debtor's assets.)

[64] This result is unaffected by the new language in Section 9–301(4),

§ 2-4. REQUIREMENT THAT THE DEBTOR HAVE "RIGHTS" IN THE COLLATERAL

The third requirement for attachment is that the debtor have "rights" in the collateral [65]—a term not defined in Article 9. Clearly the debtor has "rights" when he has full ownership and possession.[66] Possession without ownership will generally not suffice. Thus when a customer brings an appliance to a dealer merely for repairs, the dealer's inventory financer cannot assert a claim to the item.[67] But "rights" can arise without possession. It is widely accepted that a debtor obtains "rights" when he acquires a "special property interest" in goods under a contract for sale within the meaning of Section 2-501(1). Under that provision a "special property interest" arises at the time the goods are "identified" to the contract, which generally occurs: (1) when the contract is made, if the particular goods in question are in existence at that time and are described in the contract, or (2) if the contract is for the sale of future goods, when the goods are shipped, marked, or otherwise designated by the seller as the goods to which the contract refers.[68] Thus when a buyer-debtor and third-party seller enter into a contract for sale of a particular wood lathe (for example, "Serial Number 1234") then sitting in the seller's warehouse, "rights" are obtained for purposes of attachment and perfection of a security

---

discussed *infra* § 4-1 A (3). The outcome would be different if the intervening interest were that of a second secured party who took a security agreement, loaned funds, and filed on January 15: Assuming the governing priority rule to be Section 9-312(5) (discussed *infra* § 4-2 A (1)(a)), priority would go to the initial secured party by virtue of his having *filed* first, despite the fact that his interest would have been *perfected* second.

[65] 1972 U.C.C. § 9-203(1)(c); 1962 U.C.C. § 9-204(1).

[66] Thus in the ordinary case in which a bank makes a non-purchase-money loan against an automobile already owned by the debtor (as distinguished from a purchase money loan to enable the debtor to buy the auto), the "rights" requirement is satisfied at the outset.

[67] Likewise, a debtor who has stolen the property in question does not have "rights."

[68] Section 2-501(1), however, allows the parties to agree to some other time as the time for "identification."

interest taken by the debtor's equipment financer when the contract is entered into. But if the contract is for sale of *a* wood lathe of a certain type to be assembled by the seller on a future date, the debtor does not obtain "rights" until the machine is produced and tagged with his name. In either case "rights" are acquired (and thus the financer's security interest can attach and become perfected) before delivery of the machine to the debtor.

Section 9–204(2) of the 1962 Code specifies the time before which "rights" cannot be acquired in certain types of collateral; that is, no "rights" are obtainable in crops until they are planted or otherwise become growing crops, in the young of livestock until they are conceived, in fish until caught, in oil, gas, or minerals until extracted, in a contract right until the contract has been made, or in an account until it comes into existence. These guidelines, viewed by some as either self-evident,[69] unenlightening,[70] or confusing,[71] are omitted in the 1972 Code, leaving the courts to make the determination. Nevertheless, to the extent that they are helpful, these principles (albeit no longer explicitly stated) should obtain under the new Code. For instance, there can be no doubt that so long as minerals remain untouched in the ground they are part of the realty and no Article 9 security interest can attach as to them.

When does a debtor acquire "rights" in collateral covered by an after-acquired property clause?[72] At least arguably, there can be no "rights" and thus no attachment and perfection until the debtor actually acquires the item in question.[73] This does

---

[69] For example, it seems obvious that a debtor cannot have "rights" in chattels that have not yet come into existence, such as crops not yet planted.

[70] For instance, are fish swimming in a pond owned by a commercial grower "caught"? And at precisely what point in the mining process are minerals "extracted"?

[71] The statement that there can be no "rights" in an account until it comes into existence causes difficulties with regard to the vulnerability of "floating liens" to attack by a bankruptcy trustee. See § 6–3 B *infra*.

[72] Such clauses are sanctioned by Section 9–204. See § 2–2 D (2) *supra*.

[73] The "entity" theory adopted in some bankruptcy cases can be used to

not necessarily mean that the security interest is subordinated to intervening claims, however. Assume that on January 1 the secured party takes a security agreement giving him a security interest in the debtor's existing and after-acquired inventory, loans money, and files a financing statement. On January 15, an unsecured creditor obtains a judicial lien against the debtor's assets. On February 1, the debtor acquires a new item of inventory. On default, which creditor has priority with respect to the new item? If "rights" are not acquired until February 1, then attachment and perfection do not occur until then [74]—after the appearance of the lienor on the scene—and it might seem at first glance that the lienor will prevail under Section 9–301(1)(b). But it can be argued that the new item was not in existence for the lien to attach to (and hence, in essence, there was no lien with respect to the new item) until the debtor acquired it on February 1, and at the moment the new item did come into existence on that date, it was automatically covered by the perfected security interest, so that the lienor could not have satisfied the requirement of Section 9–301(1)(b) that he acquire his lien "before" perfection of the security interest; hence the secured party has priority.[75] And if the interest arising on January 15 were a competing security interest instead of a lien, the initial secured party would prevail under the first-to-file rule of Section 9–312(5).[76]

---

argue that attachment under a "floating lien" arrangement occurs at an earlier time. See § 6–3 B *infra*.

[74] The other requirements—filing, the giving of "value" and execution of the security agreement—were met on January 1.

[75] It can also be argued that the lien attaches simultaneously with perfection of the security interest—a situation not dealt with in the Code—and that therefore the lienor and secured party should share pro-rata.

For a discussion of the application of the argument in the text as a basis for upholding a "floating lien" arrangement against attack by a bankruptcy trustee, see § 6–3 B *infra*.

[76] See § 4–2 A (1)(a) *infra*. This assumes that the intervening interest is a non-purchase-money one. A purchase-money creditor would generally prevail over the initial secured party under Section 9–312(3). See §§ 4–2 B (1) and 4–2 B (2) *infra*.

3

Perfection of the Security Interest

§ 3-1. INTRODUCTION; TIMING OF PERFECTION

Section 9-303(1) states that a security interest is perfected "when it has attached and when all of the applicable steps required for perfection have been taken." In most cases, whether, and when, the security interest has been perfected determines whether the secured party has first claim on the collateral covered by the security interest as against the competing claim of a third party such as a lienor, a buyer from the debtor, another secured party or the debtor's bankruptcy trustee.[1] Although perfection does not always guarantee priority over such parties, it is usually a prerequisite thereto.

Article 9 provides for three basic methods of perfection: (1) the filing of a financing statement—the most frequent method; (2) the secured party's taking possession of the collateral—often referred to as the "pledge"; and (3) in a limited number of situations, attachment alone without the necessity of either filing or taking possession. Each of these methods (and a few other miscellaneous ones) will be discussed in this chapter. Which method or methods are appropriate in a given situation will depend on the classification of collateral, the type of transaction involved, or both.

It will be noted that perfection occurs when the requirements for attachment (in general, execution of the security agreement,

---

[1] Perfection, as distinguished from attachment, has no bearing on the secured party's rights against the debtor. See § 2-1 *supra*.

the giving of "value," and the debtor's acquisition of "rights")[2] have been met and any additional required step (for example, filing or the taking of possession) has been taken.[3] These elements may occur in any order, and perfection is accomplished when the last of them, whichever that may be, takes place. Thus when filing is appropriate, perfection takes place upon the occurrence of the last event listed in each of the following sequences: (1) filing, execution of the security agreement, the giving of "value," the acquisition of "rights"; (2) execution of the security agreement, filing, the acquisition of "rights," the giving of "value"; (3) the acquisition of "rights," execution of the security agreement, the giving of "value," filing. In the case of perfection upon attachment alone, delete filing from each of the foregoing sequences. When perfection is by possession, substitute the taking of possession for filing and omit the need for a written security agreement (although a verbal agreement is still necessary) in each of the sequences.[4]

§ 3–2. PERFECTION UPON ATTACHMENT— "AUTOMATIC" PERFECTION

In certain situations specified in Section 9–302(1), a security interest becomes perfected "automatically" when all of the requirements for attachment[5] have been satisfied, without the secured party's having to file or take possession of the collateral.

A. Purchase-Money Security Interests in Consumer Goods and Farm Equipment

The most important situation in which automatic perfection obtains is that involving a purchase money security interest in consumer goods, as referred to in Section 9–302(1)(d). Thus a department store that sells a stereo or refrigerator on credit to

---

[2] For a discussion of these requirements, see Chapter 2 *supra*.

[3] U.C.C. § 9–303(1).

[4] *See* U.C.C. §§ 9–203(1), 9–303(1), and Section 9–305, Comment 3.

[5] These requirements are found in 1962 U.C.C. § 9–204(1) and 1972 U.C.C. § 9–203(1).

Ms. Jones has a perfected security interest at the time of the sale—that is, when Ms. Jones has executed a security agreement, the store has given "value" in the form of an extension of credit, and Ms. Jones has a contractual "right" to the goods—without the necessity of filing a financing statement. This exemption from filing (or taking possession)[6] is said to be justified on the basis that the costs of requiring public notice would greatly outweigh the benefits. The costs to dealers of filing would include not only filing fees but, more importantly, personnel time spent on paperwork—costs that would often be disproportionate to the relatively small value of most consumer items and would curtail retail installment selling or increase the price to the consumer. Moreover, there is less need for public notice of financing of consumer purchases than in other situations, since it is common knowledge among creditors that consumer goods against which they may be asked to lend are likely to have been bought on secured credit and that the original seller may have a previous interest which, although unfiled, will have priority.[7]

It will be noted that Section 9–302(1)(d) permits automatic perfection only for *purchase money* security interests in *consumer* goods; that is, a secured party who has relied on automatic perfection and has not filed or taken possession may find himself unperfected and therefore subordinated to competing interests when (1) his security interest is deemed not to qualify as a "purchase money" interest under Section 9–107 or (2) he has misclassified as "consumer goods" an item which properly falls within some other category (such as "equipment") under Section 9–109. These two potential problems are discussed in

---

[6] Section 9–302(1)(d) may be referred to as simply an "exemption from filing," since the likelihood of the purchase money secured party's perfecting by taking possession of consumer goods is, practically speaking, remote.

[7] Not all states have subscribed to these rationales: A few have either entirely removed purchase money security interests in consumer goods from the list of exemptions in Section 9–302(1) or else require filing or possession when the purchase price of the goods exceeds a specified amount (for example, $1,000).

more detail elsewhere.[8] It should also be noted that automatic perfection is not available for motor vehicles for which license plates are required under state law [9] and is (depending on which version of the Code is in effect in the state) either unavailable or available only on a limited basis for fixtures. In the latter regard the 1962 Code disallows automatic perfection for security interests in fixtures in all circumstances, whereas the 1972 version of Section 9–302(1)(d) requires a fixture filing for protection against real estate claimants to the extent provided in Section 9–313 but allows automatic perfection as against other types of competing claimants.[10]

The secured party should bear in mind that there are two advantages in filing a purchase money security interest in consumer goods despite the exemption in Section 9–302(1)(d). First, under Section 9–307(2), a consumer buyer from a consumer debtor generally takes free of a security interest created by the latter, despite automatic perfection, unless the secured party has filed.[11] Second, under Section 9–306(3), filing ensures continuous perfection with respect to proceeds beyond the ten-day period after the debtor receives them.[12]

Section 9–302(1)(c) of the 1962 Code provides for automatic perfection of a purchase money security interest in farm equip-

---

[8] For a discussion of what constitutes a "purchase money" security interest, see § 4–2 B (4) infra. On distinguishing between the classifications of collateral set out in Section 9–109, see § 1–5 A (1) supra.

[9] U.C.C. § 9–302(1)(d). This is the meaning of the phrase "required to be licensed" under the 1962 Code version as well as the phrase "required to be registered," which was substituted for the former in the 1972 Code. Presumably the change was made because "licensed" appears nowhere else in the Code, whereas "registered" is the term used in 1972 Section 9–103 (2)(b). In most states a security interest in a vehicle required to be registered can be perfected only by compliance with the state certificate of title act. See §§ 3–3 A and 5–3 infra.

[10] See §§ 4–4 C (2)(b)(iii) and 4–4 F infra.

[11] See § 4–3 A (2)(b) infra.

[12] See § 4–3 B (4)(b) infra.

ment having a purchase price not in excess of $2,500.[13] This provision is omitted in the 1972 Code because it has proved more detrimental than beneficial to the farmer: Under it, creditors have been reluctant to lend against farm equipment for fear of subordination to a pre-existing purchase money security interest, whose existence would not be revealed by a filing search.[14]

B. *Temporary Perfection with Respect to Instruments, Documents, and Proceeds*

Section 9–302(1)(b) provides for automatic perfection of "a security interest temporarily perfected in instruments or documents without delivery under Section 9–304 or in proceeds for a 10 day period under Section 9–306." The ten-day period for proceeds is discussed in a subsequent chapter.[15] The present discussion focuses on temporary perfection under Section 9–304 —more specifically subsections (4) and (5) thereof, which provide for perfection in certain cases for a 21-day period even though the secured party has not filed and has allowed the debtor temporarily to have possession of the collateral.[16]

Section 9–304(4) states: "A security interest in instruments or negotiable documents is perfected without filing or the taking of possession for a period of 21 days from the time it attaches to the extent that it arises for new value given under a written security agreement." Encompassed within this provision are the so-called "day loans" made by banks to stockbrokers against corporate securities being traded on the market.[17] The lender

---

[13] Exceptions are made for fixtures and for vehicles required to be licensed.

[14] Such a security interest would have priority under Section 9–312(5).

[15] §§ 4–3 B (4)(a) and 4–3 B (5)(b) *infra.*

[16] Comment 4 to Section 9–304 observes that the reason for this temporary automatic perfection is that "no useful purpose would be served by cluttering the files with records of such exceedingly short term transactions."

[17] Such loans are typically made and repaid on the same day. It will be recalled that investment securities (for example, stocks and bonds) are within the definition of "instrument" in Section 9–105.

never takes possession of the stock certificates but rather leaves them in the stockbroker's hands so that the requirements of transfer from sellers to buyers can be effected—a practice sanctioned by Section 9–304(4), which, unlike Section 9–304(5), does not require that the secured party have already perfected its security interest [18] before the debtor takes possession. Section 9–304(4) would also cover the type of situation in which a bank that has acquired a security interest in a negotiable bill of lading by honoring drafts drawn by a seller of goods under a letter of credit turns the bill of lading over to the buyer-debtor so that the latter can obtain the goods. In such a case, however, the lender might wish to bring its transaction within Section 9–304(5) (as further discussed below) rather than Section 9–304(4) because of the difference between the sections with regard to the time of commencement of the 21-day period: Under Section 9–304(4) the period commences upon attachment of the security interest, whereas under Section 9–304(5) it does not begin to run until the document is turned over to the debtor.[19] Since the time of attachment may precede the time of turnover,[20] the lender may find itself with considerably less than 21 days left by the time the document is released to the debtor.

It will be noted that Section 9–304(4), unlike Section 9–304(5), imposes no limitation on the purpose for which the debtor is in possession but does require that the secured party have given new value under a written security agreement.

Subsection (5) of Section 9–304 provides that when a secured party who already has a perfected security interest in an instrument, negotiable document, or goods held by a bailee who has

---

[18] In the case of instruments, such perfection would necessitate the secured party's taking possession. U.C.C. § 9–304(1).

[19] U.C.C. § 9–304, Comment 4.

[20] Attachment will occur when the debtor has executed a security agreement, the secured party has made or contracted to make the loan, and the debtor has a contractual right to receive the goods from the seller. On the latter element, see § 2–4 *supra*.

issued a non-negotiable document [21] turns the collateral over to the debtor for one of the purposes specified in subsection (5)(a) or (5)(b), the security interest remains perfected for 21 days after the turnover without filing or possession.

Under subsection (5)(a) when goods or documents covering the goods are involved the turnover must be for a purpose looking toward sale by the debtor.[22] As noted previously, this provision embraces the type of situation in which a buyer obtains an advance for the purchase price of goods by persuading his bank to issue a letter of credit to the seller authorizing the latter to draw drafts on the bank.[23] When the bank in effect pays the seller for the goods by honoring the drafts, it obtains possession of the negotiable bill of lading issued by the carrier with whom the goods are shipped. Under Sections 9–305 and 9–304(2), the bank now has a perfected security interest in the document and the goods. The bank may wish to retain its perfected interest against the possibility of the buyer's failing to repay the loan; but at the same time the parties may anticipate that the buyer will make repayment with the proceeds obtained from reselling the goods within a short period of time, necessitating release of the bill of lading to the buyer so that he can obtain the goods. Section 9–304(5)(a) allows all of this to be accomplished, giving the bank a perfected interest for 21 days in the absence of filing or possession.[24]

---

[21] Perfection is accomplished by possession in the case of an instrument (Section 9–304(1)), by possession or filing in the case of a negotiable document (Sections 9–304(1) and 9–305), or by one of the three methods specified in Section 9–304(3) in the case of goods covered by a non-negotiable document. When perfection is by filing, the protection afforded by Section 9–304(5) is not needed.

[22] Subsection (5)(a) requires that the turnover be "for the purpose of ultimate sale or exchange or for the purpose of loading, unloading, storing, shipping, transshipping, manufacturing, processing or otherwise dealing with them in a manner preliminary to their sale or exchange."

[23] See U.C.C. § 9–304, Comment 4; U.C.C. § 9–303, Comment 2; and § 1–5 B (2)(a) *supra*.

[24] A cross-reference to Section 9–312(3) has been added to the 1972 Code version of Section 9–304(5)(a) for the reason discussed in § 4–2 B (2)(d)(iv) *infra*.

Subsection (5)(b) of Section 9–304 affords automatic perfection for 21 days in the case of an instrument delivered to the debtor "for the purpose of ultimate sale or exchange or of presentation, collection, renewal or registration of transfer." This provision would, for instance, enable a bank that holds shares of preferred stock as collateral to release the certificates temporarily to the owner-debtor for exchange with the issuer for common stock. Or the exchange might be for shares in another corporation in the case of a merger.

It will be noted that the automatic perfection afforded by Sections 9–304(4) and 9–304(5) is only temporary; at the end of the 21-day period, perfection ceases unless the secured party has satisfied the ordinary requirements of filing or taking possession.[25] It will also be noted that perfection under Section 9–304(4) or 9–304(5) is not necessarily proof against subordination: If the debtor transfers the collateral to a party in the nature of a bona fide purchaser of the sort protected under Section 9–309 [26] or Section 9–307(1),[27] the latter may take priority despite the fact that the security interest is perfected.

C. Isolated Assignments of Accounts

Under Section 9–302(1)(e) of the 1972 Code, a security interest is automatically perfected upon attachment without filing in the case of "an assignment of accounts which does not alone or in conjunction with other assignments to the same assignee transfer a significant part of the outstanding accounts of the assignor."[28] The courts have taken several factors into con-

---

[25] These requirements must be met before the end of the 21-day period in order for perfection to be continuous thereafter. U.C.C. § 9–303(2).

As stated in Comment 4 to 1972 Section 9–304, if the instruments, documents, or goods are sold during the 21-day period, perfection of the security interest in the proceeds is thereafter governed by the 10-day rule of Section 9–306(3). See § 4–3 B (4) infra.

[26] See § 4–3 A (4) infra.

[27] See § 4–3 A (2) infra.

[28] The only change from the 1962 Code is the elimination of the reference to "contract rights" in conformity with the change in Section 9–106, discussed supra § 1–5 C (1)(a).

sideration in determining what constitutes a "significant part" of the assignor's outstanding accounts under this language: (1) whether the assignment in question (taken in conjunction with other assignments to the same assignee) represents a substantial percentage of the total outstanding accounts of the assignor; [29] (2) whether the assignor was, or reasonably should have been, aware that the assignment was of a substantial percentage of the assignor's accounts; (3) whether the assignment was an "isolated" one (for example, the only assignment made by this assignee to this assignor) or was part of a regular course of financing; [30] and (4) whether the assignee is a professional financer in the business of taking assignments, such as a bank or finance company,[31] as opposed to a nonprofessional—in which case the exemption is less likely to apply. An assignment of a very large percentage of outstanding accounts may, however, be deemed outside the exemption even though made to a nonprofessional. In view of the uncertainty regarding the outcome in litigation in this area, the safest course is for the secured party to file.

It should be kept in mind that under Section 9–104(f) certain transfers of accounts, such as an assignment for the purpose of collection only, are entirely excluded from the coverage of Article 9.[32] In these cases non-Code law governs priority conflicts and Article 9 filing rules and exemptions therefrom are irrelevant. When there is doubt as to the applicability of the Section 9–104 exclusion, however, prudence dictates filing.

---

[29] There is no clear rule about what percentage suffices. The cutoff point may be as low as 20 per cent.

[30] Comment 5 to Section 9–302 refers to "casual or *isolated* assignments" as coming within the exemption and observes that "[a] person who *regularly* takes assignment of any debtor's accounts should file." (Emphasis added.)

[31] Comment 5 to Section 9–302 refers to "*casual* or isolated assignments" as falling within the exemption and observes that "[a]ny person who regularly takes assignments of *any* debtor's accounts should file." (Emphasis added.)

[32] See § 1–4 F (6) *supra*.

D. *Other Situations Involving Automatic Perfection*

Section 9–302(1)(f) exempts from filing a security interest of a collecting bank created under Section 4–208 [33] and a security interest arising under Article 2 on Sales.[34]

Two new automatic-perfection categories have been added in the 1972 version of Section 9–302(1): (1) a security interest created by an assignment of a beneficial interest in a trust or a decedent's estate,[35] and (2) "an assignment for the benefit of all creditors of the transferor and subsequent transfers by the assignee thereunder." [36] The first category was added with the awareness that a debtor's interest in property held in trust under a will or deed of trust is often not thought of as a type of collateral covered by Article 9,[37] and thus the filing requirement in the 1962 Code (the proper Article 9 classification being "general intangibles" under Section 9–106)[38] served as a trap for unsophisticated lenders. The exemption from filing for assignments for the benefit of creditors recognizes that these arrangements are not really financing transactions and that a debtor in this situation will not ordinarily be engaging in further credit transactions.[39]

---

[33] Assume that a depositary bank (Section 4–105) takes a check on deposit and permits the depositor to withdraw funds against the deposit before it (the depositary bank) collects from the drawee bank. If the drawee bank then dishonors the check, Section 4–208(1) gives the depositary bank a security interest which, under Section 4–209, enables it to assert holder-in-due-course status in suing the drawer and thereby overcome most defenses the drawer might assert (for example, that the check was given to the payee-depositor for merchandise which turned out to be defective). *See* U.C.C. §§ 3–307 and 3–305.

[34] See the discussion of Section 9–113 in § 1–4 E *supra.*

[35] 1972 U.C.C. § 9–302(1)(c).

[36] 1972 U.C.C. § 9–302(1)(g).

[37] 1972 U.C.C. § 9–302, Comment 5.

[38] Filing would be required under the 1962 Code. U.C.C. § 9–305, Comment 1.

[39] U.C.C. § 9–302, Comment 5.

§ 3–3. PERFECTION BY FILING

A. When Filing Is or Is Not Required or Permitted: Types of Collateral; National Filing or Registration Systems; Certificate of Title Laws

Security interests are most commonly perfected by the filing of a financing statement in the appropriate state or county office. Section 9–302 prescribes in a general way the situations in which filing is necessary; namely, for all security interests other than (1) those perfected by possession under Section 9–305,[40] (2) those perfected automatically upon attachment alone,[41] and (3) those subject to a non-Code filing, registration, or certificate of title system.[42] More specifically, filing is or is not required or permitted as follows: It is the only permissible method of perfecting a security interest in accounts,[43] contract rights (under the 1962 Code), and general intangibles—perfection by possession being unavailable for these types of collateral.[44] Filing is permissible as an alternative to possession for perfecting security interests in goods, negotiable documents, and chattel paper.[45] Filing is not available to perfect security interests in instruments (negotiable instruments and investment securities)—concerning which (except for temporary automatic perfection under Section 9–304(4), 9–304(5), or 9–306(3))[46] only possession will suffice.[47] Under Sections 9–302(3) and 9–302(4), filing under Article 9 is also ineffective when the security interest is subject to a federal statute providing for a non-Code national filing or registration system (for example, for interests in ships, certain

---

[40] U.C.C. § 9–302(1)(a).

[41] 1972 U.C.C. § 9–302(1)(b)–(g); 1962 U.C.C. § 9–302(1)(b)–(f). On situations involving automatic perfection, see § 3–2 *supra*.

[42] U.C.C. § 9–302(3) and (4).

[43] The exception in Section 9–302(1)(e) allowing automatic perfection with respect to isolated assignments of accounts is discussed *supra* § 3–2 C.

[44] U.C.C. § 9–304, Comment 1; U.C.C. § 9–305, Comment 1.

[45] U.C.C. §§ 9–305 and 9–304(1).

[46] See § 3–2 B *supra*.

[47] U.C.C. § 9–304(1).

motor vehicles operated interstate, railroad rolling stock, aircraft, copyrights, patents, and trademarks)[48] or covers a motor vehicle for which a certificate of title must be obtained under a state statute.[49] Compliance with such a statute is (for example, for purposes of the Article 9 priority rules) equivalent to the filing of a financing statement under the Code.[50]

B. Contents of the Financing Statement

(1) In General; Minor Errors Not Seriously Misleading

The requirements regarding what must be filed in order for the secured party's interest to be perfected by filing are set out in Section 9–402. The vast majority of filings—whether in a local or central office—are made on a standard-form financing statement called "Form UCC-1," which has been approved for use in filing offices in a great many states. When both a local and central filing are to be made, "Form UCC-2"—which, at least in states that still have the 1962 Code in force, is usually virtually identical to Form UCC-1 [51]—may be used for the local filing. In states that have adopted the 1972 Code, there will be at least a few changes in Form UCC-1 and perhaps extensive changes in Form UCC-2,[52] with the latter possibly being the only standard form for local filing. A typical form UCC-1 in use

---

[48] For citations to, and brief discussions of, the relevant federal legislation, see the footnotes to § 1–4 F (1) *supra*. To the extent that aspects of the security transaction other than filing (for example, priorities and rights on default) are not covered by the federal statute, the rules of Article 9 remain applicable. See the last sentence of 1972 Section 9–302(4).

[49] Article 9 filing remains necessary, however, for security interests in vehicles held by a dealer as inventory (which interests are, in any event, excluded from most certificate of title laws). On the operation of certificate of title acts (which sometimes extend to pleasure boats and mobile homes), see § 5–3 *infra*. In respects other than perfection (for example, priorities and default), Article 9 rules continue to control.

[50] 1972 U.C.C. § 9–302(4).

[51] Form UCC-2 usually has fewer carbon copies.

[52] The changes in Form UCC-2 particularly reflect the new language in 1972 Section 9–402(5), discussed *infra* § 3–3 B (6).

under the 1962 Code is set out in Figure 1; examples of forms UCC-1 and UCC-2 in use under the 1972 Code are set out in Figures 2 and 3, respectively.[53] The relative brevity of these forms reflects the Code's adoption of a "notice" filing system whereunder what is required to be filed is not the entire security agreement (although Section 9–402(1) *permits* filing of a copy of the security agreement in lieu of a financing statement)[54] but only a short notice containing just enough information to alert file searchers that a security interest *may* exist in the collateral in question and that further inquiry should be made of the parties to ascertain the complete state of affairs.[55] Section 9–402 requires that the financing statement contain the following:

(1) Names of the debtor and secured party

(2) Addresses of the debtor and secured party

(3) Signature of the debtor and, under the 1962 Code, of the secured party, and

(4) A description of the collateral covered by the security

---

[53] Standard-form financing statements, if properly filled in, contain the information required in Section 9–402, as outlined in Section 9–402(3).

[54] If the secured party avails himself of this option, care must be taken to see that the security agreement contains all of the information and the signatures required in a financing statement. Items that will most commonly need to be added to bring the ordinary security agreement into compliance are the addresses of the parties and, where the 1962 Code is in effect, the signature of the secured party. Because a copy of the security agreement will be on larger-sized paper than a Form UCC-1 (thereby necessitating special storage facilities) and will often be lengthier, many filing officers charge extra for such a filing. See the reference to "standard form" filings in 1972 Section 9–402(5).

[55] U.C.C. § 9–402, Comment 2. Section 9–208 provides the mechanism for further inquiry: The prospective creditor or purchaser may ask the debtor to obtain from the secured party information concerning the amount of unpaid indebtedness, the items of collateral covered by the security interest, or both—information that the secured party is required to give to the debtor (but, in the interest of restricting information to parties with a legitimate need to know, not to anyone else).

UNIFORM COMMERCIAL CODE—FINANCING STATEMENT—FORM UCC-1 [1962 Code]

INSTRUCTIONS

1. PLEASE TYPE this form. Fold only along the perforation for mailing.
2. Remove Secured Party and Debtor copies and send other 3 copies with interleaved carbon paper to the filing officer. Enclose filing fee of $4.00.
3. When filing is to be with more than one office, Form 2 may be placed over this set to avoid double typing.
4. If the space provided for any item(s) on the form is inadequate the item(s) should be continued on additional sheets, preferably 5″ x 8″ or 8″ x 10″. Only one copy of such additional sheets need be presented to the filing officer with a set of three copies of the financing statement. Long schedules of collateral, indentures, etc., may be on any size paper that is convenient for the secured party.
5. If collateral is crops or goods which are or are to become fixtures, describe generally the real estate and give name of record owner.
6. When a copy of the security agreement is used as a financing statement, it is requested that it be accompanied by a completed but unsigned set of these forms, without extra fee.
7. At the time of original filing, filing officer should return third copy as an acknowledgment. At a later time, secured party may date and sign Termination Legend and use third copy as a Termination Statement.

This STATEMENT is presented to a filing officer for filing pursuant to the Uniform Commercial Code.

1 Debtor(s) (Last Name First) and address(es)	2 Secured Party(ies) and address(es)	3 Maturity date (if any):
		For Filing Officer (Date, Time, Number, and Filing Office)

4 The financing statement covers the following types (or items) of property:

ASSIGNEE OF SECURED PARTY

Check ☒ if covered: ☐ Proceeds of Collateral are also covered ☐ Products of Collateral are also covered No. of additional Sheets presented:

Filed with:

By: ....   By: ....

Signature(s) of Debtor(s)   Signature of Secured Party

(STANDARD)

(1) FILING OFFICER COPY—ALPHABETICAL

Figure 1.

STATE OF ILLINOIS

UNIFORM COMMERCIAL CODE—FINANCING STATEMENT—FORM UCC-1   [1972 Code]

INSTRUCTIONS:

1. PLEASE TYPE this form. Fold only along perforation for mailing.
2. Remove Secured Party and Debtor copies and send other 3 copies with interleaved carbon paper to the filing officer. Enclose filing fee.
3. If the space provided for any item(s) on the form is inadequate the item(s) should be continued on additional sheets, preferably 5″ x 8″ or 8″ x 10″. Only one copy of such additional sheets need be presented to the filing officer with a set of three copies of the financing statement. Long schedules of collateral, indentures, etc., may be on any size paper that is convenient for the secured party.

This STATEMENT is presented to a filing officer for filing pursuant to the Uniform Commercial Code.

Debtor(s) (Last Name First) and address(es)

Secured Party(ies) and address(es)

For Filing Officer
(Date, Time, Number, and Filing Office)

ASSIGNEE OF SECURED PARTY

1. This financing statement covers the following types (or items) of property:

2. ☐ Products of Collateral are also covered.

___ Additional sheets presented.
___ Filed with Office of Secretary of State of Illinois.
___ Debtor is a transmitting utility as defined in UCC § 9-105.

By: ....
        Signature of (Debtor)   (Secured Party)*

* Signature of Debtor Required in Most Cases:
  Signature of Secured Party in Cases Covered by UCC § 9-402(2)

(1) FILING OFFICER COPY—ALPHABETICAL   This form of financing statement is approved by the Secretary of State.
STANDARD FORM—UNIFORM COMMERCIAL CODE—FORM UCC-1—REV. 1975

Figure 2.

STATE OF ILLINOIS

UNIFORM COMMERCIAL CODE—FINANCING STATEMENT—FORM UCC-2   [1972 Code]

INSTRUCTIONS:

1. PLEASE TYPE this form. Fold only along perforation for mailing.
2. Remove Secured Party and Debtor copies and send other 3 copies with interleaved carbon paper to the filing officer. Enclose filing fee.
3. If the space provided for any item(s) on the form is inadequate the item(s) should be continued on additional sheets, preferably 5″ x 8″ or 8″ x 10″. Only one copy of such additional sheets need be presented to the filing officer with a set of three copies of the financing statement. Long schedules of collateral, indentures, etc., may be on any size paper that is convenient for the secured party.

This STATEMENT is presented to a filing officer for filing pursuant to the Uniform Commercial Code.

Debtor(s) (Last Name First) and address(es)	Secured Party(ies) and address(es)	For Filing Officer (Date, Time, Number, and Filing Office)
		ASSIGNEE OF SECURED PARTY

1. This financing statement covers the following types (or items) of property:

2. (If collateral is crops) The above described crops are growing or are to be grown on:
   (Describe Real Estate)

3. (If applicable) The above goods are to become fixtures on (The above timber is standing on . . .) (The above minerals or the like (including oil and gas) or accounts will be financed at the wellhead or minehead of the well or mine located on . . .) (Strike what is inapplicable) (Describe Real Estate)

   and this financing statement is to be filed in the real estate records. (If the debtor does not have an interest of record) The name of a record owner is

4. ☐ Products of Collateral are also covered.

—— Additional sheets presented.
—— Filed with Recorder's Office of .... County, Illinois.

By: ....
Signature of (Debtor)   (Secured Party)*

* Signature of Debtor Required in Most Cases:
  Signature of Secured Party in Cases Covered by UCC § 9-402(2)

(1) FILING OFFICER COPY—ALPHABETICAL   This form of financing statement is approved by the Secretary of State.
STANDARD FORM—UNIFORM COMMERCIAL CODE—FORM UCC-2—REV. 4-73

Figure 3.

interest and, in certain cases, of the real estate with which
the collateral is associated.

Great care should be taken to fill in each of these items properly,
since a failure to comply with the requirements of Section 9–402
may invalidate the filing, precluding perfection, and resulting
in subordination of the security interest to the claims of third
parties. If a mistake has been made, however, it should be kept
in mind that the secured party has a possible defense based on
the language of the last subsection of Section 9–402: "A financing statement substantially complying with the requirements of
this section is effective even though it contains minor errors
which are not seriously misleading." [56] As stated in the comment, the intent of this language is "to discourage the fanatical
and impossibly refined reading of . . . statutory requirements
in which courts have occasionally indulged themselves." [57]
Many courts have heeded this admonition.

(2) Names of the Parties

Section 9–402(1) requires that the financing statement show
the names of the debtor and the secured party. [58] Of the two,
accuracy in the debtor's name is the more critical: Since financing statements are indexed in filing offices alphabetically by the
last names of debtors, [59] an error therein may cause the filing
officer to insert the statement in the wrong place in the files,
with the result that a person searching the records may miss the
filing and extend credit against the collateral or purchase it on

---

[56] 1972 U.C.C. § 9–402(8); 1962 U.C.C. § 9–402(5).

[57] 1972 U.C.C. § 9–402, Comment 9; 1962 U.C.C. § 9–402, Comment 5.

[58] Blank spaces for the name and address of the debtor and of the
secured party are provided at the top of Form UCC-1. See Figures 1 and 2,
§ 3–3 B (1) *supra.* The name requirement is not expressly stated in the
1962 version of Section 9–402(1), but it is implied; *see* 1962 U.C.C.
§ 9–402(3).

[59] Thus the debtor's name (as well as the secured party's) should be listed
in "last name first" order—a requirement that, although not explicit, seems
inherent in the system and is reflected in the instructions on Form UCC-1.

the erroneous assumption that it is unencumbered. Indeed, the degree of likelihood that a party examining the files with reasonable care would find the financing statement serves (or at least should serve) as the basis for a court's deciding whether the defect in question is fatal or is merely a "minor error not seriously misleading." Thus a misspelling of the debtor's last name that results in misindexing is likely to cause the filing to fail; whereas an error in the first name is less likely to do so.[60] But even an error in the last name in the name-and-address block may be excused when the name *is* correctly reflected in the signature and the filing officer, catching the discrepancy, indexes under the correct name.

An error commonly resulting in invalidation of the financing statement is the use of a trade name for a sole proprietorship instead of the debtor-owner's individual name—for example, "Carolyn's Fashion Shop" instead of "Carolyn Hill."[61] The rule that a trade name is insufficient, applied by courts under the 1962 Code even though not expressly stated therein, is made explicit in the first sentence of Section 9-402(7) of the 1972 Code: "A financing statement sufficiently shows the name of the debtor if it gives the individual, partnership or corporate name of the debtor, whether or not it adds other trade names or names of partners."[62] The new Code provides for the *addition* of a

---

[60] It may be assumed that a near-miss ("Jon" for "John") is less likely to be fatal than a complete misstatement ("George" for "John"), particularly in a small community.

[61] An error in a trade name/ assumed name/ fictitious name/ "d.b.a." name that is listed *in addition* to the correct individual name is, however, likely to be considered inconsequential.

[62] The reasoning is that "[t]rade names are . . . too uncertain and too likely not to be known to the . . . person searching the record." 1972 U.C.C. § 9-402, Comment 7. An argument can be made that the statutory language does not *forbid* the use of a trade name alone, but the language of Comment 7 ("contemplates filing only in the individual name, not in a trade name") and the similar use of the word "sufficient" in Section 9-402(1), the language of which is universally considered mandatory, indicate that the use of a trade name alone is impermissible.

trade name (for example, "Carolyn Hill, d/b/a Carolyn's Fashion Shop"), however, at the secured party's option.[63] The quoted language also points out that the name of a partnership rather than the names of the partners or trade names should be used for a partnership debtor and that the exact corporate name of a corporate debtor should be shown.[64]

In order to clear up uncertainty under the 1962 Code regarding the need for a new filing after a change in the debtor's name, identity, or corporate structure (as when a proprietorship or partnership incorporates or a corporation is absorbed in a merger),[65] Section 9–402(7) of the 1972 Code provides that when the change renders a previously filed financing statement seriously misleading a new filing showing the new name and so forth must be made concerning collateral acquired more than four months after the change.[66] The old financing statement will continue to protect collateral acquired before the change (and during the four-month period), however, so that refiling is required only in "floating lien" type arrangements when the collateral turns over, not in "one shot" financing situations.

The last sentence of Section 9–402(7) of the 1972 Code answers a question much debated under the 1962 Code by providing that when collateral is transferred by the debtor there need not be a new filing naming the transferee—even when the

---

[63] 1972 Section 9–403(5) provides for indexing under the trade name in addition to the individual name if the secured party wishes.

[64] However, the omission or incorrect spelling or abbreviation of a suffix such as "Company" or "Incorporated" is likely to be deemed a "minor error not seriously misleading." See § 3–3 B (1) *supra*. But the use of the name of a division of a corporate debtor is highly perilous.

[65] Under the 1962 Code, which is silent on the question, courts have generally held that a refiling is not necessary except when the creditor knew at the outset of the security transaction that the debtor's name would later be changed.

[66] In order to enjoy continuous perfection, the secured party must make the new filing before the end of the four-month period. The new statement may be signed by the secured party instead of the debtor. 1972 U.C.C. § 9–402(2).

secured party "knows of or consents to" the transfer.[67] This relieves the secured party of the necessity of constantly checking on whether the debtor has disposed of the collateral and imposes on prospective creditors the burden of ascertaining the existence of a prior owner and searching the files under that name.[68] To the extent that the words "or consents to" in the quoted phrase are inconsistent with the rule in Section 9-306(2) that a security interest is terminated by the secured party's authorization to the debtor to dispose of the collateral,[69] they should be ignored as an error in drafting.

Errors in the secured party's name on the financing statement are less likely to be deemed fatal than errors in the debtor's name, since, as noted, indexing is based on the latter. As long as what *is* disclosed would lead a reasonably diligent searcher to the creditor's identity, the defect should be regarded as a "minor error not seriously misleading."[70] A question not expressly dealt with by either version of the Code is whether it is sufficient for the financing statement to show the name of a nominee creditor or agent acting on behalf of multiple lenders. The courts have answered in the affirmative, citing the "mere notice calling for further inquiry" function of Code filing.[71] The Code also makes it clear that when a secured party assigns a perfected security interest to another, the latter need not refile in order to maintain perfected status against creditors of, and transferees from, the original debtor.[72]

---

[67] This provision applies, for instance, when a partnership or proprietorship incorporates and transfers encumbered assets to the resultant corporation.

[68] The apparent harshness to lenders who extend credit without having discovered the existence of a security interest created by a former owner is mitigated by Sections 9-307(1) and 9-308, under which certain purchasers of goods and chattel paper, respectively, take free of a security interest irrespective of its perfected status. See §§ 4-3 A (2)(a) and 4-3 A (3) *infra.*

[69] See § 4-3 A (1) *infra.*

[70] On "minor errors not seriously misleading," see § 3-3 B (1) *supra.*

[71] See § 3-3 B (1) *supra.*

[72] U.C.C. § 9-302(2).

The 1972 Code contains a new provision, Section 9–408, which permits a lessor or consignor to file a financing statement using the terms "consignor," "consignee," "lessor," "lessee," or the like, instead of the "secured party" and "debtor" labels called for in Section 9–402, in leases or consignments not intended as security.[73]

(3) Addresses

Section 9–402(1) requires that the financing statement show "an address of the secured party from which information concerning the security interest may be obtained" and "a mailing address of the debtor." Here inaccuracies are likely to be considered "minor errors not seriously misleading,"[74] so long as the information given would ultimately put a reasonably diligent searcher in touch with the party in question. Thus a former address, a post-office box number, an address from which mail is forwarded, and even the name of a city alone (when the city was small and the debtor was a one-of-a-kind organization) have been held sufficient. On the other hand, courts have generally invalidated the filing when the address of one or both parties was completely omitted.[75]

(4) Signatures

Section 9–402(1) of the 1962 Code requires that both the debtor and the secured party sign the financing statement. The purpose of requiring the debtor's signature is to guard against an unwarranted filing giving the misleading appearance that the debtor's property is encumbered. But the requirement that the secured party sign serves no purpose other than to ensnare the occasional unwary creditor who inadvertently fails to com-

---

[73] See 1972 U.C.C. § 9–408, Comment 2 and §§ 1–4 B and 1–4 C supra.

[74] 1972 U.C.C. § 9–402(8); 1962 U.C.C. § 9–402(5). See § 3–3 B (1) supra.

[75] A few cases have upheld the financing statement even in the face of a complete omission when the address in question was or should have been known to third parties.

ply.[76] Consequently, the 1972 Code eliminates the need for the secured party's signature, and even under the 1962 Code the majority of courts have excused omission of the secured party's signature as a "minor error not seriously misleading." [77] The absence of the debtor's signature, however, is one of the surest grounds for invalidation of the financing statement under either version of the Code.

As to what is meant by "signed," the term is broadly defined in Section 1–201(39) to include "any symbol executed or adopted by a party with present intention to authenticate a writing." The accompanying comment observes that a signature need not be complete and, so long as adopted with intent to authenticate, may be printed, stamped, or written, may consist of initials or a thumbprint, and may be on any part of the document including a billhead or letterhead.[78] In accordance with this permissive language, courts have, for instance, upheld as a valid signature the name of a debtor-corporation typed or handwritten on the signature line without any accompanying agent's signature and, obversely, the manual signature of an agent with no showing of representative capacity or of the corporation's name on the signature line.[79] Signatures in such form are, of course, not recommended. The signature of an organization is ordinarily made by typing the name of the organization and placing underneath it the word "by" followed by the manually inscribed signature of the agent and a designation of his office or representative capacity ("by John Jones, Presi-

---

[76] According to the Reasons for 1972 Change following Section 9–402 of the 1972 Code, this requirement "has sometimes misled secured parties, who are accustomed to pre-Code practice and real estate practice under which only the debtor . . . need sign such instruments as chattel mortgages and real estate mortgages."

[77] See § 3–3 B (1) *supra.*

[78] U.C.C. § 1–201, Comment 39. There is no need for acknowledgement before a notary public, for witnesses, or for affidavits of good faith. U.C.C. § 9–402, Comment 3.

[79] In the latter instance, however, the name was shown in the name and address blank.

dent"). It will be noted that the validity of a signature made by an agent hinges not only on authentication but also on the existence of authority to sign for the principal under the rules of agency law.[80]

The last sentence of Section 9–402(1) of the 1972 Code contains a new provision permitting the filing of a photocopy of a financing statement or security agreement "if the security agreement so provides or if the original has been filed in this state," [81] overturning a holding under the 1962 Code that such a copy was not "signed."

In a few special situations listed in Section 9–402(2), the debtor need not sign the financing statement; the secured party's signature suffices. This is true under both the 1962 and 1972 versions of the Code: (1) when collateral already subject to a security interest in one state is removed to another,[82] and (2) when a filing regarding proceeds is necessary under Section 9–306(3) if the security interest in the original collateral was perfected.[83] Three new instances in which the secured party alone may sign are added in the 1972 Code: (1) when the debtor's location is changed to another state,[84] (2) when a new filing is necessitated by lapse of the initial filing,[85] and (3) when a new filing is required under 1972 Section 9–402(7) because of

---

[80] *See* U.C.C. § 1–103.

[81] This relieves a secured party who has obtained only one signed original and then later discovered the need for multiple filings (as in two or more counties) of the necessity of going back to a possibly uncooperative debtor for further signing.

[82] U.C.C. § 9–402(2)(a). The fact that the collateral was brought into the new state must be stated on the financing statement. On the need for filing in the new state, see Section 9–103, discussed in Chapter 5 *infra*.

[83] U.C.C. § 9–402(2)(b). The financing statement must describe the original collateral. On Section 9–306(3), see § 4–3 B (4) *infra*.

[84] 1972 U.C.C. § 9–402(2)(a). That such a change has occurred must be specified in the financing statement. The new provision meshes with 1972 Section 9–103(3), discussed *infra* § 5–4 B.

[85] 1972 U.C.C. § 9–402(2)(c). On the subject of lapse under Section 9–402(2), see § 3–3 F *infra*.

a change in the debtor's name, identity, or corporate structure.[86] In all of these situations the debtor may be unavailable or, having already obtained the credit he desires, may be unjustifiably uncooperative about signing the new financing statement.

(5) Description of Collateral

Section 9–402(1) requires that the financing statement contain a statement "indicating the types or describing the items of collateral." As is true with respect to the collateral description required in the security agreement,[87] defects in this regard may consist of a complete omission of the description, a misclassification or erroneous identification of the collateral, or an overly broad description. The complete absence of a description—as when the secured party sets out on a separate page a list of property too lengthy to fit on a Form UCC-1 and then neglects to attach the page to the Form UCC-1—is virtually certain to cause invalidation of the filing, resulting in loss of perfection. Also likely to be fatal is a misclassification of the property under the Article 9 collateral categories (for example, "equipment" versus "inventory")[88] or a major inaccuracy in identifying the collateral (for example, "generator" versus "drill press"). These defects, of course, mislead credit searchers concerning what property is encumbered. An insubstantial error, however, such as a misstatement of one digit in an eleven-digit serial number, is likely to be excused as a "minor error not seriously misleading." [89]

Insofar as claims of overbroadness are concerned,[90] the key

---

[86] 1972 U.C.C. § 9–402(2)(d). See § 3–3 B (2) *supra*.

[87] U.C.C. § 9–203(1). See § 2–2 C *supra*.

[88] For a discussion of the various categories of collateral under Article 9, see § 1–5 *supra*. On distinguishing between the subcategories of goods listed in Section 9–109, see § 1–5 A (1) *supra*.

[89] 1972 U.C.C. § 9–402(8); 1962 U.C.C. § 9–402(5). See § 3–3 B (1) *supra*.

[90] The two basic difficulties with an overly broad description are (1) that it may create a cloud on the debtor's property, impairing his ability to obtain financing elsewhere and that (2) it may reflect creditor overreaching by way of an attempt to claim more security vis-à-vis third parties than is warranted.

provision is Section 9–110, which provides: "For the purposes of this Article any description of personal property . . . is sufficient whether or not it is specific if it reasonably identifies what is described." [91] Also of importance is the fact that Section 9–402 contemplates only "notice filing," with the financing statement serving merely to put credit searchers on notice that the secured party "*may* have a security interest in the collateral described" and that "[f]urther inquiry will be necessary to disclose the complete state of affairs." [92] Hence although descriptions such as "all assets" or "all personal property of the debtor" are likely to be struck down,[93] descriptions couched in terms of the Article 9 collateral categories are generally deemed acceptable. This is particularly true of references to "all accounts" or "all inventory" (assuming the security agreement indeed contemplates coverage of "all")—types of collateral that turn over under "floating lien" arrangements.[94] Also although there are holdings to the contrary, the weight of authority recognizes the validity of "all equipment" descriptions. More doubtful, however, are references to "all consumer goods."

It will be noted that when the collateral description in the security agreement differs from that in the financing statement —as when the latter refers to "all" equipment or inventory, whereas the former lists only some items of equipment or perhaps only one or two lines of inventory—the less inclusive de-

---

[91] The Comment to Section 9–110 observes that the quoted language was intended to overrule cases under pre-Code chattel security laws that required descriptions "of the most exact and detailed nature."

[92] U.C.C. § 9–402, Comment 2 (emphasis added).

[93] Such descriptions are too general to fit within the "items"/"types" language of Section 9–402(1).

[94] The reasoning is that accounts or inventory not yet in existence are not capable of description at the time of initial filing and that it would be unduly burdensome to expect the secured party to refile on each new item when the collateral changes on a daily basis. *See* U.C.C. § 9–402, Comment 2. Note that the same comment points out the absence of any need for a reference to after-acquired property in the financing statement (although such a reference may be necessary in the security agreement, as discussed *supra* § 2–2 D (2)). On "floating liens," see § 2–2 D (2) *supra*.

scription is generally determinative, leaving the secured party unprotected against the claims of third parties concerning the excess.

(6) Description of Real Estate and Other Requirements for Filings Covering Realty-Associated Collateral; Mortgage as Fixture Filing

Section 9–402(1) of the 1962 Code requires that a financing statement covering crops or fixtures describe not only the chattels but also the real estate involved. The 1972 Code retains unchanged the requirement of a realty description for crop filings.[95] But new Section 9–402(5) establishes more extensive requirements for financing statements filed against fixtures [96] and applies those requirements to financing statements covering timber to be cut, minerals (including oil and gas), and accounts arising from the sale of minerals at the wellhead or minehead [97] as well. Under the new requirements the financing statement must (1) state that it covers whichever of the foregoing types of collateral is involved, (2) specify that it is to be filed in the real estate records, (3) describe the real estate, and (4) show the name of a record owner of the real estate (in addition to the name of the debtor) if the debtor does not have an interest of record in the realty. These requirements mesh with the new provision in 1972 Section 9–403(7) requiring the filing officer to index financing statements covering realty-related collateral in the real estate records [98] (as distinguished from the ordinary UCC filing

---

[95] 1972 U.C.C. § 9–402(1).

[96] On the subject of fixtures, see § 4–4 *infra*. On fixture filings, defined in 1972 Section 9–313(1)(b), see § 4–4 F *infra*. Fixture filings when the debtor is a transmitting utility are excluded from Section 9–402(5) because of the provision for central filing in this situation in Section 9–401(5), discussed *infra* § 3–3 C (4).

[97] The minerals and accounts referred to are those subject to 1972 Section 9–103(5), as discussed *infra* § 5–6.

[98] The section does not require that financing statements covering crops be so indexed, however, there being no requirement in Section 9–401(1) that crop filings be made in the real estate records. This explains why the

records) in the same fashion as a real estate mortgage would be indexed—the purpose being to ensure that the filing will be found by one conducting a real estate search (for example, a prospective purchaser or mortgagee of the realty who might not think to check the chattel records). The requirement of naming a record owner ensures that the financing statement will be discovered even though the debtor's name is not found in the real estate chain of title.[99]

Unless the state in question has adopted the optional language in 1972 Section 9–402(5) requiring that the real estate description be "sufficient if it were contained in a mortgage of the real estate to give constructive notice of the mortgage under the law of this state," the description need not be a formal "legal description" (for example, by metes and bounds) of the sort used in conveyancing; a street address in a city ("1234 South Elm Street, Birmingham, Alabama"), a general description in a rural area ("Farm of Samuel H. Jones, four miles south of Winston, Douglas County, Georgia"), a guide to a recorded map or plat ("Lot 273 of Woodland Hills No. 7 as recorded in Plat Book 9 at page 37 in the Probate Office of Tuscaloosa County, Alabama"), or incorporation by reference to a deed or mortgage containing a legal description will suffice.[100] On the other hand, an unduly vague description of the real estate, or the total absence thereof, will invalidate the filing.

---

reference to crops is found in Section 9–402(1) and not in Section 9–402(5). A real estate description in connection with crops is simply a useful method of describing fungible collateral (that is, of indicating which crops are covered).

[99] 1972 Section 9–403 (7) requires the filing officer to index the financing statement in the real estate records under the name of any record owner shown therein. Under 1972 Section 9–313(4)(a) and (b), a fixture filing is effective against real estate claimants even though the debtor does not have an interest of record if he is in possession. See § 4–4 C (2)(b)(i) and 4–4 C (3)(b) *infra*.

[100] See Comment 5 to 1972 Section 9–402 and Reasons for 1972 Change to that section. See also Section 9–110, which provides that "any description of . . . real estate is sufficient whether or not it is specific if it reasonably identifies what is described."

Section 9–402(6) of the 1972 Code contains a new provision recognizing that a real estate mortgage [101] duly recorded under real property law which contains language creating a security interest in a fixture may serve double duty as a fixture filing under Article 9, provided that the contents of the mortgage satisfy the normal requirements for a financing statement covering a fixture.[102]

(7) Need for Reference to Proceeds, Products, Future Advances, and After-Acquired Property

Section 9–306(3)(a) of the 1962 Code requires that the secured party assert a claim in the financing statement to proceeds the debtor may obtain from sale of the original collateral as a condition to having an automatically perfected interest in the proceeds beyond the ten-day period after the debtor receives them.[103] This requirement is reflected in the reference to "proceeds" in the last paragraph of the list of required contents for the financing statement in 1962 Section 9–402(3) and is manifested on the typical standard-form financing statement (Form UCC-1)[104] as a "proceeds" box to be checked. The 1972 Code, on the other hand, omits from Section 9–306(3) the requirement of claiming proceeds in the financing statement [105] and omits the reference thereto in Section 9–402(3), with the result that the

---

[101] The term "mortgage" is defined in 1972 Section 9–105(1)(j) as "a consensual interest created by a real estate mortgage, a trust deed on real estate, or the like." There is no definition in the 1962 Code.

[102] These requirements are set forth in Sections 9–402(1) and 9–402(5). For further discussion, see § 4–4 G *infra*. In view of the long-term nature of financing under the typical real estate mortgage, the effective life of a fixture filing via mortgage recordation is not limited to the usual five-year period; under 1972 Section 9–402(6), the filing is good for the duration of the obligation. See § 3–3 F *infra* and 1972 U.C.C. § 9–403, Comment 2.

[103] For further discussion, see § 4–3 B (4)(b)(i) *infra*.

[104] See § 3–3 B (1) *supra*.

[105] On the reasoning behind the change, see § 4–3 B (4)(b)(ii) *infra*. For a discussion of the parallel change in regard to the need for making reference to proceeds in the security agreement, see § 2–2 D (1) *supra*.

Form UCC-1 used under the new Code no longer contains a "proceeds" box to be checked.

Under Section 9–315(1)(b) of both the 1962 and 1972 versions of the Code, a secured party who finances goods that are to be manufactured, processed, assembled or commingled with other goods to form a finished product without losing their identity and who wishes his security interest to carry over into the product must assert a claim to products in the financing statement.[106] This requirement is reflected in the reference to "products" in the last paragraph of the list of required contents for the financing statement in Section 9–402(3) and is manifested on Form UCC-1 as a "products" box to be checked.

Comment 5 to 1972 Section 9–204 and Comment 2 to 1972 Section 9–402 clearly state what is widely recognized under the 1962 Code: There is no need to refer to after-acquired property or future advances in the financing statement.[107]

C. *Place of Filing*

Determining the proper place to file the financing statement is just as important to the secured party as properly drafting it: A filing in the wrong place will (except in the limited circumstances set out in Section 9–401(2)) be ineffective to perfect the security interest, usually resulting in loss of priority to third-party claimants.[108] Accordingly, cautious practitioners follow the rule: When in doubt about the proper place of filing, file in all places that *might* be appropriate.

It will be noted that the present discussion focuses only on the place for filing *within* the state, as prescribed in Section 9–401; the question of *what* state is the appropriate one in which to file—a matter primarily governed by Section 9–103—will be taken up in a later chapter.[109]

---

[106] See § 4–6 *infra.*

[107] A reference to after-acquired property may be necessary in the security agreement, however. See § 2–2 D (2) *supra.*

[108] On priority conflicts, see Chapter 4 *infra.*

[109] Chapter 5 *infra.*

(1) The Alternative Versions of Section 9–401

In an effort to accommodate differing views among the states concerning the degree to which "local" versus "central" filing should be required ("local" usually meaning with the County Clerk, Recorder of Deeds, or similar county official; "central" usually referring to filing with the Secretary of State in the state capital), both the 1962 and 1972 Official Texts offer three alternative versions of subsection (1) of Section 9–401, leaving it to each state to adopt the version it prefers.[110]

(a) First Alternative

This version, enacted in the smallest number of states, calls for the greatest degree of central filing.[111] Paragraph (a) requires local filing (in the office where a mortgage on the real estate would be filed or recorded) only for fixtures under the 1962 Code and only for fixtures, timber to be cut, minerals, and accounts arising from the sale of minerals at the wellhead or minehead under the 1972 Code.[112] In all other cases (consumer goods, equipment, farm products including crops, inventory, documents, chattel paper, accounts, and general intangibles) subsection (b) requires central filing.

(b) Second Alternative

This version of Section 9–401(1), enacted in the largest number of states,[113] establishes two different categories of local filing:

---

[110] For a discussion of the arguments for and against requiring local versus central filing, see Comment 1 to Section 9–401.

[111] The First Alternative, with variations, has been enacted in approximately seven states. (The author will hedge with the term "approximately," since some jurisdictions have rewritten the Official Text of Section 9–401(1) so extensively as to render it virtually unrecognizable.) Counsel should carefully check the version in force in his state.

[112] The latter items were added in the 1972 Code after a number of states had enacted nonuniform amendments covering them.

[113] Approximately 24 states have adopted the Second Alternative, with variations.

First, under paragraph (a), financing statements covering farm-related collateral (equipment used in farming operations,[114] farm products including crops, and accounts or general intangibles arising from the sale of farm products by a farmer) and consumer goods must be filed in the ordinary chattel filing records in the county of the debtor's residence.[115] (When the collateral is crops growing in a county other than that of the debtor's residence, filing is required in both counties.) Second, under paragraph (b), filings concerning real estate-related collateral (fixtures under the 1962 Code; fixtures, minerals, and accounts arising from the sale of minerals at the wellhead or minehead under the 1972 Code) are to be made locally in the office where a mortgage on the real estate would be filed or recorded.[116] In all cases other than the foregoing (that is, for financing statements covering equipment, inventory, documents, chattel paper, accounts, and general intangibles—essentially business collateral),[117] central filing is required under paragraph (c). Described another way (at least insofar as the 1972 Code is concerned), the Second Alternative requires local

---

[114] On what constitutes "equipment used in farming operations," see § 1–5 A (3) *supra*.

[115] In order to resolve uncertainty under the 1962 Code as to what constitutes the "residence" of a corporate farm-debtor, the 1972 Code provides in new Section 9–401(6) that "the residence of an organization is its place of business if it has one or its chief executive office if it has more than one place of business."

If the debtor is not a resident of the state, filings with respect to the collateral listed in the text are to be made in the county where the goods are kept.

[116] Timber, minerals, and accounts relating to minerals were added in the 1972 Code after a number of states had enacted nonuniform amendments covering these items.

The 1972 Code contains new language in Section 9–403(7) requiring the filing officer to *index* financing statements covering items listed in the text in the real estate records. On the significance of this new language, see § 4–4 F infra; on the tie-in with new Section 9–402(5), see § 3–3 B (6) *supra*.

[117] Filing is not permitted for instruments. U.C.C. § 9–304(1).

filing (1) for farm collateral, (2) for consumer goods, and (3) for realty-connected collateral; whereas the First Alternative requires local filing only for realty-connected collateral.

(c) Third Alternative

This version of Section 9–401(1) merely repeats the language of the Second Alternative [118] except that when central filing is required under paragraph (c), a local filing is also necessary: (1) if the debtor has a place of business in only one county in the state (in which case filing is to be made in that county), or (2) if the debtor has no place of business in the state (in which case filing is to be made in the county of his residence).[119] As regards what constitutes a "place of business" for purposes of this dual filing requirement—a question not dealt with in the Code— the weight of authority applies a "notoriety" test, whereunder the determination rests on how widely known as a place of business the place in question is.[120] Thus when the debtor has a well-known office in one county but does his paperwork at his residence in another, the argument that a central filing alone suffices because places of business exist in multiple counties may fail. Another question that has arisen under the Third Alternative is whether the location of the debtor's residence or the location or number of his place(s) of business is determined (1) at the time of filing or (2) at the time of attachment of the security interest.[121] The case law under the 1962 Code is mixed

---

[118] Approximately 14 states have enacted the Third Alternative, with variations.

[119] The provision for dual filing saves local persons wishing to conduct a credit search the trouble and expense of checking central files located in another part of the state. It should be noted that, except when Section 9–401(2) applies (see § 3–3 C (2) *infra*), a filing in only one of the two required places is ineffective to perfect the security interest.

[120] The fact that a particular address is specified in the corporate charter is not necessarily determinative nor is the amount of paperwork, correspondence, telephone calls, and so forth associated with a given location.

[121] With respect to residence, the question is also relevant under paragraph (a) of the Second Alternative.

in this regard. Under the 1972 Code, Comment 4 to Section 9–401 indicates that the "last event" test set out in Section 9–103(1)(b) is relevant.[122]

It will be noted that ascertainment of the proper place to file hinges on counsel's ability to correctly identify the category of collateral involved (for example, "equipment" versus "consumer goods")—a matter previously discussed.[123]

(2) Filing in Good Faith in an Improper Place

Even when a place-of-filing rule under Section 9–401(1) has been violated, perfection may still be salvaged in the limited circumstances set out in Section 9–401(2), which provides that a filing made in good faith in the wrong place or not in all of the prescribed places (that is, when dual filing is required),[124] is nevertheless effective: (1) with respect to any collateral concerning which the filing *is* proper and (2) against any person who "has knowledge of the contents" of the filed financing statement.[125] The first part of the rule simply means that when a financing statement covering, say, both inventory and consumer goods is filed centrally under the Second or Third Alternative versions of Section 9–401(1), perfection is good with respect to the inventory (for which central filing is proper) but not with respect to the consumer goods (for which local filing is required).

The second part of Section 9–401(2) would, under the preceding facts, validate the filing with respect to the consumer goods also if the competing claimant had seen the incorrectly

---

[122] On the "last event" test, see § 5–2 B (1) *infra*. A number of commentators have urged application of the time-of-filing test.

[123] For a discussion of each type of collateral, see § 1–5 *supra*. On distinguishing between the subcategories of goods in Section 9–109, see § 1–5 A (1) *supra*.

[124] Dual filing is required in paragraph (a) of the Second Alternative and paragraph (c) of the Third Alternative of Section 9–401(1). See §§ 3–3 C (1)(b) and 3–3 C(1)(c) *supra*.

[125] Section 9–401(2) will not save the secured party when the filed statement fails adequately to describe the collateral or when no filing is made at all.

filed statement in a search of the central records (or perhaps learned of its contents in response to a request for information from the filing officer). In such a case the actual-knowledge requirement of Section 9–401(2) would be satisfied.[126] Less clear, however, are situations in which the competing claimant learns of the *security interest* but not of the filed financing statement. The case law is divided on whether Section 9–401(2) can be invoked in such cases.

(3) Change in Debtor's Residence or Place of Business or in Use or Location of the Collateral

Suppose a financing statement is initially filed in the proper place under Section 9–401(1) but then the debtor's residence or place of business or the location of the collateral, whichever controlled the place of filing, is thereafter changed to another county. Under the standard version of Section 9-401(3), refiling in the new county is not necessary; the original filing remains effective.[127] In the handful of jurisdictions that have adopted the Alternative version of Section 9–401(3), however, the original filing remains effective only for four months after the change; a refiling must be made in the new county within the four-month period in order to ensure continuous perfection beyond that period.[128]

When the use of the collateral changes after an initially proper filing, as when goods that are initially consumer goods (for which local filing is usually required) are later used for business purposes, thereby becoming equipment (for which cen-

---

[126] It does not suffice that a reasonable person *should* have known of the filing. See the definition of "knowledge" in Section 1–201(25), and see Comment 5 to Section 9–401.

[127] Section 9–401(3) pertains only to changes occurring *within* the state; changes from one state to another come under Section 9–103, as discussed in Chapter 5 *infra*.

[128] See the discussion of the analogous provisions relating to *inter*state changes in 1962 Section 9–103(3) and 1972 Sections 9–103(1)(d)(i) and 9–103 (3)(e) in §§ 5–2 C and 5–4 B *infra*.

tral filing is usually required),[129] the original filing remains effective under both the standard and Alternative versions of Section 9–401(3).

(4) Collateral of a "Transmitting Utility" Debtor

Section 9–401(5) of the 1972 Code establishes a new rule calling for central filing with respect to collateral of a debtor that is a "transmitting utility"[130]—a term defined in 1972 Section 9–105(1)(n) to include organizations such as electric, gas and telephone companies, and railroads.[131] The rule is aimed particularly at easing the filing burden of financers with respect to widely dispersed fixtures such as electrical pylons, telegraph poles, pipelines, and signalling systems, concerning which, under the ordinary local-filing rule in Section 9–401(1), filings might have to be made in counties all over the state.[132]

Financing statements covering fixtures of transmitting utilities are exempted from the realty description and other requirements to which filings covering real estate-related collateral are normally subject under 1972 Section 9–402(5).[133] Moreover, since financings of utilities tend to be long term, Section 9–403(6) of the 1972 Code makes filings against these debtors effective indefinitely rather than just for the usual five-year period allowed under Section 9–403(2).[134]

---

[129] For a discussion of the classifications of goods under Section 9–109, see § 1–5 A *supra*.

[130] Some states had enacted nonuniform provisions of a similar nature dovetailing with 1962 Section 9–302(3)(b).

[131] The definition covers "any person primarily engaged in the railroad, street railway or trolley bus business, the electric or electronics communications transmission business, the transmission of goods by pipeline, or the transmission or the production and transmission of electricity, steam, gas or water, or the provision of sewer service."

[132] It is expected that the special nature of the debtor will alert credit searchers to check the central rather than the local filing records.

[133] See § 3–3 B (6) *supra*.

[134] See § 3–3 F *infra*.

D. *When To File; When Filing Is Deemed To Occur and Effect Thereon of Mistake by Filing Officer*

Insofar as the proper time for filing the financing statement is concerned, two important things should be kept in mind: First, under Section 9–402(1), a filing may be made before the security interest attaches (for instance, before the loan proceeds are paid out)[135] and even before the security agreement is executed—in other words, while the parties are still engaged in negotiations. Second, the secured party's failure to file promptly may result in subordination of the security interest to the rights of third-party claimants, as discussed in succeeding chapters.[136]

Assuming the financing statement is correctly filled out in accordance with Section 9–402, is legible, and is accompanied by the appropriate fee, the time when filing is deemed to occur [137] is the time of presentation to the filing officer—not a time arbitrarily determined by the officer or the time of proper indexing by him.[138] In other words, the filing will be deemed to take place even though the filing officer (1) rejects the statement for an incorrect reason [139] or (2) accepts it but then delays in indexing it or makes a mistake in indexing not caused by the secured party, and a credit searcher is thereby misled.[140]

---

[135] On the subject of attachment, see Chapter 2 *supra.*

[136] See Chapter 4 (priority conflicts with competing creditors of, and buyers from, the debtor) and Chapter 6 (conflict with debtor's bankruptcy trustee) *infra.*

[137] As will be seen in Chapters 4 and 6 *infra,* the time of filing can be crucial in a priority dispute.

[138] *See* U.C.C. § 9–403, Comment 1. Except when the filing officer improperly refuses to take the statement, the time of filing will be evidenced by the date and hour marked on the statement (see the box in the upper right-hand corner of Form UCC–1, § 3–3 B (1) *supra*) by the officer as required in Section 9–403(4).

[139] Failure of the financing statement to comply with Section 9–402 (see § 3–3 B *supra*), illegibility (which can cause erroneous indexing), and tender of an inadequate fee (see § 3–3 J *infra*) are widely regarded as justifiable reasons for rejection by the officer.

[140] *See* U.C.C. § 9–407, Comment 1. Depending on state law relating to the liability of government officials, a third party may be able to recover

E. Amendments

After a financing statement has been filed, it may be necessary to file an amendment thereto.[141] The form generally used for this purpose is Form UCC-3, an example of which is set out in a subsequent section.[142] Amendments are most commonly filed to add a new type or types of collateral not described in the original financing statement—as when the original filing covers only inventory and a security interest is later taken in equipment as well.[143]

The only language in Article 9 dealing with amendments is found in Section 9–402(4), which provides that the term "financing statement" as used in Article 9 refers to the original financing statement *and* any amendments and that an amendment covering additional collateral is effective with respect to this collateral only from the time of filing of the amendment.[144] Also new language added in the 1972 Code makes explicit what was implicit under the 1962 version: (1) that an amendment must be signed by both the debtor and the secured party[145] and

---

against the filing officer for the officer's negligence—as when the third party lends in reliance on not having found a statement that was misplaced in the files and then loses in a priority conflict with the secured party whose financing statement was misindexed.

[141] An amendment is filed in the same office as the financing statement to which it relates.

[142] § 3–3 F *infra.*

[143] An amendment is not needed, however, when the new collateral consists only of additional units of a classification already described in the original financing statement—as when the original statement covers "all inventory" and the debtor later acquires a new line of inventory not carried at the time of initial filing. See 1972 U.C.C. § 9–402, Comment 4.

[144] In other words, priority with respect to the added collateral does not "relate back" to the time of the initial filing under a provision like Section 9–312(5), discussed *infra* § 4–2 A (1).

[145] The dual signature requirement applies under 1962 Section 9–402(1) to a "financing statement," which is defined in 1962 Section 9–402(4) to include an amendment. The requirement that the secured party sign an amendment is retained in the 1972 Code, despite elimination of the similar requirement in Section 9–402(1) with respect to the financing statement, so as to guard against the debtor's adversely affecting the interest of the

(2) that an amendment does not extend the period of effectiveness of the original financing statement.[146]

F. Duration of Effectiveness of Filing; Continuation

Under Section 9–403(2), a filed financing statement normally has an effective life of five years from the date of filing. Thereafter the filing lapses and the security interest becomes unperfected (except when perfection obtains even in the absence of filing)[147] unless a continuation statement is filed pursuant to Section 9–403(3) prior to the lapse. Occasionally, however, one of the exceptions to the five-year duration rule applies.

Under Section 9–403(2) of the 1962 Code, when the secured obligation has a maturity date of five years or less and the financing statement so specifies, the filing is effective until 60 days after the stated date. In recognition that the secured party can evade what was intended to be a limitation by simply not noting the maturity date on the financing statement when the loan agreement provides for a less-than-five-year maturity, the 1972 Code eliminates this special provision.[148]

New language has been added in the 1972 version of Section 9–403(2) to the effect that when the five-year period expires during insolvency proceedings, the filing remains effective until 60 days after termination of the proceedings. Although the

---

secured party, for instance, by filing an amendment subtracting collateral. *See* 1972 U.C.C. § 9–402, Comment 4.

[146] The filing of a continuation statement pursuant to Section 9–403(2) and (3) (see § 3–3 F *infra*) is the only method of extension sanctioned by Article 9.

[147] The words "unless it is perfected without filing" have been added in the fourth sentence of Section 9–403(2) of the 1972 Code to make it clear that interests automatically perfected under Section 9–302 (see § 3–2 *supra*), such as a purchase-money security interest in consumer goods, remain perfected irrespective of the status of a financing statement filed with respect thereto.

[148] See the Reasons for 1972 Change to Section 9–403. In any event, the virtually universal practice under the 1962 Code has been not to specify a maturity date in the financing statement.

weight of authority under the 1962 Code holds that the situation is frozen during bankruptcy, with the secured party being relieved of the necessity of filing a continuation statement, decisions to the contrary have left the matter unclear.[149] The new provision resolves the issue by codifying the majority rule under the old Code.

In two special situations that tend to involve long-term financing, Section 9–403(6) of the 1972 Code essentially makes the filing good for the life of the obligation secured rather than just for five years: [150] first, if the debtor is a transmitting utility [151] and the financing statement so states, the filing remains valid until a termination statement is filed; and second, when a real estate mortgage serves as a fixture filing under 1972 Section 9–402(6),[152] the period of effectiveness for Article 9 purposes continues until the mortgage is released, satisfied, or its effectiveness terminates regarding the real estate.

What happens when a conflicting interest intervenes between the time of initial filing and lapse? Assume the following chronology: (1) SP₁ files, (2) SP₂ files, and (3) SP₁'s filing lapses, the five-year period having expired without his having filed a continuation statement. Assuming both security interests are non-purchase-money ones, SP₁ has priority *during* the five-year

---

[149] See the Reasons for 1972 Change to Section 9–403. Assume, for instance, the following sequence: (1) SP₁ files, (2) SP₂ files, (3) bankruptcy proceedings are commenced, and (4) during the proceedings the five-year period for SP₁'s financing statement expires without SP₁'s having filed a continuation statement. Assuming that both security interests are non-purchase-money ones, the majority of courts applying the 1962 Code would award priority to SP₁ under Section 9–312(5) (discussed *infra* § 4–2 A (1)); but a minority would reach the opposite result, on the theory that SP₁'s interest lapsed, whereupon SP₂'s initially subordinate interest "rose to the top."

[150] There is no counterpart in the 1962 Code.

[151] See the definition in 1972 Section 9–105(1)(n). Other provisions relating to transmitting utilities are discussed *supra* § 3–3 C (4).

[152] See § 3–3 B (6) *supra*.

period by virtue of the first-to-file rule of Section 9–312(5).[153] But upon lapse does SP₂'s interest remain subordinate or does it "rise to the top" and prevail? The answer is uncertain under the 1962 Code.[154] Section 9–403(2) of the 1972 Code resolves the question in favor of SP₂ by providing that a security interest that becomes unperfected upon lapse will be deemed to have *been* unperfected "as against a person who became a purchaser[155] or lien creditor before lapse."[156]

In order to prevent the effectiveness of a filed financing statement from lapsing (and the security interest from thereby becoming unperfected) at the end of the five-year period specified in Section 9–403(2), the secured party must, pursuant to Section 9–403(3), file a continuation statement[157] within 60 days prior to the expiration of the five-year period.[158] The form generally used for a continuation statement (as well as for other purposes discussed subsequently) is Form UCC-3, reproduced in Figure 4. It appears that a continuation statement filed

---

[153] See § 4–2 A (1)(a) *infra*.

[154] See the discussion of the similar "rising to the top" problem in connection with Section 9–103, *infra* § 5–2 C (2).

[155] The holder of an Article 9 security interest comes within the definition of "purchaser" in Section 1–201(32) and (33).

[156] For reasons that are not clear, the reference to "lien creditor" is not found in the comparable "rising to the top" provision in 1972 Section 9–103(1)(d)(i), discussed *infra* § 5–2 C (2).

[157] The continuation statement must be signed by the secured party (the debtor's signature not being required), identify the original financing statement by file number, and state that the original statement is still effective. In addition, the 1972 Code contains new language requiring that a continuation statement signed by a person other than the secured party of record be accompanied by a separate written statement of assignment signed by the secured party of record and complying with Section 9–405(2), discussed *infra* § 3–3 I.

[158] With regard to a financing statement specifying a maturity date of the secured debt of five years or less, Section 9–403(3) of the 1962 Code requires that the continuation statement be filed within six months before, and 60 days after, the stated date. The 1972 Code omits this provision, consistent with the elimination from Section 9–403(2) of the special rule allowing a stated maturity date to control the duration of effectiveness.

STATE OF ILLINOIS
UNIFORM COMMERCIAL CODE
STATEMENTS OF CONTINUATION, PARTIAL RELEASE, ASSIGNMENT, ETC.—FORM UCC-3

INSTRUCTIONS:

1. PLEASE TYPE this form. Fold only along perforation for mailing.
2. Remove Secured Party and Debtor copies and send other 3 copies with interleaved carbon paper to the filing officer.
3. Enclose filing fee.
4. If the space provided for any item(s) on the form is inadequate the item(s) should be continued on additional sheets, preferably 5" x 8" or 8" x 10". Only one copy of such additional sheets need be presented to the filing officer with a set of three copies of Form UCC-3. Long schedules of collateral, etc., may be on any size paper that is convenient for the secured party.
5. At the time of filing, filing officer will return third copy as an acknowledgement.

This STATEMENT is presented to THE FILING OFFICER for filing pursuant to the Uniform Commercial Code.

For Filing Officer
(Date, Time, Number, and Filing Office)

Debtor(s) (Last Name First) and address(es)   Secured Party(ies) and address(es)

This Statement refers to original Financing Statement No. ....
Date filed: ...., 19..........   Filed with ....

A. ☐ CONTINUATION .... The original financing statement between the foregoing Debtor and Secured Party, bearing the file number shown above, is still effective.

B. ☐ PARTIAL RELEASE .... From the collateral described in the financing statement bearing the file number shown above, the Secured Party releases the property indicated below.

C. ☐ ASSIGNMENT .... The Secured Party certifies that the Secured Party has assigned to the Assignee whose name and address is shown below, Secured Party's rights under the financing statement bearing the file number shown above in the property indicated below.

D. ☐ TERMINATION .... The Secured Party certifies that the Secured Party no longer claims a security interest under the financing statement bearing the file number shown above.

E. ☐ AMENDMENT .... The financing statement bearing the above file number is amended.
   ☐ To show the Secured Party's new address as indicated below;
   ☐ To show the Debtor's new address as indicated below;
   ☐ As set forth below:

.... (Secured Party)

.... (Debtor)

Dated: ...., 19..........   By: ....

(Signature of Debtor, if required)   (Signature of Secured Party)

(1) FILING OFFICER COPY—ALPHABETICAL

This form of Financing Statement is approved by the Secretary of State.

STANDARD FORM—UNIFORM COMMERCIAL CODE—FORM UCC-3 REV.

Figure 4.

either (1) before the 60-day period preceding lapse or (2) after lapse will be ineffective. In the former situation the secured party will have to wait until commencement of the 60-day period; [159] in the latter, a new financing statement will have to be filed. If a continuation statement is filed in a timely manner, the effectiveness of the original financing statement is extended for five years beyond the date on which it would have become ineffective, whereupon it will lapse unless another continuation statement is filed in the same manner as discussed above and so on. Thus a series of continuation statements can be used to continue the effective life of the original filing indefinitely.

G. Release of Collateral

When a secured party releases all or a part of the collateral covered by a filed financing statement, he may make this fact a matter of record by filing a statement of release as provided in Section 9–406. The statement must be signed by the secured party, describe the collateral being released, give the name and address of the debtor and of the secured party, and show the file number of the financing statement to which the release pertains.[160] The standard form used for this purpose is Form UCC-3, reproduced previously.[161] The filing of a statement of release is appropriate only while the financing arrangement is still in effect; upon conclusion of the arrangement, a termination statement should be filed pursuant to Section 9–404.[162]

---

[159] In other words, the 60-day period has been interpreted as being mandatory rather than permissive.

[160] The 1972 Code adds a requirement that a statement of release signed by a person other than the secured party of record be accompanied by a separate written statement of assignment signed by the secured party of record and complying with Section 9–405(2), discussed *infra* § 3–3 I.

[161] § 3–3 F *supra*. As this form is also used for other purposes, the "release" box must be checked.

[162] See § 3–3 H *infra*. A statement releasing all collateral should not be confused with a termination statement: The former would be used when all the original collateral is released but is to be replaced with new collateral (in which case, as in other cases involving the addition of collateral,

There is no requirement that a statement of release be filed when a release occurs, but by so doing the secured party may reduce the number of inquiries made by credit searchers.

H. Termination

Upon conclusion of the financing arrangement—that is, when there is no longer an outstanding secured obligation and no commitment to make advances, incur obligations, or otherwise give value—Section 9–404(1) requires that the secured party, on written demand by the debtor, send the debtor a termination statement to the effect that he (the secured party) no longer claims a security interest under the financing statement.[163] Either Form UCC-3 (with the "termination" box checked)[164] or the third carbon copy of Form UCC-1 or Form UCC-2 (which the secured party will have received back from the filing officer)[165] may be used for this purpose. Upon receipt of the termination statement the debtor may file it, so as to have the fact of discharge noted in the records and the financing statement (and thus the cloud on his property) removed therefrom.[166]

---

an amendment should also be filed—see § 3–3 E *supra*). In most cases, statements of release are filed to record partial releases.

[163] The financing statement must be identified by file number. The 1972 Code adds language to Section 9–404(1) explicitly requiring that a termination statement be sent for each filing officer with whom the financing statement was filed. The new Code also requires that a termination statement signed by a person other than the secured party of record be accompanied by a separate written statement of assignment signed by the secured party of record and complying with Section 9–405(2), discussed *infra* § 3–3 I. Under the 1962 Code, such a termination statement must "include or be accompanied by the assignment or a statement by the secured party of record that he has assigned the security interest to the signer of the termination statement."

[164] Form UCC–3 is reproduced in § 3–3 F *supra*.

[165] The third carbon copy, unlike the other copies, has a block on the bottom captioned "Termination Statement," with blanks for the date of termination and signature.

[166] For evidentiary purposes, the 1972 version of Section 9–404(2) requires that the filing officer retain the financing statement for one year after

The 1972 Code version of Section 9–404(1) contains a new provision creating an exception to the general rule that the secured party need only send the termination statement to the debtor (rather than file it) and need not even do that unless the debtor demands it:[167] If the financing statement covers consumer goods, then within one month after conclusion of the financing arrangement in the absence of a demand by the debtor, or within ten days after a written demand, the secured party must himself file a termination statement.[168]

A secured party who fails to transmit a termination statement to the debtor upon demand under either the 1962 or 1972 Code or who fails to file a termination statement with respect to consumer goods in the manner required by the 1972 Code is liable to the debtor for $100 and, in addition, for any loss suffered by the debtor by reason of such failure.[169]

I. Assignment of the Security Interest

When the secured party assigns his interest, Section 9–405 provides two procedures for having the assignment noted of record. The first, set out in Section 9–405(1), applies when the security interest is assigned before the original financing statement is filed—as when a dealer who sells goods on secured credit immediately assigns the conditional sale contract (chattel paper) to *his* financer. When the financing statement is then filed, Section 9–405(1) provides for notation of the assignment thereon either by specification of the name and address of the assignee (Forms UCC-1 and UCC-2 provide a blank for this purpose)[170]

---

receipt of the termination statement unless a microfilm record is kept. The 1962 Code provides for immediate removal.

[167] Even without a termination statement, the financing statement will eventually lapse (Section 9–403(2)) and be removed from the records (Section 9–403(3)). See § 3–3 F *supra.*

[168] The financing statement must be identified by file number. A termination statement must be filed with each filing officer with whom the financing statement was filed.

[169] U.C.C. § 9–404(1).

[170] See § 3–3 B (1) *supra.*

or by the inclusion of an assignment itself or a copy thereof on the face or back of the statement. The language in the 1962 Code to the effect that either the original secured party (for example, the dealer) or the assignee (for example, the dealer's financer) may sign the statement as the secured party is omitted in the 1972 version, consistent with the elimination from Section 9–402(1) of the requirement that a financing statement be signed by the secured party.[171] Upon the filing of a financing statement disclosing the assignment in the above manner, the assignee becomes the secured party of record, pursuant to Section 9–405(3).

The second procedure for noting an assignment on the records comes into play when the assignment occurs after a financing statement has already been filed by the assigning creditor. In such a case Section 9–405(2) provides for the filing (in the place where the original financing statement was filed)[172] of a separate statement of assignment containing (1) the signature of the secured party of record (the assignor), (2) the names of the secured party of record and the debtor, (3) the file number and date of filing of the original financing statement, (4) the name and address of the assignee, and (5) a description of the collateral assigned. The standard form normally used for this purpose is Form UCC-3 (with the "assignment" box checked),[173] but a copy of the assignment itself is sufficient if it sets forth the items listed above. Upon the filing of a statement of assignment, the assignee becomes the secured party of record, pursuant to Section 9–405(3).

Language has been added in the 1972 Code version of Section 9–405(2) to the effect that an assignment of record of a security interest in a fixture created in a real estate mortgage serving as a fixture filing under Section 9–402(6) may be made

---

[171] See § 3–3 B (4) *supra*.

[172] The requirement of filing in the same place as the original financing statement is made explicit in the 1972 Code; it was implicit in the 1962 version.

[173] Form UCC–3 is reproduced in § 3–3 F *supra*.

only by an assignment of the mortgage in compliance with non-Code real property law.

It should be noted that the two procedures for filing an assignment outlined above are permissive, not mandatory: Under Section 9–302(2), an assignment of a perfected security interest need not be filed to continue perfection as against creditors of and transferees from the debtor. Nevertheless, the filing of an assignment may prove beneficial in several respects. First, Section 9–302(2) does not protect against creditors of, and transferees from, the *assignor* (for example, against the bankruptcy trustee of an assigning dealer). The filing of an assignment may provide such protection.[174] Second, a secured party who assigns his interest may wish to have the fact noted of record so that subsequent inquiries from credit searchers will be addressed not to him but to the assignee.[175] Third, after the filing of an assignment the assignee becomes the secured party of record[176] and may thereafter file a continuation statement, termination statement, or statement of release[177] without a separate statement of assignment signed by the assignor.

The general rule applicable to priority conflicts between an assignee of a security interest and third-party claimants to the

---

[174] The word "may" is used advisedly. Although some commentators opine that the filing of an assignment suffices for perfection as against creditors of, and transferees from, the assignor, the author feels that the safest course is to file a new financing statement, so that there will be something in the records showing the assignor as a debtor. An assignee who perfects by taking possession of chattel paper need not worry about this, however.

[175] U.C.C. § 9–405, Comment. The assignor thereby avoids the risk of liability for failing to respond properly to a request for information under Section 9–208 or to a demand for a termination statement under Section 9–404(1).

[176] U.C.C. § 9–405(3). The word "disclosure" in Section 9–405(3) refers to the filing of the original financing statement with a notation of the assignment thereon, as provided in Section 9–405(1).

[177] See U.C.C. §§ 9–403(3) (§ 3–3 F *supra*), 9–404(1) (§ 3–3 H *supra*), and 9–406 (§ 3–3 G *supra*), respectively.

collateral is that the assignee enjoys whatever priority the assignor had.[178]

The rules in Section 9–318 governing rights between the original debtor and an assignee of a security interest have previously been discussed.[179]

J. Fees; Information from Filing Officer

Various sections of Article 9 impose fees for the filing of documents previously described: Section 9–103(5) (financing statements and continuation statements), Section 9–406 (statements of release), Section 9–404(3) (termination statements), Section 9–405(1) (financing statements with an assignment noted thereon), and Section 9–405(2) (separate statements of assignment). Language has been added in the 1972 Code to each of the sections just listed imposing an extra fee for filing a statement that is not on a standard form prescribed by the filing officer. Given the fact that a filing is not deemed to occur until tender of the correct fee,[180] that the amount of fees periodically increase, and that fee computations can be complex, the filing party (particularly if he is a novice) will be well advised to check the requisite amount in advance with the filing officer. Tender of an inadequate fee is a valid basis for rejection of the statement by the filing officer.[181] And during the delay between a rejection and a proper refiling, a third-party claim may arise (for example, a competing secured party may file) and attain priority.

A credit searcher (for example, a prospective creditor or buyer) may obtain information concerning filings that have been made against a particular debtor in one of two ways. First, he may go to the appropriate filing office (as determined by

---

[178] On priorities, see Chapter 4 *infra*.

[179] § 1–5 C (1)(c) *supra*. The term "account debtor" used in Section 9–318 is defined to include a person obligated under a security interest assigned via an assignment of chattel paper.

[180] See § 3–3 D *supra*.

[181] *Id*.

Section 9–401)[182] and conduct his own search of the records. Pursuant to Section 9–403(4), the filing officer will have indexed each filed financing statement alphabetically by the last name of the debtor and will have marked on the statement a file number and the hour and date of filing.[183] If the credit searcher wishes more information than is disclosed on the filed statement, he may contact the debtor and follow the procedure outlined in Section 9–208.

The second method of obtaining information, which is useful when it is inconvenient for the credit searcher to go to the filing office himself (as when the records to be searched are located in a distant part of the state) is to invoke Section 9–407(2) —an optional provision enacted in all but a handful of states. Under this section the inquiring party may send an information request (with the requisite fee) to the filing officer, essentially asking the latter to conduct the search for him. The officer will then send back a certificate listing the date and hour of filing and the name and address of the secured party shown on any presently effective financing statement on file against a specified debtor and any statement of assignment thereof.[184] Or, for what usually is a considerably larger fee, the inquiring party may request actual photocopies of the statements on file. The standard form often used for either type of request is Form UCC-11, an example of which is set forth below.

---

[182] See § 3–3 C *supra*.

[183] Other provisions governing the filing officer's handling of various statements include Section 9–406 (statements of release), Section 9–404(2) (termination statements), Section 9–405(1) (financing statements with an assignment noted thereon), Section 9–405(2) (separate statements of assignment), and Section 9–403(4) (continuation statements). Rules concerning removal from the files and destruction of lapsed financing statements are set forth in Section 9–403(3).

[184] The disadvantage of using this procedure, as opposed to conducting the search in person, is that some filing offices are understaffed and a considerable delay may ensue between the sending of the request and receipt of the certificate. If the timing of the certificate is crucial (as in the case of a closing), this should be discussed with the filing officer beforehand.

STANDARD FORM—UNIFORM COMMERCIAL CODE—FORM UCC-11
Approved by The Secretary of State of Alabama

UNIFORM COMMERCIAL CODE REQUEST FOR INFORMATION OR COPIES—FORM UCC-11

REQUEST FOR COPIES OR INFORMATION Present in Triplicate

DEBTOR(S) (LAST NAME FIRST) AND ADDRESS(ES)	PARTY REQUESTING COPIES OR INFORMATION	FOR FILING OFFICER USE

☐ (1) COPY REQUEST: Filing officer please furnish exact copies of all financing statements and statements of assignment listed below, which are on file with your office. Upon receipt of these copies, the undersigned party agrees to pay to the Filing Officer $.50 for each page of each financing statement or statement of assignment furnished by the Filing Officer.

....
(Signature of Requesting Party)

FILE NO.	DATE AND HOUR OF FILING	NAME AND ADDRESS OF SECURED PARTY

The undersigned filing officer hereby certifies that the attached .... copies are true and exact copies of all available financing statements or statements of assignment listed in the above request. Additional fee required $..............

Dated this .... day of ...., A.D., 19 ....

....
(Signature of Filing Officer)

☐ (2) INFORMATION REQUEST: Filing officer please furnish certificate showing whether there is on file as of ...., 19 ...., at .... .M. any presently effective financing statement, or any statement of assignment thereof, naming the above debtor, give the date and hour of filing of each such statement, and the names and addresses of each party named therein. Enclosed is the statutory fee of $1.00. The undersigned party further agrees to pay to the Filing Officer, upon receipt of the above certificate, the sum of $.50 for each financing statement and each statement of assignment reported on the certificate.

....
(Signature of Requesting Party)

FILE NO.	DATE AND HOUR OF FILING	NAME AND ADDRESS OF SECURED PARTY

The undersigned filing officer hereby certifies that the above listing is a record of all presently effective, financing statements and statements of assignment which name the above debtor, and which are on file in my office as of ...., 19 ...., at .... .M. Additional fee required $..............
Dated this .... day of ...., A.D., 19 ....

....
(Signature of Filing Officer)

UNIFORM COMMERCIAL CODE—STATE OF ALABAMA

(1) TO BE RETURNED WITH COPIES OR INFORMATION

It will be noted that the credit searcher, rather than the creditor who has properly filed, bears the risk that the filing officer will make a mistake and fail to disclose the existence of a filed statement.[185]

§ 3–4. PERFECTION BY POSSESSION—THE PLEDGE

A. *In General; When Perfection by Possession Is Appropriate; What Constitutes "Possession"*

In a number of instances Article 9 permits or requires perfection of a security interest by the secured party's (or his representative's) taking possession of the collateral—the so-called "pledge" or possessory security interest—in lieu of filing a financing statement.[186] The basic rationale behind recognition of this device is that, at least with respect to some types of collateral, the debtor's lack of possession serves the same purpose as filing: It alerts a prospective creditor or buyer that the property in question may be encumbered and that further inquiry is necessary. Under the combination of Sections 9–302(1)(a), 9–305, and 9–304(1), the extent to which the pledge is permitted or required may be analyzed as follows.

The taking of possession is a permissible alternative to filing for perfection of security interests in goods, chattel paper,[187] and negotiable documents of title (for example, bills of lading or terminal warehouse receipts).[188] The latter two items, although not tangibles, are embodied in "indispensable paper," such that enforcement of the property right depends on possession; [189]

---

[185] See § 3–3 D *supra.*

[186] Also it will be recalled that under Section 9–203(1)(a) a written security agreement is not required for creation of a possessory security interest. See § 2–2 A *supra.*

[187] Possession is the preferable means of perfection for chattel paper in terms of risk of subordination to a competing claimant. See the discussion of Section 9–308, *infra* § 4–3 A (3). For a general discussion of chattel paper, see § 1–5 B (3) *supra.*

[188] For a discussion of documents of title, see § 1–5 B (2) *supra.*

[189] See the discussion at the beginning of § 1–5 B *supra.*

hence the absence of possession in the debtor should put third parties on inquiry.[190] In contrast to chattel paper and negotiable documents (and instruments, as discussed *infra*), possessory security interests in goods such as equipment or inventory are infrequent, since the debtor usually needs to retain possession of these items himself in order to keep his business operating or to make sales or both.[191] A special type of pledge employing a field warehousing arrangement is feasible for financing of inventory, however, as previously discussed.[192]

Under Sections 9-305 and 9-304(1), security interests in money and in instruments (for example, promissory notes, stock certificates, and bonds) may be perfected *only* by the secured party's taking possession (except when temporary perfection is allowed pursuant to Sections 9-304(4) and 9-304(5) or Sections 9-306(2) and 9-306(3)):[193] regarding these items, filing is not

---

[190] Under Section 9-304(2), during the period that goods are in the possession of the issuer of a negotiable document therefor (for example, a terminal warehouseman; see § 1-5 B (2)(b) *supra*), perfection of a security interest in the document automatically perfects an interest in the goods themselves; and a security interest perfected directly in the goods during this period is subordinated thereto—the notion being that title to the goods is "locked up" in the negotiable document. *See* U.C.C. § 9-304, Comment 2. On the other hand, title to goods covered by a *non*-negotiable document (such as a receipt issued by a field warehouseman; see § 1-5 B (2)(b) *supra*) is not regarded as "locked up" in the document. Consequently, under Section 9-304(3), perfection with respect to such goods may be accomplished (1) by filing with respect to them, (2) by the issuance of a non-negotiable document in the name of the secured party, or (3) by the bailee's receipt of notification of the secured party's interest. Under Section 9-305, the last-mentioned method is regarded as equivalent to the secured party's taking possession, without the necessity of consent by the bailee. *See* U.C.C. § 9-304, Comment 3, and U.C.C. § 9-305, Comment 2.

[191] Pledges of certain consumer goods, such as jewelry, with a pawnbroker are not uncommon, however.

[192] § 1-5 B (2)(b) *supra*.

[193] For a discussion of temporary perfection with respect to instruments under Section 9-304(4) and (5), see § 3-2 B *supra*. On temporary perfection with respect to proceeds under Section 9-306(3), see § 4-3 B (4)(a) *infra*. The 1972 Code adds a reference to Section 9-306 in Section 9-304(1)

permissible. An explicit reference to "money" has been added in Sections 9–304(1) and 9–305 of the 1972 Code to make it clear that money is not (as might be argued under the 1962 Code) classified as general intangibles, for which filing, rather than possession, would be appropriate.[194] The rule limiting perfection of security interests in instruments to possession accords with the long-established commercial practice of taking these items in pledge when loans are made against them.[195] Since, as is true with respect to chattel paper and documents of title, the property right represented by an instrument is embodied in "indispensable paper,"[196] the debtor's lack of possession should alert third parties to the possibility of an encumbrance.

Security interests in "pure intangibles"—accounts, contract rights (under the 1962 Code), and general intangibles—may be perfected only by filing:[197] Regarding these items, taking possession is not permissible.[198] Since property rights of this sort are not embodied in any particular piece of paper the possession of which is required for enforcement of the right, there is nothing the lack of possession of which would indicate the possibility of an encumbrance.

The third sentence of Section 9–305 speaks to the timing of perfection by possession by providing that this perfection commences at the time possession is taken, "without relation back."[199] This rule rejects the theory adopted at common law

---

in order to make it clear that temporary perfection can be had with respect to cash proceeds without the secured party's taking possession of them.

[194] For the same reason, language excluding money from the definition of general intangibles has been added in Section 9–106 of the 1972 Code. Note that money held for numismatic value, such as a rare coin collection, is "goods" (rather than "money"), for which either filing or possession is appropriate.

[195] See U.C.C. § 9–304, Comment 1.

[196] See the discussion at the beginning of § 1–5 B supra.

[197] Isolated assignments of accounts, for which automatic perfection is allowed under Section 9–302(1)(e), are an exception. See § 3–2 C supra.

[198] U.C.C. § 9–304, Comment 1; U.C.C. § 9–305, Comment 1.

[199] The security interest may attach, unperfected, at an earlier time, however, pursuant to Section 9–204. See U.C.C. § 9–305, Comment 3.

in some jurisdictions that the taking of possession relates back to the date of the original security agreement.[200] The same sentence of Section 9–305 provides that perfection by possession terminates whenever the secured party relinquishes possession— the sole exception being the 21-day period of temporary perfection provided for in Sections 9–304(4) and 9–304(5).[201]

A question of obvious significance is: what constitutes "possession"? Beyond the obvious situation in which the creditor has the collateral safely locked away on his premises, the answer is by no means clear. The term is not defined in the Code,[202] although Comment 2 to Section 9–305 does observe that possession may be taken either by the secured party himself or by an agent on his behalf and that the debtor or a person controlled by him cannot qualify as the creditor's agent.[203] Further guidance must be drawn from the caselaw. The courts have held, for instance, that the possession requirement for perfection was not met when a landlord-secured party had the right, unexercised, to retake premises on which collateral owned by the tenant-debtor was located; when the secured party briefly boarded a boat, removed some equipment, and prepared the boat for winter; when the secured party retained possession of the registration certificates for arabian horses; when, at the

---

[200] U.C.C. § 9–305, Comment 3. Thus, for instance, a secured party who obtains a security agreement prior to the 90-day preference period preceding the filing of a bankruptcy petition but who does not take possession of the collateral until after commencement of the period cannot defeat the trustee's claim of voidable preference by arguing that perfection occurred, via "relation back," prior to the period. For a discussion of voidable preferences under the Bankruptcy Act, see § 6–3 *infra*.

[201] *See* U.C.C. § 9–305, Comment 3.

[202] Section 9–305 does provide that if collateral other than goods covered by a negotiable document (for example, goods covered by a non-negotiable document) is held by a bailee, the secured party is deemed to have possession from the time the bailee receives notification of the secured party's interest, even though the bailee has not consented to hold on the secured party's behalf. *See* U.C.C. § 9–305, Comment 2. Corresponding language is found in Section 9–304(3).

[203] Thus the appointment of the debtor as his agent for collection of an instrument will not suffice to give the secured party "possession."

time in question, employees of the secured party had arrived at the debtor's premises but had not begun loading the collateral on the creditor's truck; and when the secured party took possession of the keys to a safe deposit box containing the collateral, but the debtor, who rented the box, could still gain access to it. On the other hand, by the majority view, perfection of a security interest in instruments can be accomplished by an escrow agent's taking possession thereof, despite the fact that such an agent acts on behalf of the debtor as well as the creditor.

B. The Secured Party's Duties with Respect to Pledged Collateral—Section 9–207

Although not an aspect of perfection, it is relevant at this point to consider the duties imposed by Section 9–207 on a secured party with respect to collateral in his possession. These duties apply regardless of whether the creditor has possession by virtue of a pre-default pledge arrangement or as the result of repossession after default.[204]

Section 9–207(1) requires that a secured party "use reasonable care in the custody and preservation of collateral in his possession." This duty would be violated, for example, when a creditor repossessed a piece of machinery and then allowed it to depreciate badly. Conversely, the courts have held that a secured party is not obligated to preserve the value of pledged securities by selling them in a falling market.[205] In the absence of contributory negligence on the debtor's part, an exculpatory clause in the security agreement, or both, however, the courts tend to hold the secured party accountable for neglecting to take advantage of the opportunity to convert pledged debentures into common stock of greater value. A finding of contributory

---

[204] See U.C.C. § 9–501(1), (2). Repossession is discussed in § 7–4 A infra.

[205] This assumes good faith on the creditor's part. It is unclear whether the debtor's having requested a sale would change the outcome. But contributory negligence on the debtor's part in knowing of the declining market and failing to request a sale presents an even stronger case for excusing the creditor.

negligence is more likely when the debtor is a knowledgeable investor. Insofar as exculpatory language is concerned, the duty of reasonable care imposed by Section 9–207(1) may not be disclaimed *per se,* but the parties are free to agree to reasonable standards by which the duty of care is to be measured.[206] Language in the pledge agreement relieving the secured party of the duty of converting debentures arguably falls within the latter category.[207]

The second sentence of Section 9–207(1) declares that when the pledged (or repossessed) collateral consists of an instrument (for example, a note, stock certificate, or bond) or chattel paper, the creditor's duty of care encompasses "taking necessary steps to preserve rights against prior parties unless otherwise agreed." These steps would, for instance, include proper presentment of a promissory note to the maker for payment on the maturity date and giving notice of dishonor to indorsers so as to retain the right to recover against them upon nonpayment by the maker.[208] The secured party can avoid the responsibility of taking steps against prior parties, however, either (1) by including a clause to that effect in the security agreement[209] or (2) by simply notifying the debtor of any act that must be taken and allowing the debtor to perform such act himself.[210]

Under Section 9–207(2)(a), expenses incurred in the custody, preservation, use, or operation of collateral in the secured

---

[206] U.C.C. § 1–102(3).

[207] Security agreements commonly assign the burden of taking action in preservation of pledged instruments to the debtor.

[208] *See* U.C.C. §§ 3–501 through 3–511.

[209] Since the second sentence of Section 9–207(1), unlike the first, contains the qualifying phrase "unless otherwise agreed," such a clause does not run afoul of Section 1–102(3) and is clearly valid.

[210] U.C.C. § 9–207, Comment 1. Significant in this regard is Section 9–304(5)(b), which allows the secured party temporarily to relinquish possession of an instrument to the debtor without loss of perfection if the purpose is to enable the latter to make presentment or collection (in the case of a negotiable instrument) or renewal or registration of transfer (in the case of a stock certificate). See § 3–2 B *supra.*

party's possession are chargeable to the debtor and may be added to the secured debt, as long as such expenses are reasonable and unless the parties agree otherwise. Included are payments for insurance, taxes, and such items as storage and maintenance.[211]

Under Section 9–207(2)(b), unless the parties agree otherwise, the risk of loss of, or damage to, pledged or repossessed collateral is on the debtor [212]—but only to the extent of any deficiency in the secured party's insurance coverage. In other words, when the secured party's interest is insured and the debtor's is not, the risk of loss is on the secured party to the extent of his coverage. Thus the secured party may not collect twice—once from his insurance company and again from the debtor.[213]

Section 9–207(2)(c) provides that any increase (such as the young of animals or stock dividends) or profits other than money received from pledged or repossessed collateral may be held by the secured party and added to the collateral as security for the debt.[214] Money profits (such as cash dividends on pledged securities or interest payments on bonds), however, may not be held but must either be applied in reduction of the debt or remitted to the debtor.[215]

Section 9–207(2)(d) imposes on the secured party the duty to keep non-fungible collateral identifiable, but commingling of

---

[211] Upon repossession after default, Section 9–504(1)(a), discussed *infra* § 7–4 C (1), also applies.

[212] Section 1–102(3) would prevent the secured party from contractually disclaiming responsibility for negligence on his part, however.

[213] It is unclear whether the insurer, having paid the secured party, may recover on the debt from the debtor via the equitable doctrine of subrogation. Arguably it may not because Section 9–207(2)(b) discharges the debt, so that there is nothing for the insurer to be subrogated to.

[214] The parties may, by agreement, however, require that any increase or profits be turned over to the debtor.

[215] In the absence of specification in the security agreement, the secured party may choose between the two alternatives.

fungible collateral (such as oil in a storage tank or grain in a silo)[216] is permitted.

Section 9–207(2)(e) permits a secured party in possession of pledged collateral to repledge it with a third party as security for his own debt (as when a stockbroker holding his customer's stock in pledge repledges it with a bank as security for a loan)— but only on terms that do not impair the debtor's right to redeem the collateral. Thus the creditor acts improperly if he repledges for an amount greater than the original debt or for a period exceeding the duration of the original pledge: In either case, the debtor will be hampered in getting his property back on the terms for which he originally pledged it.[217]

Section 9–207(4) authorizes the secured party to use or operate pledged or repossessed collateral in three specified circumstances.[218] First, use or operation is permissible when required for preservation of the collateral or its value, as when a piece of machinery will deteriorate unless kept in use.[219] Second, the collateral may be used or operated "pursuant to the order of a court of appropriate jurisdiction"—presumably referring to an order issued in insolvency proceedings. Finally, use or operation is authorized "in the manner and to the extent provided in the security agreement" except in the case of consumer goods.[220] Comment 4 to Section 9–207 observes: "Agreements providing for such operation are common in trust indentures securing corporate bonds and are particularly important when

---

[216] The term "fungible" is defined in Section 1–201(17).

[217] *A fortiori*, the secured party is in violation of Section 9–207(2)(e) if he *sells* pledged instruments to a holder in due course or securities to a good faith purchaser, since the debtor will be unable to retrieve the property from transferees of this sort. Although a secured party's interest is freely assignable, there must be a transfer of both the security *and* the debt.

[218] He may not, of course, use the collateral for his own benefit.

[219] This is simply the corollary of the duty imposed by Section 9–207(1) to exercise care in custody and preservation.

[220] The limitation with respect to consumer goods guards against abuse of unsophisticated debtors via adhesive language in the security agreement.

the collateral is a going business." It will be noted that profits earned in the course of use or operation must be remitted to the debtor,[221] whereas reasonable expenses incurred are chargeable to the debtor and are secured by the collateral.[222]

Under Section 9–207(3), a secured party is liable for any loss caused by his failure to fulfill the obligations imposed by Section 9–207, discussed previously, but he does not lose his security interest.

§ 3–5. PERFECTION WITH RESPECT TO PROCEEDS

The subject of perfection with respect to proceeds obtained by a debtor upon sale of the original collateral is taken up in the next chapter.[223]

---

[221] U.C.C. § 9–207(2)(c).
[222] U.C.C. § 9–207(2)(a).
[223] § 4–3 B (4) *infra.*

4

Priorities

In the majority of cases litigated under Article 9, the central question will be who has first claim on the property that is the subject of the security interest—the secured party or a competing third-party claimant. In most cases the competing claimant will be (1) a lien creditor, (2) another secured party, (3) a buyer from the debtor, (4) an owner of the real estate on which the chattel is located who asserts a claim to the chattel as a fixture, or (5) the debtor's bankruptcy trustee. The first four types of priority conflict are examined in this chapter; the fifth is treated in Chapter 6.

§ 4-1. SECURED PARTY VERSUS LIEN CREDITOR

A. Judicial Liens

(1) The General Priority Rule—Section 9-301(1)(b)

The general priority rule governing conflicts between an Article 9 secured party and a judicial lienholder [1] is Section 9-301(1)(b), the 1972 Code version of which provides that "an unperfected security interest is subordinate to the rights of . . . a person who becomes a lien creditor before the security interest is perfected." Assume, for example, that on January 1 a secured party obtains a security agreement granting him a security interest in a piece of machinery then owned by the debtor and lends funds but neglects to file a financing statement until January 8. Meanwhile, on January 4, an unsecured creditor obtains a ju-

---

[1] For a discussion of the extent to which Article 9 applies to liens, see § 1-4 F (2) *supra*.

dicial lien via judgment and levy.[2] When the debtor defaults, the lien creditor has first claim on the machine, since his lien arose before the security interest was perfected.[3] Had the secured party filed or taken possession prior to January 4, he would have priority. For further illustrations of the operation of Section 9–301(1)(b), see the previous discussions of "value" and "rights" as prerequisites to attachment.[4]

The 1962 Code version of Section 9–301(1)(b) imposes an additional requirement on the lien creditor: In order to prevail, he must not only have acquired his lien prior to perfection but must have done so "without knowledge of the security interest." Under this provision the lienor would lose in the preceding hypothetical despite later perfection of the security interest had he acquired knowledge of that interest prior to January 4. The lack-of-knowledge requirement has been dropped from the 1972 Code in view of the evidentiary difficulties associated with such a requirement and in order to make Section 9–301(1)(b) more consistent with other, "pure race to the courthouse" rules, such as Section 9–312(5).[5]

(2) The Ten-Day Grace Period for Purchase-Money Security Interests

An exception to the "first in time" rule of Section 9–301(1)(b), discussed previously, is found in Section 9–301(2), which states:

> If the secured party files with respect to a purchase money security interest before or within ten days after the debtor receives possession of the collateral, he takes priority over the rights of a transferee in bulk or of a lien creditor which arise between the time the security interest attaches and the time of filing.

Assume, for instance, that on January 1 the secured party sells a piece of machinery to the debtor on credit and takes a security

---

[2] See § 1–3 B *supra*.

[3] This assumes that the secured party did not perfect by the alternative method of taking possession prior to January 4.

[4] §§ 2–3 and 2–4 *supra*.

[5] See § 4–2 A (1)(a) *infra*.

interest therein. On the same day the machine is delivered to the debtor. Even though the secured party neglects to file until January 8, he will prevail over the interest of a judicial lien-holder arising on January 4, by virtue of Section 9–301(2).[6]

(3) Priority with Respect to Future Advances

Section 9–301(4) of the 1972 Code remedies an omission in the 1962 Code by laying down rules for resolving conflicts between a judicial lienholder and a secured party with respect to future advances made by the latter:

> A person who becomes a lien creditor while a security interest is perfected takes subject to the security interest only to the extent that it secures advances made before he becomes a lien creditor or within 45 days thereafter or made without knowledge of the lien or pursuant to a commitment entered into without knowledge of the lien.

The most important aspect of this language is the provision that the secured party has absolute priority for future advances made during the 45-day period after the lien attaches, regardless of the secured party's knowledge of the lien.[7] This rule was designed to mesh with Section 6323(d) of the Internal Revenue Code, as amended by the Tax Lien Act of 1966, which gives priority to a secured party for future advances made within 45 days after a tax lien is filed *if* the security interest is "protected under local law against a judgment lien arising, as of the time of tax lien filing, out of an unsecured obligation."[8] Assume, for instance, that on January 1 the secured party obtains a security agreement

---

[6] The ten-day grace period was established primarily with credit sales of items like equipment in mind (although the language is not so limited). These sales are frequently not negotiated beforehand, so that no advance filing is possible, and busy showroom clerks often have no opportunity to ensure that a filing is made at the time of the transaction.

[7] 1972 U.C.C. § 9–301, Comment 7.

[8] The secured party must also have had no knowledge of the tax lien filing at the time of making the future advance, and a written security agreement must have been entered into prior to the tax lien filing.

containing only an "optional" future advance clause,[9] lends $10,000, and files a financing statement. On January 15, a tax lien is filed against the property that is the subject of the security interest. On February 1, the secured party makes an optional advance of $5,000. Would the secured party have been "protected" under the 1962 Code with respect to the $5,000 future advance as against an unsecured creditor who obtained a judgment lien on January 15? As previously noted,[10] it is generally felt that the answer should be yes, on the theory that the future advance was part of a single security interest for which sufficient "value" was given at the time of the initial advance and which therefore attached and was perfected on January 1—prior to attachment of the lien—in satisfaction of Section 9-301(1)(b). Nevertheless, a contrary argument can be made that a second separate security interest was created with respect to the future advance, for which "value" was not given until February 1 and which therefore did not attach and become perfected until that date—after the lien arose.[11] Thus, in the absence of determinative language, the outcome is not certain under the 1962 Code. The 45-day provision in 1972 Section 9-301(4) was apparently designed to make certain that the secured party would prevail over the intervening lienor in this type of situation. This certainty requires that it be assumed, however, that the reference to "a person who becomes a lien creditor *while a security interest is perfected*" means "while a security interest with respect to the *initial advance* is perfected"; if it means "while a security interest with respect to the *future advance* is perfected," the situation is thrown back under the arguments made under the 1962 Code. Be that as it may, the "while a security interest is perfected" language clearly prevents the section from helping the secured party with an optional future advance clause who makes no initial advance (as when, in the hypothetical above, the creditor had

---

[9] See § 2-2 D (2) *supra.*

[10] § 2-3 *supra.*

[11] *Id.*

advanced the entire $15,000 on February 1). In such a case there can be no "value" before the inception of the lien and thus no attachment and perfection of *any* security interest prior to that time.[12]

B. *Artisans' Liens—Section 9-310*

Assume that a debtor has given a security interest in his automobile to a bank, which duly perfected the interest by notation on a certificate of title. Upon damaging the car, the debtor has it repaired by an auto dealership. The debtor then finds himself unable to pay for the repairs and defaults on his debt to the bank. The bank asserts the right to repossess the car. The auto dealership, invoking a state statute giving it a lien for repairs, asserts the right to retain possession until its bill is paid. Which party prevails?

Although Section 9-104(c) generally excludes from the coverage of Article 9 "a lien given by statute or other rule of law for services or materials,"[13] an exception is made for priority conflicts governed by Section 9-310. The latter section provides, in essence, that a lien given by statute or common law to one who furnishes services or materials[14] with respect to goods covered by a security interest prevails over the security interest (even though perfected), as long as the lienor retains possession[15] and unless the lien is created by a statute that expressly provides otherwise.[16] Thus, subject to the latter two conditions, the auto dealership in the hypothetical will prevail.

---

[12] See § 2-3 *supra*.

[13] For a discussion of the extent to which Article 9 applies to liens, see § 1-4 F (2) *supra*.

[14] A lien of the sort referred to in Section 9-310 is typically called an "artisan's" or "repairman's" lien.

[15] That is, upon giving up possession, the lienor loses his priority. Note that, apart from Section 9-310, the statute or common law rule creating this sort of lien usually requires possession as a condition of the lien.

[16] If the lien is nonstatutory or if it is created by statute but the statute is silent concerning priority against a security interest (even though decisional law has construed the statute to make the lien subordinate), the lien

§ 4-2. SECURED PARTY VERSUS SECURED PARTY

It is not uncommon for a debtor to give a security interest in the same collateral to two different lenders,[17] whereupon, when the debtor defaults on his loans, both secured parties assert a claim to the collateral.[18] In these instances the conflict between the secured parties will usually be governed by one of the provisions in Section 9–312 [19]—either the general priority rules in subsection (5), or one of the special rules in subsection (2) (pertaining to crops), subsection (3) (pertaining to conflicts involving a purchase-money security interest in inventory), or subsection (4) (pertaining to conflicts involving a purchase-money security interest in collateral other than inventory).[20]

A. General Rules of Priority

(1) Section 9-312(5)

The general rules governing priority conflicts between security interests in the same collateral are found in subsection

---

takes priority. U.C.C. § 9–310, Comment 2. The rationale for giving the lienor priority is that he has enhanced or preserved the value of the collateral. U.C.C. § 9–310, Comment 1.

[17] This may occur either through dishonesty or inadvertence. In so doing, the debtor, of course, obtains twice the amount of loan funds to which he is rightfully entitled.

[18] This will occur only if both secured parties are unpaid or partially unpaid at the time of default.

[19] Occasionally some other provision will apply; for example, Section 9–308 in some situations involving chattel paper. See § 4–3 A (3) infra.

It should be noted that Section 9–312 governs only conflicts involving two Article 9 secured parties; it does not apply to conflicts between an Article 9 secured party and some other type of competitor, such as a lienor (§ 4–1 supra) or a buyer from the debtor (§ 4–3 A infra).

[20] Subsections (3), (4) and (5) are discussed in the following sections. Subsection (2) pertaining to crops is discussed in § 4–7 infra.

The present discussion focuses on conflicts with respect to original collateral still in the hands of the debtor. If at the time of default the debtor has sold the original collateral to a buyer, the conflict may center on which secured party is entitled to the proceeds received by the debtor. The various provisions in Section 9–312 bearing on the latter type of conflict are discussed in § 4–3 B (5)(a) infra.

(5) of Section 9–312. Subsection (5) is often called the "catch-all" provision of Section 9–312 because it applies when one of the special requirements for application of subsections (2),[21] (3),[22] or (4)[23] are not satisfied. The types of situations governed by subsection (5) fall roughly into four categories, as discussed *infra*.

(a) Both Security Interests Perfected by Filing

Section 9–312(5)(a) governs situations in which both security interests are perfected by filing. To illustrate, assume the following: On Day 1, SP_1 and the debtor, a department store, begin negotiations concerning a non-purchase-money financing arrangement covering the debtor's accounts. At this time SP_1 properly files a financing statement but does not obtain a security agreement satisfying Section 9–203 [24] and does not loan any funds.[25] On Day 2, Ms. Jones, a customer of the debtor, purchases an item on unsecured credit, thereby creating an account. On Day 3, SP_2 obtains a security agreement giving it a non-purchase-money security interest in the debtor's accounts, loans money, and files. On Day 4, SP_1 (who, it will be assumed, has learned of SP_2's interest) makes its first advance to the debtor and obtains a security agreement. If the debtor defaults, which secured party wins with respect to the Jones account?

Since the conflict does not involve crops and since neither secured party is a purchase-money creditor, Sections 9–312(2), 9–312(3), and 9–312(4) do not apply. Hence the situation falls within Section 9–312(5). Since both creditors perfected their interests by filing, the applicable provision is subsection (5)(a). Under the 1962 text of subsection (5)(a), when both parties have perfected by filing, the first to *file* prevails, irrespective of which

---

[21] § 4–7 *infra*.

[22] § 4–2 B (2) *infra*.

[23] § 4–2 B (3) *infra*.

[24] On the requirements for a valid security agreement, see § 2–2 *supra*.

[25] Section 9–402(1) permits a financing statement to be filed before a security agreement is executed and before the security interest attaches.

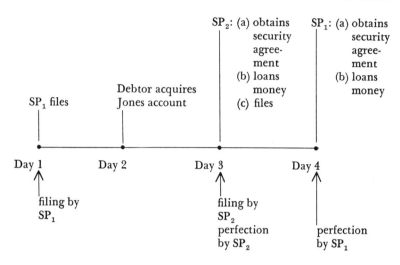

interest attached first or was perfected first.[26] Thus, under the 1962 Code, SP_1 wins, despite the fact that SP_2 perfected first (since SP_1's interest did not attach, and therefore was not perfected, until Day 4, when a security agreement was executed and "value" was given).[27] Moreover, SP_1 wins despite having had knowledge of SP_2's interest, which points up the fact that such knowledge has no bearing on the outcome under Section 9–312(5).[28]

---

[26] The first-to-file rule is said to be justified on the basis that SP_2 could have protected himself by checking the files.

[27] As discussed in Chapters 2 and 3, a security interest becomes perfected under the 1962 Code only when the last of the following four events occurs: (1) A security agreement satisfying Section 9–203(1) is executed (or the creditor has possession of the collateral); (2) the debtor has "rights in the collateral" (Section 9–204(1)) (Day 2 in the hypothetical, when the account arose); (3) the creditor has given "value" (Section 9–204(1)); and (4) a financing statement is filed, or the interest is perfected by possession (Sections 9–304 and 9–305) or automatically perfected (Section 9–302) or temporarily perfected (Section 9–304). The same is true under the 1972 Code except that requirements (2) and (3) are found in Section 9–203(1).

[28] Consequently, Section 9–312(5) is often called a "pure race" (that is, race to the courthouse) statute. Making the determinative factor an event such as the time of filing, which is capable of precise ascertainment, avoids

SP$_1$ will also prevail under the somewhat different language of 1972 Section 9–312(5)(a), which awards priority to the first secured party who either files or perfects, whichever occurs earlier; that is, in the hypothetical, the first of the two events was filing, which was accomplished by SP$_1$ on Day 1. Had SP$_1$ not filed until Day 4, the first event would have been perfection by SP$_2$ on Day 3, whereupon SP$_2$ would prevail, just as he would under 1962 Section 9–312(5)(a). The change in language in Revised subsection (5)(a) does not alter the outcome in conflicts in which both parties have perfected by filing; it is significant only in situations in which one of the parties has perfected by a means other than filing, as discussed immediately below.

(b) Both Interests Perfected, One by a Means Other than Filing

Assume the same facts as in the hypothetical just discussed except that the collateral in question is goods, rather than accounts, and on Day 3, instead of filing a financing statement, SP$_2$ perfects by taking possession. Under the 1962 Code, since the situation now involves one security interest perfected by a means other than filing, the applicable provision is subsection (5)(b), whereunder SP$_2$, the first to *perfect*, prevails—the opposite result from that reached under subsection (5)(a). The drafters of Revised Article 9 felt that this difference in outcome, hinging solely on whether the second secured party perfected by filing or possession, was unwarranted and eliminated the distinction by consolidating 1962 subsections (5)(a) and (5)(b) in the new language of 1972 subsection (5)(a), which awards priority to the first to file *or perfect*, whichever occurs earlier. Thus, under this new language, SP$_1$ would prevail regardless of whether SP$_2$ perfected by filing or possession.

Subsection (5)(b) of the 1962 Code and subsection (5)(a) of the

---

the evidentiary uncertainty associated with a showing of subjective knowledge.

1972 Code also apply when the non-filing party's interest is perfected by a means other than possession; that is, in instances involving automatic perfection under Section 9–302 [29] or temporary perfection under Section 9–304.[30] Assume, for instance, that on Day 1, SP_1 has a security interest in a negotiable document in the debtor's possession which is temporarily perfected for 21 days without filing under Section 9–304(4) or 9–304(5). On Day 2, SP_2 files and thus obtains a perfected security interest in the same document. On Day 3, SP_1 files. Under both subsection (5)(b) of the 1962 Code and subsection (5)(a) of the 1972 Code, SP_1 will prevail as the first to perfect.

(c) One Interest Perfected, the Other Not

When one security interest is perfected and the other is not, the perfected interest prevails. Although not flatly stated, this is clearly implied in Sections 9–301(1)(a)[31] and 9–312(5). Under 1962 Section 9–312(5)(b) and 1972 Section 9–312(5)(a), the perfected interest is perfected "first."

(d) Neither Interest Perfected

Subsection (5)(c) of 1962 Section 9–312—renumbered as subsection (5)(b) in the 1972 Code—provides that when neither security interest is perfected, the first to attach prevails.[32] This would be true in the hypothetical posed in Section 4–2A(1)(a) above if, for instance, SP_1's filing was in the wrong place under Section 9–401 and SP_2's financing statement was not signed by the debtor, as required by Section 9–402(1). In that case SP_2's interest, which attached first (on Day 3), would win.

---

[29] Automatic perfection is discussed in § 3–2 *supra*.

[30] Temporary perfection is discussed in § 3–2 B *supra*.

[31] *See* U.C.C. § 9–301, Comment 2.

[32] This priority rule is largely of theoretical interest, since it is difficult to imagine many disputes reaching trial without at least one of the interests being perfected; that is, upon learning of the dispute, one or both parties will dash to file (or otherwise perfect) on the theory that late perfection may be better than none at all.

(2) Future Advances

Assume that on Day 1, SP_1 obtains a security agreement giving him a security interest in equipment in the debtor's possession worth $15,000. SP_1 loans $10,000 and files a financing statement. Neither the security agreement nor the financing statement mentions mandatory future advances. On Day 2, SP_2 takes a non-purchase-money security interest in the same equipment, loans $7,000, and files. On Day 3, SP_1 advances an additional $5,000 against the same equipment. If the debtor defaults, does SP_1 have priority for the aggregate amount of the two advances—$15,000—or only for the initial $10,000 advance?

SP_1 will prevail concerning the full $15,000 under both the 1962 and 1972 versions of Section 9–312. The first sentence of new subsection (7) of the 1972 Code states what was implicit under subsection (5)(a) of the 1962 Code; namely, that a creditor has the same priority with respect to future advances as he does with respect to his initial advance under Section 9–312(5). Stated another way, priority with respect to future advances relates back to the initial time of filing. Thus, since SP_1 has first-to-file priority under subsection (5)(a) with respect to the initial $10,000 advance, he likewise prevails regarding the $5,000 future advance.[33] And this is true regardless of whether or not the initial security agreement bound SP_1 to make any future advances[34] and regardless of whether future advances were referred to in the financing statement.[35]

---

[33] The rationale for this result is that the first party to file should not have to check for later filings by others and should not himself have to make a new filing before each subsequent advance. The advantages are readily apparent in "revolving floating lien" arrangements (described in § 2–2 D (2) *supra*), in which the lender may make a multitude of future advances. Moreover, the initial filing should alert the intervening creditor to the existence of a prior claim to the collateral in question; and it is unusual for a creditor to loan against collateral that secures a prior loan. The more common practice is for the later creditor to pay off the earlier one, thus ensuring total priority.

[34] *See* 1972 U.C.C. § 9–312, Comment 7.

[35] 1972 U.C.C. § 9–204, Comment 5.

But suppose SP₁ had perfected by taking possession rather than filing. This raises a more difficult question under the 1962 Code because the situation now falls under subsection (5)(b),[36] which awards priority to the first to *perfect* rather than the first to file. And since the time of perfection hinges on the time of attachment, which, in turn, depends on when "value" was given,[37] it can be argued that SP₁ should lose with respect to the $5,000 advance, which was the subject of a separate security interest that did not attach ("value" not being given until the advance was made on Day 3) and thus was not perfected until after SP₂ perfected.[38]

Subsection (7) of the 1972 Code resolves this difficulty by stating that regardless of whether future advances are made while the security interest is perfected by filing *or by possession,* the secured party's priority concerning future advances will be the same as the priority to which he is entitled with respect to his initial advance under the "first to file or perfect" rule of subsection (5)(a). Thus, in the immediately preceding illustration, since SP₁ would prevail under 1972 subsection (5)(a) with respect to his initial advance (by virtue of being the first to perfect), he would likewise prevail concerning the subsequent advance.

It should be noted that 1972 subsection (7) applies the "relation back" rule only when the future advance in question is made "while a security interest is perfected by filing or the taking of possession." The second and third sentences of subsection (7) apply a different rule in the rare situation in which future advances are made while the security interest is perfected automatically (Section 9–302) or temporarily (Section

---

[36] One interest is perfected by a means other than filing. See § 4–2 A (1)(b) *supra.*

[37] 1962 U.C.C. § 9–204(1).

[38] The general view under the 1962 Code seems to be that this argument is invalid and that the $5,000 should instead be deemed part of a single continuous security transaction for which sufficient "value" was given in the form of the initial $10,000 advance. U.C.C. § 1–201(44)(d).

9–304); namely, that priority dates only from the time of the advance unless the secured party committed to make it while the interest was perfected by filing or possession.[39] To illustrate: Assume that on Day 1, SP_1 takes a security interest in a negotiable document, makes an advance, and perfects by taking possession of the document. On Day 2, SP_2 takes a security interest in the same document and perfects by filing. On Day 3, SP_1 turns the document over to the debtor for one of the purposes specified in Section 9–304(5)(a). On Day 4, SP_1 makes a further advance. Although SP_1 will prevail concerning the initial advance, he will lose with respect to the advance on Day 4, which was made after SP_2 perfected. Had SP_1 *committed* on Day 1 to make the future advance, however, he would have priority concerning both advances.

Although the phrase "for the purposes of subsection (5)" in 1972 subsection (7) might seem to suggest that the "relation back" rule is confined to situations governed by subsection (5) and that some other rule applies when the special purchase-money provisions in subsections (3) and (4) govern, in actuality the same rule—that a secured party's priority with respect to future advances is the same as with respect to his initial advance—applies under the latter subsections; the only difference is that the rule operates negatively. Assume that on Day 1, SP_1 and Debtor enter into a typical inventory "floating lien" arrangement,[40] wherein SP_1 is to make non-purchase-money future advances against incoming items of inventory. SP_1 makes an initial advance and files. On Day 2, Debtor acquires a new item of inventory with funds loaned by SP_2, who takes a purchase-money security interest, files, and otherwise complies with the requirements of Section 9–312(3). On Day 3, SP_1 makes a sub-

---

[39] The theory is that the initial secured party's filing or taking of possession (that is, absence of possession in the debtor) will sufficiently alert the prospective intervening party to the existence of a prior claim, but automatic or temporary perfection, which involve neither filing nor possession, will not.

[40] Floating liens are discussed in § 2–2 D (2) *supra*.

sequent advance against the new item. If Debtor defaults, to what extent does each creditor have a claim to the new item of inventory?

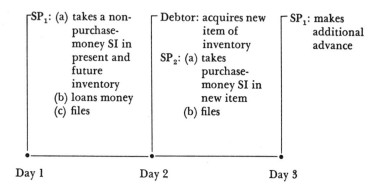

SP$_1$: (a) takes a non-purchase-money SI in present and future inventory (b) loans money (c) files	Debtor: acquires new item of inventory SP$_2$: (a) takes purchase-money SI in new item (b) files	SP$_1$: makes additional advance
Day 1	Day 2	Day 3

Under Section 9–312(3), SP$_2$ has priority with respect to the new item free of SP$_1$'s claim for either advance.[41] In other words, SP$_1$ has the same *lack* of priority with respect to its future advance as with respect to its initial advance.[42] This is true under both the 1962 and 1972 Codes; and the same result would occur under Section 9–312(4) if the collateral were equipment rather than inventory.

(3) After-Acquired Collateral

The immediately preceding hypothetical can be used to illustrate application of the rules of priority with respect to after-acquired collateral under Section 9–312(5).[43] If the security

---

[41] *See* 1972 U.C.C. § 9–312, Comment 6. This is true assuming the amount realized upon repossession and sale of the item is no more than the unpaid balance owed SP$_2$. If the item were sold for more, SP$_1$ would have a claim to the surplus.

For further discussion of the Section 9–312(3) priority rules, see §§ 4–2 B (1) and (2) *infra*.

[42] The requirement under Section 9–312(3) that SP$_2$ notify SP$_1$ is designed to warn the latter party not to make further advances.

[43] The illustration given in § 4–2 A (1)(a) *supra* also involves after-acquired collateral.

interest taken by SP_2 on Day 2 were a *non*-purchase-money one, Section 9–312(5)(a) would apply,[44] and SP_1 would prevail concerning the new item of inventory [45] (for the amount of both advances) by virtue of being the first to file.[46] This would be so despite the fact that both interests attached and thus were perfected simultaneously on Day 2 when the debtor acquired "rights in the collateral." [47] The same result would occur under both the 1962 and 1972 versions of the Code.

If, on the other hand, SP_2 took a purchase-money interest on Day 2 and otherwise satisfied the requirements of Section 9–312(3), the latter section would give SP_2 priority concerning the new item (with respect to both advances),[48] as indicated above.[49]

B. Special Rules of Priority—Conflicts Involving a Purchase-Money Security Interest

As noted, the general rule governing conflicts between secured parties, set forth in Section 9–312(5), awards priority on a first-in-time (that is, first to file or otherwise perfect) basis. Special situations exist, however, in which the second secured party on the scene is given priority by virtue of having a purchase-money security interest. These are situations governed by Sections 9–312(3) and 9–312(4).[50]

---

[44] Subsection (5) would likewise apply if SP_2 had taken a purchase-money interest but one of the other requirements of subsection (3) was not satisfied.

[45] This discussion assumes that SP_1 had a valid security interest in after-acquired collateral, as discussed in § 2–2 D (2) *supra*.

[46] *See* 1972 U.C.C. § 9–312, Comment 6.

[47] 1962 U.C.C. § 9–204(1); 1972 U.C.C. § 9–203(1)(c). The time when a debtor acquires "rights" is discussed in § 2–4 *supra*.

[48] The same would be true with respect to collateral other than inventory under Section 9–312(4).

[49] § 4–2 A (2) *supra*.

[50] The special rule in Section 9–312(2) pertaining to crops is discussed in § 4–7 *infra*.

(1) In General—Special Preemptive Priority

In general, both subsections (3) and (4) of Section 9–312 apply to the following basic type of situation: On Day 1, SP_1 takes a security interest in Debtor's presently owned and after-acquired property and properly perfects (usually by filing). On Day 2, Debtor acquires a new item of property of the type covered by SP_1's security interest, using credit extended by SP_2, to whom Debtor (intending also to obtain an advance against the new item from SP_1) dishonestly gives a purchase-money security interest.[51] SP_2 perfects. When Debtor defaults, the question arises whether SP_1 or SP_2 has priority with respect to the new item.

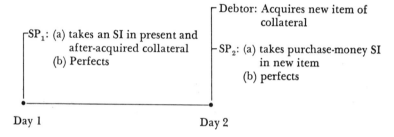

If the general rule of Section 9–312(5) were applied, SP_1, being the first to file or otherwise perfect, would prevail. But here, since SP_2 has a purchase-money security interest, he will prevail even though second in time, assuming he has satisfied the requirements of subsection (3) or (4) of Section 9–312.

The rationale for this special preemptive priority is often described in shorthand terms as "the encouragement of new money." Basically it protects the debtor from the initial secured party's after-acquired collateral clause: The initial creditor may not be committed to, and may not wish to, loan the debtor additional funds on some date subsequent to the initial advance when the debtor needs to expand and buy additional inventory or needs to purchase a new item of equipment to keep his busi-

---

[51] The later security interest may well be given as a matter of inadvertence rather than dishonesty.

ness running profitably. The special priority given by subsections (3) and (4) of Section 9–312 enables the debtor to attract
new credit for these purposes by offering a later purchase money
lender first claim on the new property. In order to enjoy this
priority, however, the later secured party must carefully thread
his way through the various requirements imposed by subsection
(3) or (4) of Section 9–312, whichever is applicable, as discussed
next.

(2) Purchase-Money Security Interest in Inventory—Section 9–312(3)

If the secured party attempting to claim preemptive priority
with respect to inventory collateral fails to comply with any one
of the following requirements embodied in subsection (3) of
Section 9–312, the dispute will come within subsection (5),
whereunder priority will usually be lost to the prior perfected
security interest.[52]

(a) Purchase-Money Requirement

Only a security interest that can be characterized as "purchase-
money" within the definition of Section 9–107 can invoke the
special priority of Section 9–312(3). The requirements for
purchase-money status are discussed in a succeeding subsection.[53] Moreover, subsection (3) only applies to a conflict between a purchase-money interest and a prior *non*-purchase-
money interest. The status of multiple purchase-money
interests is discussed below.[54]

(b) Time of Perfection

Under both the 1962 and 1972 Codes, Section 9–312(3) can
be invoked only if "the purchase money security interest is perfected at the time the debtor receives possession of the inven-

---

[52] Priorities under Section 9–312 (5) are discussed in § 4–2 A *supra*.

[53] § 4–2 B (4) *infra*.

[54] § 4–2 B (5) *infra*.

tory." The term "receives possession" refers to the time the goods are actually physically delivered to the debtor and not to the possibly earlier time when the debtor acquires "rights in the collateral" (as when the goods are "identified to the contract" under Section 2–501 at the time the debtor contracts to purchase them for later delivery).[55]

In order to ensure satisfaction of the subsection (3) perfection requirement, the purchase-money party should file well in advance of his transaction with the debtor. Unlike subsection (4), subsection (3) does not afford a ten-day grace period for filing *after* the debtor acquires possession of the goods.

(c) "Inventory"

Section 9–312(3) applies only to purchase-money security interests in *inventory,* as that term is defined in Section 9–109(4).[56] Less strict requirements are imposed by Section 9–312(4) on creditors with purchase money interests in collateral other than inventory. Thus a purchase-money party who is uncertain whether his collateral qualifies as "inventory" should comply with the requirements of subsection (3), thereby ensuring satisfaction of subsection (4) should a court later deem the latter provision to be applicable.

(d) Notification Requirement

(i) Purpose. The typical situation for which Section 9–312 was designed involves an initial financer who takes a

---

[55] Acquisition of "rights in the collateral" as one of the prerequisites to attachment is discussed in § 2–4 *supra.* It should be noted that perfection is not required "before" the debtor obtains possession of the goods. The "at the time" language takes into account the type of situation in which the purchase-money party has already filed, has obtained a security agreement, and has "given value" by extending credit. If the debtor immediately takes possession of the goods at the time of purchase, the last event for attachment, and therefore for perfection—the debtor's acquisition of "rights in the collateral"—occurs *simultaneously* with the debtor's taking possession. In such a case the perfection requirement of Section 9–312(3) is satisfied.

[56] For a discussion of what constitutes inventory, see § 1–5 A (5) *supra.*

"floating lien" security interest in a merchant-debtor's presently owned and after-acquired inventory, contemplating that as the debtor sells present items to customers and acquires new replacement items, further advances will be made against the new items.[57] A key requirement of both the 1962 and 1972 versions of Section 9–312(3) is that the purchase-money party notify the initial financer of the new security interest. Unless warned of the new encumbrance, the initial financer will make advances against the new items without being aware that his rights have been preempted by an intervening creditor.[58] A purchase money party who fails to give notification in the proper form, at the proper time, and to the proper person, will generally lose the benefit of Section 9–312(3) and be subordinated to the earlier creditor under Section 9–312(5).

(ii) Form. Both the 1962 and 1972 versions of Section 9–312(3) require notification that the purchase-money party "has or expects to acquire a purchase-money security interest in inventory of the debtor, describing such inventory by item or type." Under the 1962 Code it is generally felt that the notification can be oral. In the interest of greater evidentiary certainty, 1972 Section 9–312(3)(b) requires that the notification be "in writing."

(iii) Duration of Effectiveness. The 1962 Code is unclear about whether a secured party who anticipates more than one purchase-money transaction with the debtor must notify the earlier creditor only once or at the time of each transaction. The 1972 version of Section 9–312(3)(c) makes it clear that the purchase-money party need only give notice once; thereafter, for a period of five years, he may enter into any number of transactions without the need for additional notifications.[59]

(iv) Interests Temporarily Perfected Under Section 9–304(5). The 1962 version of Section 9–312(3) leaves uncer-

---

[57] "Floating lien" arrangements are discussed in § 2–2 D (2) *supra*.

[58] *See* 1972 U.C.C. § 9–312, Comment 3.

[59] The five-year period of effectiveness was chosen by analogy to the duration of financing statements under Section 9–403(2).

tain the status of a purchase-money financer who pays against a negotiable document of title (such as a bill of lading) covering a new item of inventory, releases the document to the debtor to enable him to obtain possession of the goods, and, instead of filing, relies on the temporary perfection allowed for 21 days after release of the document under Section 9–304(5).[60] The financer has no problem satisfying the requirement that his interest in the inventory be perfected before the debtor receives possession thereof; [61] the question is whether he must give notification to the earlier filed secured party in order to prevail. Under one line of reasoning Section 9–312(3) of the 1962 Code governs the priority of a creditor of this sort, and notification must be given. But another line of argument holds that this situation is governed by Section 9–309, which provides that "a holder to whom a negotiable document of title has been duly negotiated . . . take[s] priority over an earlier security interest even though perfected." The latter provision requires no notification. Essentially, the problem results from the lack of any reference in Section 9–312(3) to interests temporarily perfected under Section 9–304(5) and the lack of any reference in Section 9–304(5) to Section 9–312(3). The drafters of the 1972 Code have clarified the situation, adopting the first line of reasoning, by inserting both references. Thus under 1972 Section 9–312 (3)(b)(ii) the purchase-money party who relies on the 21-day period of temporary perfection must give notification to earlier filed secured parties. Unfortunately, however, as discussed be-

---

[60] A typical sequence of events leading up to the financer's possession of the document is described in the last paragraph of § 1–5 B (2)(a) *supra*.

[61] Under Section 9–305 possession of the document perfects the security interest therein; under Section 9–304(2) perfection of an interest in the document also perfects the interest in the goods themselves; under Section 9–304(5), when the creditor releases the document to the debtor, his interest is perfected without either filing or possession for 21 days; and under Section 9–303(2), "[i]f a security interest is originally perfected in any way permitted under this Article and is subsequently perfected in some other way . . . the security interest shall be deemed to be perfected continuously for the purposes of this Article."

low,[62] it is not entirely clear *when* that notification must be given.

(v) When and to Whom Notification Must Be Given. The 1962 version of Section 9–312(3) states that the purchase-money creditor must give notification to earlier creditors who either (a) filed prior to the time of the purchase-money party's filing or (b) did not file but were nevertheless "known" to the purchase-money party; and it is required that the notification be "received" before the debtor obtains possession of the new item of inventory. Thus the 1962 Code clearly specifies both *who* must be notified and the *time* for notification.

It is likewise clear that the 1972 Code has removed one category from the "who" requirement; namely, in the interest of greater evidentiary certainty, it will no longer be necessary for the purchase-money party to notify earlier creditors "known" but not on file.[63]

Apart from the foregoing, however, it is unclear under the 1972 Code *who* must be notified and *when* that notification must be given.[64] The interpretive difficulty with the notification requirement imposed by paragraph (3)(b) of 1972 Section 9–312 centers on whether subparagraphs (i) ("before the date of the filing made by the purchase money secured party") and (ii) ("before the beginning of the 21 day period where the purchase money security interest is temporarily perfected [under] subsection (5) of Section 9–304") refer only to the phrase "if the

---

[62] § 4–2 B (2)(d)(v) *infra.*

[63] There were two additional reasons for this deletion: (1) The provision has no real effect anyway, since even though the purchase-money party (having properly perfected) fails to give notification and therefore loses the benefit of Section 9–312(3), he will nevertheless prevail over a prior *unfiled* creditor under Section 9–312(5) as the first to file; and (2) when two or more prior creditors exist, the 1962 Code might be read to deny priority against a prior creditor who has properly been notified unless the purchase-money party has also given notice to all other creditors entitled thereto.

[64] As discussed in § 4–2 B (2)(d)(vi) *infra,* it is also unclear whether the notification need only be "given" or must actually be "received."

holder had filed" or only to the phrase "the purchase money secured party gives notification" or to both phrases. Various commentators have given conflicting interpretations.

One possible interpretation is that subparagraphs (i) and (ii) modify only the phrase "if the holder had filed" and make no reference to the words "the purchase money secured party gives notification." In other words, the sole purpose of paragraph (3)(b) is to specify *who* must be given notification (earlier creditors who filed prior to the times stated in subparagraphs (i) and ii)), with no statement about the *time* for giving notice. The time for notification would then be specified by paragraph (3)(c), which, aside from the reference to the five-year duration,[65] states that the earlier secured party must "receive the notification . . . before the debtor receives possession of the inventory." In the author's view this interpretation—that the purchase-money creditor need only notify earlier creditors who had filed prior to the times specified in subparagraphs (i) and (ii) of paragraph (3)(b) and that the deadline for the giving (and receipt)[66] of notification is the time the debtor obtains possession of the goods—is the correct one. For one thing, this was quite clearly the rule under the 1962 version of Section 9–312(3), and no statement can be found in the legislative history of 1972 Section 9–312 evidencing any intent to institute a change. Moreover, sound policy supports setting the cutoff point by which the earlier creditor must be on file at the time the purchase-money party normally searches the record, that is, when he makes his own filing; and no policy reason appears for changing the time of the debtor's obtaining possession of the inventory as the deadline for notification, since it is the debtor's acquisition of the goods that prompts the earlier creditor to make an advance against them unless he is warned of the purchase-money interest.

For these reasons the author rejects the other two possible

---

[65] Discussed in § 4–2 B (2)(d)(iii) *supra*.

[66] The "gives" versus "receives" question is discussed in § 4–2 B (2)(d)(vi) *infra*.

interpretations: (1) that subparagraphs (i) and (ii) of 1972 paragraph (3)(b) refer both to the phrase "if the holder had filed" and the phrase "the purchase money secured party gives notification"—that is, that the purchase-money creditor must notify earlier secured parties who have filed before the date of filing by the purchase-money creditor or before the beginning of the 21-day period, whichever is appropriate, and that the notification must be given by whichever of those times applies—and (2) that subparagraphs (i) and (ii) of 1972 paragraph (3)(b) refer only to the phrase "the purchase money secured party gives notification"—that is, that the notification must be given before the date of filing by the purchase-money creditor or the beginning of the 21-day period, whichever is appropriate, but that Section 9–312(3) leaves unspecified the time by which the earlier creditor must be on file in order to be entitled to notification.

Since it is highly likely that 1972 paragraph (3)(b) *does* dictate when the earlier creditor must be on file in order to be entitled to notification (and thus answers the "*who* must be notified" question), the major question centers on the *time* for notification. Whereas, as noted, the author supports a reading which would only require receipt of the notice before the debtor obtains the inventory, careful practice requires that the purchase-money party ensure, whenever possible, that the notification is given and received before the earlier times specified in subparagraphs (i) (before the date of filing by the purchase-money party) or (ii) (before the beginning of the 21-day period) of paragraph (3)(b)), until the ambiguity is resolved judicially or by amendment to the Code.

(vi) "Giving" Versus "Receipt" of Notification. An additional ambiguity in 1972 Section 9–312(3) arises from the use of the words "gives notification" in paragraph (3)(b), as compared with the words "receives notification" in paragraph (3)(c);[67] that is, is 1972 Section 9–312(3) satisfied only if the earlier secured party actually *receives* the notification before the

---

[67] The differing definitions of "gives notification" and "receives notification" are set forth in Section 1–201(26).

requisite time [68] or is it sufficient for the purchase-money creditor to *send* the notification by the deadline, regardless of whether it is received thereafter (as when it is lost or delayed in the mails)? Since the 1962 version of Section 9–312(3) quite clearly requires "receipt," and no statement can be found in the legislative history of 1972 Section 9–312(3) evidencing any intent to change this requirement, the author believes that the 1972 Code also requires that the earlier secured party actually *receive* the notification by the deadline. In light of this ambiguity prudence dictates that the purchase-money party send the notification well in advance of the deadline. And, as noted above, prudence dictates assuming that the deadline is the date of filing by the purchase-money party or the beginning of the 21-day period, whichever is appropriate.

(e) Proceeds

The 1962 version of Section 9–312(3) leaves in doubt the extent to which the preemptive priority given a purchase-money financer in inventory as original collateral extends to proceeds received by the debtor when he sells the inventory. This has caused particularly troublesome questions when the proceeds consist in an account and the competing claimant is an earlier accounts financer. The drafters of the 1972 Code have resolved the issue in favor of the accounts financer by inserting language in 1972 Section 9–312(3) clearly stating that the purchase-money party's priority extends only to "identifiable *cash* proceeds" and therefore not to accounts. This is discussed in detail in a subsequent section.[69]

(f) Future Advances

Priority with respect to future advances in a situation governed by Section 9–312(3) has previously been discussed.[70]

---

[68] The ambiguity with regard to what constitutes the deadline (which, in the author's view, is the time the debtor obtains possession of the new item) is discussed in §4–2 B (2)(d)(v) *supra*.

[69] §4–3 B (5)(a)(i) *infra*.

[70] §4–2 A (2) *supra*.

(g) Analogous Rules Applied to Consignments

As previously discussed in detail,[71] the 1972 Code leaves it uncertain whether a consignor who is not deemed to have an Article 9 security interest but is nevertheless required to file under Section 2–326(3) must give a Section 9–312(3) notification to an earlier financer of the consignee. The drafters of the 1972 Code have resolved the question by inserting a new provision, 1972 Section 9–114, which requires the consignor to give the same notice as a purchase-money secured party in order to attain priority over the earlier-filed security interest in inventory. It should be observed that the notification language in 1972 Section 9–114 is virtually identical to that of 1972 Section 9–312(3) and therefore the same ambiguities discussed previously in connection with the latter provision [72] also obtain under the former.

(3) Purchase-Money Security Interests in Collateral Other than Inventory—Section 9–312(4)

Section 9–312(4) governs conflicts between a creditor with a security interest in after-acquired collateral *other* than inventory and a subsequent creditor who takes a purchase-money security interest therein.[73] As is true under Section 9–312(3), the purchase-money party must carefully comply with the requirements imposed by Section 9–312(4) if he is to enjoy the preemptive priority afforded by that section. These requirements, discussed next, are considerably less stringent, however, than those imposed by Section 9–312(3).

(a) Purchase-Money Requirement

Only a security interest that can be characterized as "purchase-money" within the definition of Section 9–107 can invoke the special priority of Section 9–312(4). The requirements for

---

[71] § 1–4 C *supra.*

[72] § 4–2 B (2)(d)(v) and (vi) *supra.*

[73] The basic conflict, and the purpose for favoring the purchase-money party, is described in § 4–2 B (1) *supra.*

purchase-money status are discussed in a succeeding subsection.[74] Moreover, subsection (4) only applies to a conflict between a purchase-money interest and a prior *non*-purchase-money interest. The status of multiple purchase-money interests is discussed *infra*.[75]

(b) Time of Perfection

Under both the 1962 and 1972 Code, Section 9–312(4) can be invoked only if "the purchase-money security interest is perfected at the time the debtor receives possession of the collateral or within ten days thereafter." The term "receives possession" refers to the time the goods are physically delivered to the debtor, as explained previously.[76] It is noteworthy that Section 9–312(4), unlike Section 9–312(3),[77] gives the purchase money party a ten-day grace period *after* the debtor obtains possession of the collateral within which to perfect.[78] This difference conforms to the business practice of filing on purchase-money security interests in collateral other than inventory after delivery of the collateral to the debtor.

(c) "Collateral Other than Inventory"

The types of collateral covered by Section 9–312(4) are fewer than the language "collateral other than inventory" might first suggest, being restricted largely to equipment and to farm products (such as livestock) purchased by a farmer. That is, the section applies only when there is a purchase money interest, which essentially rules out accounts, chattel paper, and instruments;[79] it applies only when the initial financer has an after-

---

[74] § 4–2 B (4) *infra*.

[75] § 4–2 B (5) *infra*.

[76] § 4–2 B (2)(b) *supra*.

[77] § 4–2 B (2)(b) *supra*.

[78] A similar grace period is afforded *all* purchase-money creditors, as against lienors, by Section 9–301(2). See § 4–1 A (2) *supra*.

[79] Purchase-money security interests in these types of collateral are virtually nonexistent; although it is conceivable that a financer might lend funds to enable a broker dealing in these items to purchase them.

acquired property interest, which virtually rules out consumer goods;[80] and it does not apply to conflicts between real estate claimants and purchase money security interests in fixtures.[81]

As previously noted, a purchase money secured party who is unsure whether his collateral is inventory within Section 9–312(3) or collateral other than inventory within Section 9–312(4) should comply with the more stringent requirements of the former section, so as to be protected under both provisions.

(d) No Notification Required

Unlike Section 9–312(3), Section 9–312(4) does not require that the purchase-money party give notification to the earlier financer.[82] The significance of this is that the initial secured party should have serious reservations about making future advances against collateral other than inventory.

(e) Proceeds

Both the 1962 and 1972 versions of Section 9–312(4) clearly give the subsequent purchase-money creditor priority concerning the original collateral, but the 1962 Code makes no mention of whether the preemptive priority extends to proceeds. Section 9–312(4) of the 1972 Code states that it does and, unlike 1972 Section 9–312(3), places no limitation on the type of proceeds. This is discussed in more detail *infra*.[83]

(f) Future Advances

Priority with respect to future advances in a situation governed by Section 9–312(4) has previously been discussed.[84]

---

[80] 1962 U.C.C. § 9–204(4)(b); 1972 U.C.C. § 9–204(2). See § 2–2 D (2) *supra*.

[81] Conflicts of this sort are governed by Section 9–313. See § 4–4 *infra*.

[82] Comment 3 to Section 9–312(4) explains that "an arrangement for periodic advances against incoming property is unusual outside the inventory field."

[83] § 4–3 B (5)(a)(i) *infra*.

[84] § 4–2 A (2) *supra*.

(4) What Constitutes a Purchase-Money Security Interest

As noted in the preceding subsections,[85] only those security interests that can be characterized as "purchase-money" qualify for the special preemptive priority afforded by Sections 9–312(3) and 9–312(4).[86] "Purchase money" is defined in Section 9–107 (unchanged in the 1972 Code), which provides:

> A security interest is a "purchase money security interest" to the extent that it is
>
> (a) taken or retained by the seller of the collateral to secure all or part of its price; or
>
> (b) taken by a person who by making advances or incurring an obligation gives value to enable the debtor to acquire rights in or the use of collateral if such value is in fact so used.

(a) Seller-Creditor—Section 9–107(a)

Subsection (a) of the foregoing definition refers to a secured party seller [87] who sells goods on credit to a debtor-buyer and takes a security interest to secure all or part of the unpaid purchase price.[88]

Subsection (a) has caused few problems except in situations in which the seller has attempted to aggregate under a single security interest a number of different items purchased at different times—as when a department store purports to take a purchase-money security interest not only in the consumer goods presently being purchased but also in those purchased in the past, in the future or both until all indebtedness to the

---

[85] § 4–2 B (2) and (3) *supra.*

[86] Purchase-money status is also important under other provisions; for example, Section 9-301(2) (ten-day grace period for filing as against a lien creditor or transferee in bulk), § 4–1 A (2) *supra;* Section 9–302(1)(d) (exemption from filing for purchase-money security interests in consumer goods), § 3–2 A *supra;* and 1972 Section 9–313(4) (fixtures), § 4–4 *infra.*

[87] In pre-UCC terminology, "conditional vendor."

[88] The "all or part" language means that a seller who receives an initial $500 cash down payment on a $3,000 item will have a security interest to the extent of the remaining unpaid balance—$2500.

store is paid.[89] Since Section 9–107(a) does not contemplate extension of a purchase-money security interest in an item to obligations other than "its" (this particular item's) price, the seller is vulnerable to losing his purchase-money status unless the security agreement sets forth some means of keeping the interest in each item separate, as, for instance, by language providing that the security interest in each item is extinguished when that particular item is completely paid for and that payments shall be applied against items in the order of their purchase (that is, "first-in, first-out"). The safest practice, of course, is for the seller to take a separate security interest in each item.

A party who takes by assignment from a secured creditor seller inherits the seller's purchase-money status, as when a financer advances money to the seller against the latter's assignment of chattel paper.[90]

(b) Nonseller-Creditor—Section 9–107(b)

Subsection (b) of Section 9–107 includes within the definition of "purchase money" transactions a security interest taken by a nonseller-creditor who advances to a buyer the purchase price to be paid by the latter to a third-party seller. Subsection (b), however, imposes several prerequisites to purchase-money status in this type of situation.

As indicated in Comment 2 to Section 9–107, the security interest will not qualify as purchase-money if it is taken "as security for or in satisfaction of a pre-existing claim or antecedent debt"; that is, new value must be given.[91] The secured party may extend credit not only by "making advances," however, but

---

[89] When the secured party has opted not to file on a supposed purchase-money security interest in consumer goods, relying on the exemption afforded by Section 9–302(1)(d) (discussed in § 3–2 A *supra*), a court's refusal to recognize purchase-money status will make Section 9–302(1)(d) inapplicable, rendering the security interest unperfected for lack of filing.

[90] *See* U.C.C. § 9–107, Comment 1.

[91] Thus the Section 9–107 requirement is somewhat narrower than the concept of "value" as defined in Section 1–201(44).

also by "incurring an obligation," which would include a contractual obligation to the buyer or to the seller (including a guaranty) to advance funds for the purchase price. And the debtor may use the funds either to acquire "rights in" or "the use of" the property, which contemplates the debtor's acquisition of rights under a lease as well as purchase of full ownership.

Subsection (b) also requires the secured party to prove (1) that his *purpose* in extending credit was to enable the debtor to acquire the item in question and (2) that the advance was *in fact so used* by the debtor. These requirements pose no problem when the debtor receives the loan funds from the secured party, walks across the street, and pays them to the seller; the difficulty arises when there is a gap between the time of the purchase and the advance, as in the following illustration: On Day 1, SP$_1$ takes a security interest in the debtor's present and after-acquired equipment and perfects by filing. On Day 2, Debtor purchases from Seller a new compressor and takes delivery. Five days later, on Day 7, SP$_2$ loans money allegedly for the purchase price of the compressor, takes an alleged purchase money security interest therein, and perfects by filing.

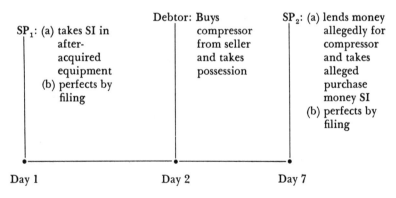

SP$_1$: (a) takes SI in after-acquired equipment (b) perfects by filing	Debtor: Buys compressor from seller and takes possession	SP$_2$: (a) lends money allegedly for compressor and takes alleged purchase money SI (b) perfects by filing
Day 1	Day 2	Day 7

SP$_2$ will claim preemptive priority under Section 9–312(4). SP$_1$ will contest the purchase-money nature of SP$_2$'s interest, arguing that priority is governed by Section 9–312(5) rather than Section 9–312(4) and that SP$_1$ therefore wins as the first to perfect.

If SP$_2$ has not followed the standard advice to pay the money directly to the seller or to give a check to the debtor made payable to the seller, he may have difficulty showing that his purpose was to enable the debtor to acquire the item in question or that the advance was "in fact so used" by the debtor or both. It can be argued that nothing in the Code requires the advance to be made prior to, or contemporaneously with, the purchase and that the security interest should qualify as purchase-money as long as the loan funds are traceable into the hands of the seller.[92] It is uncertain, however, whether courts will permit the secured party to use fictional methods of tracing.[93] And the legislative history of Section 9–107 presents a possible obstacle: The 1952 draft contained a clause permitting purchase-money status even when value was advanced within ten days after the debtor received possession of the collateral and even though the advance was not in fact used to pay the price. This clause was deleted by the Editorial Board in 1955 on the ground that it "extended the purchase-money concept too far."

It should be noted that insofar as Sections 9–312(3) and 9–312(4) are concerned, the issue of purchase-money status becomes irrelevant when the secured party has given value after the debtor's obtaining possession of the item in question (Section 9–312(3)) or after the ten-day period following the debtor's obtaining possession (Section 9–312(4)). In such cases another requirement of these sections is violated; namely, that perfection be accomplished by the prescribed deadline.[94] This would be true in the preceding hypothetical, for instance, if SP$_2$ had neither extended credit nor made a binding commitment to do so until Day 11.

---

[92] The purchase-money creditor's burden would be easier if the debtor purchased on unsecured credit from the seller and, prior to the advance, had insufficient funds in his checking account to cover the purchase price; it would be more difficult when the debtor paid cash or had sufficient funds in his account.

[93] For example, first-in, first-out; or last-in, first-out.

[94] Perfection does not occur until all three requirements for attachment under 1962 Section 9–204(1) or 1972 Section 9–203(1) have been satisfied—agreement, debtor's rights in the collateral, and value. See § 3–1 *supra*.

(5) Multiple Purchase-Money Interests

It sometimes occurs that more than one purchase money security interest is taken in the same item of collateral. This may be true (a) when each of two creditors finances a portion of the purchase price or (b) when a dishonest debtor borrows the full purchase price from each of two creditors and purports to give each a full purchase-money security interest in the item.

(a) Partial, Contributory Interests

It is not unheard of for each of two secured parties to finance a portion of the purchase price of a particular item. Assume, for instance, that the debtor contemplates purchasing a $5,000 piece of equipment. On Day 1, SP_1 loans $1,000 (20 per cent of the purchase price), takes a purchase-money security interest, and files. On the morning of Day 2, SP_2 advances $4,000 (the remaining 80 per cent), takes a purchase-money security interest, and files. On the afternoon of Day 2, the debtor purchases the item from Seller and takes possession. Or, in the alternative, assume the same facts except that the $1,000 advanced by SP_1 was a down payment and that SP_2 was the seller himself, who financed the unpaid balance of $4,000.

It should first be noted that no conflict will arise so long as the item brings the full initial purchase price upon reclamation and resale. In that case each party will simply recoup the amount of his contribution. The difficulty arises when the resale value (say, $4,000 in the aforementioned hypothetical) is insufficient to satisfy both claims.

It seems to be generally agreed that subsections (3) and (4) of Section 9–312 do not apply to situations involving multiple purchase-money interests but rather are restricted to conflicts between a purchase-money interest and a non-purchase-money one. Unfortunately, there is no unanimity about what rule does govern. On the one hand, it can be argued that there is no determinative language in the Code and that the most equitable solution is to allow the purchase-money parties to share ratably in accordance with the contribution of each. Thus, in the hypothetical, SP₁ would receive 20 per cent of the resale price and SP₂ would receive 80 per cent. On the other hand, it can be argued that subsection (5) of Section 9–312 should govern, since it expressly applies "in all situations not governed by other rules stated in this section." Under this solution, SP₁'s $1,000 claim would be satisfied first, since it would have priority as the first to be filed.[95]

(b) Full, Overlapping Interests

A dishonest debtor might borrow the full purchase price of an item from each of two different creditors and purport to give each a full purchase money interest in the item. In such a case priority should be awarded under Section 9–312(3) or 9–312(4), whichever is appropriate, to the party whose advance was "in fact so used," since only that party would qualify as a purchase-money creditor under Section 9–107.[96]

§ 4–3. SECURED PARTY'S RIGHTS UPON SALE OR OTHER DISPOSITION OF COLLATERAL BY THE DEBTOR

Preceding sections have focused on the secured party's rights against adverse claimants when the secured collateral is still in the hands of the debtor at the time of default. Suppose, however, that the debtor has sold or otherwise disposed of the collateral. Can the secured party still reach the collateral, even though it is now in the hands of a subsequent transferee? And to what extent can the secured party reach the proceeds received by the debtor in exchange for the collateral?

---

[95] If neither secured party had filed and thus neither interest was perfected, a further difficulty would arise, since under both the 1962 and 1972 versions of Section 9–312(5), when both interests are unperfected, priority is awarded to the first to attach. But in this situation both interests would have attached simultaneously on Day 2 when the debtor acquired rights in the collateral. This difficulty suggests that the easier solution is to allow the parties to share ratably in all cases.

[96] Section 9–107 is discussed in § 4–2 B (4)(b) *supra*.

The threshold provision pertaining to both questions is Section 9–306(2), which provides that should the debtor sell or otherwise dispose of collateral subject to a security interest, the secured party has potential rights in two respects. First, subject to important exceptions, the secured party has the right to follow the original collateral into the hands of the transferee from the debtor and reclaim it to satisfy the debt.[97] This right arises from the statement in Section 9–306(2) that a security interest "continues in collateral notwithstanding sale, exchange, or other disposition thereof." Second, the secured party also has the right, subject to exceptions, to take from the debtor any funds or other proceeds paid by the buyer in purchasing the collateral. This right derives from the provision in Section 9–306(2) that a security interest "also continues in any . . . proceeds . . . received by the debtor."

Note that the secured party will be in conflict with two different types of adverse claimants depending on which thing is in issue—the collateral itself or the proceeds therefrom. When the secured party is claiming the collateral itself, he will usually be in conflict with the buyer from the debtor.[98] When the secured party is claiming a right to the proceeds received by the debtor, the adverse claimant will usually be another creditor of the debtor, such as a lienor (including a bankruptcy trustee) or a second secured party.

Subsection A of the following discussion focuses on the secured party's ability to follow the collateral itself into the hands

---

[97] Since this right is exercisable by the secured party only upon default by the debtor-seller, the buyer or other transferee is safe as long as the debtor is properly repaying the secured party.

[98] The conflict may be with a creditor of the buyer, but in that case the general rule is that the latter has no greater rights than his debtor (the buyer), so the outcome still essentially hinges on the secured party's rights versus the rights of the buyer. The secured party could also be in conflict with another creditor of the debtor, such as another secured party who is claiming the same collateral, in which case three disputes would be involved: (1) secured party versus buyer; (2) competing creditor versus buyer; and (3) secured party versus competing creditor.

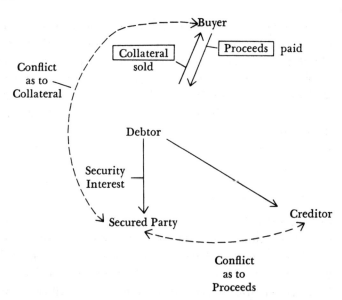

of a buyer or other transferee from the debtor; Subsection B addresses the secured party's rights to proceeds received by the debtor.

A. Rights Against Buyers and Other Transferees

Section 9–306(2) permits the secured party to reach collateral in the hands of a buyer or other transferee from the debtor with two significant exceptions: (1) when the secured party authorizes the disposition and (2) when other sections, such as 9–307, 9–308, or 9–309 "otherwise provide." The authorization exception is discussed below; other exceptions are discussed in following subsections.

(1) Authorization by Secured Party

Section 9–306(2) provides essentially that, insofar as the collateral itself is concerned, the security interest does not survive a sale or other disposition which was "authorized by the secured party in the security agreement or otherwise." [99] This means that even though the buyer does not qualify for special status under some other provision, as when a buyer of goods fails to satisfy the requirements for being a "buyer in ordinary course of business" within Section 9–307(1),[100] he nevertheless takes free of the security interest. The quoted language has also been taken to mean that the security interest is cut off, regardless of whether the secured party's authorization was express or implied.

(a) Express Authorization

Express authorizations have caused few problems. It is common for a financer holding a security interest in a debtor-retailer's inventory to state in the security agreement that the debtor is free to sell without restriction. This is hardly surprising, since such a debtor is in business to sell his merchandise and since, as discussed below,[101] Section 9–307(1) would allow most buyers of inventory to cut off the security interest in any event.

At the opposite extreme, some security agreements, particularly with regard to non-inventory collateral like equipment, expressly forbid the debtor to sell without prior permission from the secured party.[102] It should be noted that although the secured party can attempt to "persuade" the debtor not to make an unauthorized disposition by inserting a clause of this sort,[103] Section 9–311 provides that such a clause does not actually block transfer of the debtor's equity, either in a voluntary (for ex-

---

[99] The security interest in the proceeds received by the debtor does survive, however. See § 4–3 B *infra*.

[100] See § 4–3A (2)(a) *infra*.

[101] § 4–3 A (2)(a) *infra*.

[102] Such a provision can be envisioned even in the case of inventory when the collateral consists of a small number of large items, like sailing yachts—a situation in which the small turnover would make the seller's applying for permission before each sale feasible. The advantage would lie in the secured party's being alerted before each sale of the need to police the debtor's application of the proceeds.

[103] The clause frequently makes violation an event of default.

ample, sale) or involuntary (for example, judicial lien) disposition. This means, for instance, that the secured party would be foreclosed from claiming that the debtor's violation of a "prior permission" clause subordinated a buyer in ordinary course who would otherwise prevail under Section 9–307(1).[104]

(b) Implied Authorization

A tougher question concerning authorization is whether the secured party can be deemed to have *impliedly* authorized disposition. Authority is divided on this issue, some courts having held that implied authorization can arise even when the security agreement expressly forbade sale without prior permission if, on repeated prior occasions, the secured party knew about and failed to object to the debtor's selling the collateral without permission.

(2) Buyers of Goods

Even if the secured party has not authorized the sale, a buyer of goods may take free of the security interest under the circumstances set forth in Sections 9–307 and 9–301(1)(c).[105]

(a) Buyers in Ordinary Course of Business—Section 9–307(1)

The most important provision in Section 9–307 is subsection (1) (unchanged in the 1972 Code), which provides that "[a] buyer in ordinary course of business . . . takes free of a security interest created by his seller even though the security interest is perfected and even though the buyer knows of its existence." This language was designed to protect those who purchase from merchants holding goods for sale. These buyers, particularly

---

[104] Nor could a secured party with an unperfected security interest maintain that such a clause subordinated a Section 9–301(1)(b) lienor.

[105] When the secured party *has* authorized disposition by the debtor, buyers take free even if the requirements of Sections 9–307 or 9–301(1)(c) are not satisfied.

consumer buyers, would not expect the goods to be sold subject to encumbrances and would therefore not think to check for a filed financing statement. Section 9–307(1) therefore gives the buyer title free of the security interest and does so even if the security interest was previously perfected [106] *if* the requirements therein are satisfied; namely, (1) that the buyer qualifies as a "buyer in ordinary course of business" and (2) that the security interest was "created by his seller."

(i) Section 1–201(9) Requirements. In order to qualify as a "buyer in ordinary course of business" within Section 9–307(1), the buyer must satisfy the criteria set forth in Section 1–201(9), which requires that the goods be acquired (a) in good faith and without knowledge that the sale violated a term of the security interest; (b) from a person in the business of selling goods of the kind in question; and (c) not in bulk or as security for, or in satisfaction of, a debt.

The requirement that the buyer have purchased without knowing that the sale violated the security interest is not, as might first appear, inconsistent with the statement in Section 9–307(1) itself that the buyer takes free even if he knows of the existence of the security interest. As Comment 2 to Section 9–307 indicates, these two provisions taken together mean that a buyer who only knows the security interest *exists* takes free; [107] whereas a buyer who *also* knows that the security agreement forbade the sale violates the Section 1–201(9) requirement and thus takes subject to the security interest.

Whereas Section 9–307(1) runs either to consumer buyers or merchant buyers, the *seller* must be "a person in the business of selling goods of that kind." [108] This requirement would be

---

[106] *A fortiori,* a buyer who qualifies under Section 9-307(1) will also take free of an unperfected security interest.

[107] This stands to reason if one assumes a general awareness that most inventory secured parties authorize the seller-debtor to sell, thereby relinquishing their right to follow the collateral into the buyer's hands. See § 4-3 A (1)(a) *supra.*

[108] New language has been added to the 1972 version of Section 1–201(9)

satisfied when an auto dealer sold an automobile but not when he sold his accounts processing machine. Nor would it be satisfied when a car rental agency occasionally sold off its old cars to make way for newer models.

The requirement that the sale not be in bulk precludes the purchaser of an entire business from claiming "buyer in ordinary course" status under Section 9–307(1) with respect to goods included in the sale. And the requirement that the transaction not be as security for, or in satisfaction of, a debt excludes from the protection of Section 9–307(1) the taker of a security interest [109] or a buyer who takes the goods in cancellation of a debt owed him by the seller.

Conflicts with buyers who do not qualify for "buyer in ordinary course" status and therefore cannot invoke Section 9–307(1) are governed by Section 9–301(1)(c), whereunder the buyer will prevail only by giving value and receiving delivery of the collateral without knowledge of the security interest and before it is perfected. In other words, perfection before the purchase or the buyer's knowledge of the existence of the security interest will not protect the secured party when Section 9–307(1) applies but will protect him under Section 9–301(1)(c).

(ii) The "Created by His Seller" Requirement and the Shelter Doctrine. Assume the following situation: Debtor, a consumer,[110] purchases an automobile on secured credit from an auto dealer (Secured Party). Debtor then sells the auto to another dealer (Dealer$_2$), who, in turn, sells to another consumer (Consumer$_2$). When Debtor defaults, Secured Party claims the auto in the hands of Consumer$_2$.

---

making it clear that a person buying from an investor-seller of oil, gas, or other minerals at the wellhead or minehead (who might otherwise not be deemed "in the business of selling goods of that kind") qualifies as a buyer in ordinary course of business.

[109] The conflict between such a party and the original secured party would be governed by Section 9–312.

[110] As used here, the term "consumer" refers to a person not in the business of selling automobiles.

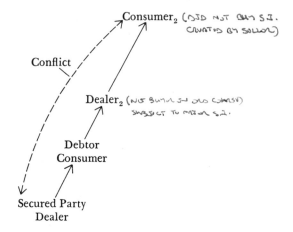

If Secured Party perfected at the time of the sale to Debtor,[111] then Dealer$_2$, who did not purchase from a person in the business of selling automobiles, will not qualify as a "buyer in ordinary course of business" within Section 1–201(9), cannot invoke Section 9–307(1), and therefore takes subject to the prior perfected security interest under Section 9–301(1)(c). Consumer$_2$, although satisfying the requirements for a buyer in ordinary course of business under Section 1–201(9) (having purchased from a person in the business of selling autos), is not protected by Section 9–307(1) because the latter section frees a buyer only from a security interest "created by his seller"—that is, one given by the buyer's immediate seller—and not from one, as in this case, given by a prior seller in the chain (Debtor).

Suppose, on the other hand, that Secured Party did not properly perfect before the sale by Dealer$_2$ to Consumer$_2$. In that case, assuming Dealer$_2$ gave value and took delivery without knowledge, Dealer$_2$ takes free of the security interest under

---

[111] In many states, perfection of a security interest in an automobile sold to a consumer requires that the secured party comply with the state certificate of title act rather than file an Article 9 financing statement. *See* Sections 9–302(3) and (4) and the discussion at §§ 3–3 A and 5–3 *infra*. But other aspects of the secured transaction, including priority conflicts, will usually be governed by Article 9 rules, such as Section 9–307.

Section 9–301(1)(c). Then, concerning Consumer$_2$, although
Section 9–307(1) is still of no assistance (because of the "created
by his seller" language), Consumer$_2$ nevertheless takes free of
the security interest because his seller (Dealer$_2$) did, under the
common law "shelter" doctrine. This doctrine, which is analogous to the shelter rule imposed on transfers of negotiable
instruments by UCC Section 3–201(1),[112] essentially holds that
a buyer receives as good a title as his seller had.[113]

(iii) Exclusion for Buyers of Farm Products. There is
one exclusion from the rule set forth in Section 9–307(1);
namely, a party "buying farm products from a person engaged
in farming operations" [114] cannot invoke the special priority
given by Section 9–307(1) to buyers in ordinary course and will
therefore prevail only if the purchase is made without knowledge and before the security interest is perfected, pursuant to
Section 9–301(1)(c).[115] Although this exclusion has been criticized on the ground that it places buyers of farm products in
a position inferior to that of buyers of inventory, the drafters of
the 1972 Code refused to remove it in the face of threats from
government agencies to stop financing farmers unless this protection against buyers was retained.

(b) Consumer-to-Consumer Sales—Section 9–307(2)

Subsection (2) of Section 9–307 (both the 1962 and 1972 versions) states:

> In the case of consumer goods, a buyer takes free of a security
> interest even though perfected if he buys without knowledge of

---

[112] The exceptions to application of the doctrine are also essentially
those set forth in Section 3–201(1).

[113] Under the shelter doctrine, when Section 9–307(1) permits the buyer
in question to take free of a prior security interest, a creditor (including a
secured creditor) of the buyer also takes free.

[114] "Farm Products" are defined in Section 9–109(3). See § 1–5 A (4)
supra.

[115] In order to make applicability of the latter section clearer, the drafters of the 1972 Code have inserted an express reference to buyers of farm
products in 1972 Section 9–301(1)(c).

the security interest, for value and for his own personal, family or household purposes, unless prior to the purchase the secured party has filed a financing statement covering such goods.[116]

The dual reference to consumer goods ("consumer goods" and "for personal, family or household purposes")[117] means that Section 9–307(2) only applies when the collateral can be characterized as consumer goods *both* in the hands of the seller-debtor *and* in the hands of the buyer; that is, applicability is limited to consumer-to-consumer sales.

Assume that a conditional seller takes a security interest in Ms. Smith's washing machine. Ms. Smith sells the machine to Ms. Jones. Under Section 9–307(2), the secured party cannot follow the machine into Ms. Jones's hands unless the security interest was perfected *by filing* prior to the sale to Ms. Jones (or unless Ms. Jones took with knowledge of the existence of the security interest). In other words, a retailer-conditional seller cannot rely on automatic perfection of its purchase money security interest in consumer goods per Section 9–302(1)(d)[118] to follow the collateral into the hands of a consumer buyer from a consumer debtor.[119] Section 9–307(2) recognizes that a consumer buyer from another consumer is more likely to be aware of the possibility of a security interest than is a consumer buyer from a merchant and is therefore more likely to check for a filed financing statement. But such a buyer cannot be expected to be aware of the possibility of a security interest automatically perfected without filing.

---

[116] The language bringing buyers of farm equipment having a purchase price not in excess of $2500 within 1962 Section 9–307(2) has been omitted from the 1972 version in conjunction with the elimination of the provision in 1962 Section 9–302(1)(c) allowing perfection of a purchase-money security interest in such farm equipment without filing. See § 3–2 A *supra*.

[117] See the definition of consumer goods in Section 9–109(1).

[118] For a discussion of Section 9–302(1)(d), see § 3–2 A *supra*.

[119] This is one reason why a retailer-conditional seller might wish to file a financing statement despite the exemption from filing afforded by Section 9–302(1)(d). Another reason, having to do with perfection with respect to proceeds beyond the ten-day period after the debtor receives them, is discussed in § 4–3 B (4)(b) *infra*.

(c) Future Advances Made After the Sale

Under both the 1962 and 1972 Code, a buyer in ordinary course of business [120] who satisfies the requirements of Section 9–307(1) takes entirely free of a prior security interest, including any future advances made by the secured party to the debtor-seller after the sale.[121]

Under the 1962 Code, since there is no statutory language to the contrary, it appears that a buyer *not* in ordinary course of business who does not purchase until after the security interest is perfected (or does not comply with one of the other requirements of Section 9–302(1)(c)) takes subject to all future advances. The 1972 Code partially changes this result by adding new language in Section 9–307(3) to the effect that a buyer not in ordinary course of business

> takes free of a security interest to the extent that it secures future advances made after the secured party acquires knowledge of the purchase or more than 45 days after the purchase, whichever first occurs, unless made pursuant to a commitment entered into without knowledge of the purchase and before the expiration of the 45 day period.

To illustrate: Assume that on January 1 the secured party loans $10,000 and takes a properly perfected security interest in all equipment of the debtor, an office supply company, including the latter's delivery truck. The security agreement permits the secured party, at its option, to make future advances. On February 1, the debtor sells the truck to a truck dealer. On March 1, the secured party advances an additional $5,000 to the debtor and then makes a further advance of $6,000 on April 1.

Since the buyer did not purchase from a person in the business of selling trucks, as required by Section 1–201(9), he cannot invoke Section 9–307(1) and is therefore subject to the previously perfected security interest to the extent of the debtor's initial indebtedness ($10,000), pursuant to Section 9–301(1)(c).

---

[120] See § 4–3 A (2)(a)(i) *supra*.

[121] Priority as to future advances is only relevant, of course, if the resale value of the repossessed goods exceeds the amount of the initial advance.

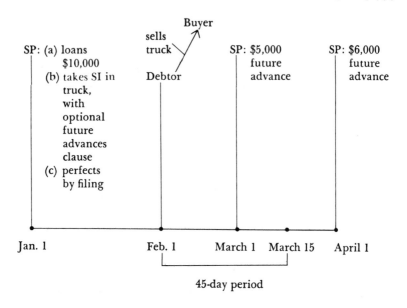

Under 1972 Section 9–307(3), the buyer is also subject to the $5,000 future advance, which was made within 45 days after the sale; but the buyer takes free of the $6,000 advance made beyond the 45-day period. Thus if the secured party repossesses the truck and sells it for $21,000, the buyer will be entitled to the $6,000 surplus. If the secured party had acquired knowledge of the sale on February 2, the buyer would take free of both future advances and would be entitled to $11,000. But if the secured party had initially (or at any time before the end of the 45-day period after the sale), without knowledge of the sale, entered into a binding commitment to make the future advances, the buyer would be entitled to nothing.

(3) Purchasers of Chattel Paper

Another provision preventing a secured party from following collateral into the hands of a taker from the debtor is found in

Section 9–308, which, in certain circumstances, gives priority to purchasers of chattel paper. As previously discussed, chattel paper typically appears in situations in which a consumer who buys goods on credit from a dealer gives the dealer a security agreement covering the goods and a note promising to repay the price in installments.[122] The combination of the two, when sold or assigned as security by the dealer to a financer, constitutes "chattel paper."[123] If the dealer then dishonestly (or inadvertently) sells or assigns the same chattel paper to a second financer, the resultant priority conflict will, in many instances, be governed by Section 9–308.

Section 9–308 differentiates between two types of security interests in chattel paper held by the initial secured party:

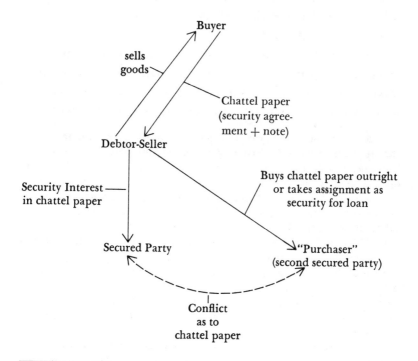

---

[122] § 1–5 B (3) *supra*.
[123] Section 9–105.

Subsection (a) (first sentence of 1962 Section 9–308)[124] governs conflicts between a secured party with a security interest taken in chattel paper as *original collateral* and a subsequent "purchaser" (meaning a second Article 9 secured party).[125] The initial secured party will have a claim to chattel paper as original collateral when he finances only the dealer's receivables and not his inventory.[126] Subsection (b) (second sentence of 1962 Section 9–308), on the other hand, governs conflicts between a secured party with a security interest in chattel paper "claimed merely as proceeds of inventory" and a subsequent purchaser. The initial secured party will have a claim to chattel paper "merely as proceeds of inventory" when he has engaged in "floor plan" financing of a dealer's inventory.[127] The present discussion focuses on the first of these two situations; the second, involving chattel paper claimed merely as proceeds, will be discussed at a later point.[128]

Section 9–308(a) (first sentence of 1962 Section 9–308) provides that as between a secured party with an initial security interest in chattel paper as original collateral and a subsequent purchaser, the subsequent purchaser prevails, even though the

---

[124] Although no substantive changes have been made with respect to chattel paper in the 1972 version of Section 9–308 (the change relating to instruments is discussed in § 4–3 B (5)(c) *infra*), the section has been subdivided so that the first and second sentences of the 1962 version have become subsections (a) and (b), respectively, of the 1972 version. For the sake of convenience, the present discussion will be phrased in terms of the subdivisions in the 1972 version.

[125] The term "purchaser" includes an Article 9 secured party. (Sections 1–201(32) and (33), although not explicit on this, are universally deemed to so provide.) Moreover, a person is an Article 9 secured party regardless of whether he takes chattel paper by outright sale or by assignment as security. (See the definition of "secured party" in Section 9–105 and the discussion in § 1–4 D *supra*.) Thus Section 9–308, in essence, governs conflicts between two Article 9 secured parties.

[126] With respect to whether an inventory financer claiming chattel paper as proceeds might be able to invoke subsection (a), see § 4–3 B (5)(b) *infra*.

[127] "Floor plan" financing is discussed in § 1–5 B (3) *supra*.

[128] § 4–3 B (5)(b) *infra*.

initial secured party perfected first [129] if all of the following requirements are met:

1. The purchaser must give "new value," meaning that he must loan directly against, or pay a purchase price directly for, the chattel paper. If the second secured party (the "purchaser") claims the chattel paper merely because it is proceeds of another form of collateral (such as inventory) in which he took a security interest, the lack of "new value" will take the conflict out of Section 9–308.[130]

2. The purchaser must take possession of the chattel paper (that is, the security agreement and note).

3. Possession must be taken "in the ordinary course of [the purchaser's] business," meaning that only professional dealers in chattel paper, such as banks and finance companies, can invoke Section 9–308.

4. Possession must be taken "without knowledge [on the purchaser's part] that the . . . paper . . . is subject to a security interest"; that is, without knowledge of the prior secured party's interest.

Failure to comply with one or more of these requirements will prevent the subsequent purchaser from invoking Section 9–308, bringing the conflict within Section 9–312, whereunder the purchaser will usually lose to the prior secured party who perfected before the "purchase." [131] Thus when SP_1 takes a security interest in chattel paper as original collateral and per-

---

[129] This means that financers can acquire chattel paper without having to check the filing records or otherwise inquire into the existence of prior claims. The effect is to promote the marketability of chattel paper, a major source of credit in the modern economy, by giving it the same sort of negotiability as that afforded negotiable instruments under Article 3.

[130] For an illustration of this type of situation, see § 4–3 B (5)(b) *infra*.

[131] Assuming the subsequent purchaser perfected, either by filing (Section 9–304(1)) or taking possession (Section 9–305)), he would not need to invoke Section 9–308 when the initial secured party failed to perfect first, since he would win in any event under Section 9–312(5).

fects by filing on Day 1, and on Day 2 the debtor transfers the chattel paper to SP_2, SP_2 prevails if he takes possession and otherwise satisfies the above requirements; otherwise, SP_1 wins under Section 9–312(5) as the first to file.

The initial secured party with a security interest in chattel paper as original collateral can protect himself from subordination under Section 9–308(a) (first sentence of 1962 Section 9–308) either (1) by requiring the debtor to deliver the chattel paper to him immediately upon receipt from the buyer [132] (as is done in "direct collection" arrangements, when the secured party collects from account debtors), thereby preventing the subsequent purchaser from taking possession, or (2) if the chattel paper is left in the hands of the debtor for collection (as is often done in "indirect collection" arrangements), by stamping a notice of the security interest on the face of the paper, thereby ensuring that the subsequent purchaser obtains knowledge.

(4) Purchasers of Instruments

Section 9–309 (unchanged in the 1972 Code) provides that the taker of a negotiable instrument, such as a check or promissory note,[133] who qualifies under Section 3–302 as a holder in due course has priority over a prior perfected security interest in the instrument.[134] Section 3–302 requires that the subsequent party

---

[132] A clause in the security agreement making failure to do this an event of default will not, of course, protect the secured party when the debtor goes ahead and transfers the chattel paper—see the discussion of Section 9–311 in § 4–3 A (1)(a) *supra*—but will diminish the likelihood of such an occurrence.

[133] Instruments as collateral are discussed in § 1–5 B (1) *supra*. It should be noted that an instrument which is part of chattel paper, such as a promissory note given by a buyer in combination with a security agreement (as discussed in § 1–5 B (3) *supra*), will be governed by the Article 9 rules relating to chattel paper (§ 4–3 A (3) *supra* and § 4–3 B (5)(b) *infra*) rather than those relating to instruments.

[134] Section 9–309 similarly subordinates the interest of a prior secured party to good faith purchasers for value of investment securities and negotiable documents.

have taken possession,[135] for value, in good faith, and without notice that someone else (like a prior secured party) has a claim to the instrument. Since the subsequent party must have taken possession, meaning that the prior security interest will not be perfected by possession, and since filing is not an available means of perfecting an interest in instruments,[136] the type of prior perfected security interest referred to in Section 9–309 is a nonpossessory one perfected in one of three ways: (1) automatically perfected for ten days after the debtor receives the instrument as proceeds, under Section 9–306(3); [137] (2) temporarily perfected for 21 days under Section 9–304(4), when new value has been given and a written security agreement obtained; or (3) temporarily perfected for 21 days under Section 9–304 (5)(b), when the secured party, who originally perfected by possession, returns the instrument to the debtor for purposes such as presentment or collection from the maker or drawer.

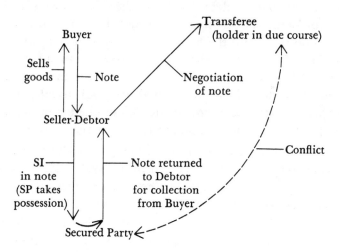

---

[135] In order to be a holder in due course under Section 3–302, the subsequent taker must be a "holder," defined in Section 1–201(20) as a person in possession.

[136] U.C.C. § 9–304(1).

[137] Conflicts concerning instruments as proceeds are discussed in § 4–3 B (5)(c) *infra*.

To illustrate the operation of Section 9–309, assume that a seller has sold an item on open account to a buyer, who gave the seller a promissory note for the purchase price. The secured party takes a security interest in the note and initially perfects by taking possession, but then returns the note to the debtor-seller for collection from the buyer. Instead of presenting the note to the buyer, the debtor negotiates it to Transferee (to whom the seller owes money), who takes possession within 21 days after the note was returned to the debtor and without notice of the security interest. Pursuant to Section 9–309, Transferee will prevail over the secured party, despite the latter's prior perfection under Section 9–304(5)(b).

B. Proceeds

(1) Introduction

In the event that the debtor sells or otherwise disposes of the secured collateral, the secured party is not limited to following the collateral itself into the hands of the buyer; he may also be able to claim the funds or other proceeds received by the debtor in exchange for the collateral.[138] Here, since the proceeds are in the hands of the debtor, the secured party will usually be in conflict with another creditor of the debtor (lienor or second secured party) or the debtor's bankruptcy trustee.[139]

The basic provision giving the secured party a claim to proceeds is Section 9–306(2) (unchanged in the 1972 Code), which states: "Except where this Article otherwise provides, a security interest continues in collateral notwithstanding . . . disposition . . . *and also continues in any identifiable proceeds* including collections received by the debtor." [140] This right exists irrespective of whether the security agreement contains a clause

---

[138] The secured party's total recovery under either or both routes may not, of course, exceed the unpaid balance of the obligation secured.

[139] Conflicts that may occasionally arise with noncreditor transferees of proceeds are discussed in § 4–3 B (5)(e) *infra*.

[140] Emphasis added.

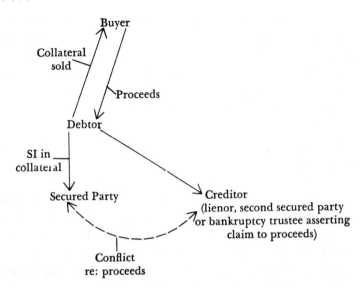

forbidding the debtor to sell the original collateral and irrespective of whether the secured party's interest in the original collateral becomes subordinate to the rights of another upon sale by the debtor.[141]

The secured party's right to proceeds is most often important in the context of inventory, accounts, and chattel paper financing. Since the very nature of inventory [142] generally presupposes its disposition to buyers in ordinary course of business,[143] the secured party's right to repossess the goods themselves will usually be terminated by Section 9-307(1) at the time of sale,[144] leaving as his sole recourse the right to proceeds. Likewise, accounts and chattel paper, as such, have little value apart from

---

[141] Subordination by virtue of authorization to sell is discussed in § 4-3 A (1) *supra*. Subordination under Section 9-307 is discussed in § 4-3 A (2) *supra*.

[142] "Inventory" is defined in Section 9-109(4) as basically goods held for sale.

[143] That is, those who buy from a person in the business of selling goods of the kind in question. U.C.C. § 1-201(9). See § 4-3 A (2)(a) *supra*.

[144] § 4-3 A (2)(a) *supra*.

their proceeds—that is, the "collections" on them referred to in Section 9–306(2). By contrast, the right to proceeds of consumer goods or equipment is less frequently of importance, since such collateral is rarely sold to a buyer in ordinary course of business,[145] and the secured party can therefore usually follow the collateral itself into the hands of the buyer.

In order to ascertain whether the secured party will prevail over competing parties claiming proceeds, one must consult the relevant priority rules, such as Section 9–301(1)(b) (pertaining to conflicts with lienors) or Section 9–312 (pertaining to conflicts with other Article 9 secured creditors). The outcome under these rules may, in turn, hinge on the type of proceeds involved, as defined in Section 9–306(1), on whether the proceeds are identifiable, and on whether and when the secured party's interest in proceeds was perfected, as determined by Section 9–306(3). These interrelated subjects—definition, identifiability, perfection, and priorities—are discussed next.[146]

(2) Definition

Section 9–306(1) of the 1972 Code defines "proceeds" as follows:

> Proceeds includes whatever is received upon the sale, exchange, collection or other disposition of collateral or proceeds. Insurance payable by reason of loss or damage to the collateral is proceeds, except to the extent that it is payable to a person other than a party to the security agreement. Money, checks, deposit accounts, and the like are "cash proceeds". All other proceeds are "non-cash proceeds".

The words "or proceeds" in the first sentence of the foregoing language means "or proceeds of proceeds"; for example, when a

---

[145] U.C.C. § 1–201(9). For example, a manufacturer of widgets would seldom be "in the business" of selling equipment such as the machinery used in its plant.

[146] It should be noted that a special set of rules, stated in Section 9–306 (4), covers the situation in which insolvency proceedings have been instituted by or against the debtor. These rules are discussed in § 6–9 *infra*.

debtor who has given a security interest in inventory (the original collateral) sells the inventory for cash (first-generation proceeds) and then uses the cash to purchase equipment (second-generation proceeds), the secured party's right to proceeds extends to the equipment.

(a) Insurance Proceeds

The second sentence of the above-quoted language was added in the 1972 version to resolve a controversy under the 1962 Code about whether a security interest in original collateral extends to insurance payable by reason of loss of, or damage to, the collateral. Suppose a perfected security interest exists in goods covered by a casualty insurance policy naming the debtor as beneficiary. The goods are destroyed by fire. Thereafter a third party obtains a judgment lien against the debtor's assets. One might assume that the insurance proceeds, which stand as a substitute for the destroyed collateral, are "proceeds" within Section 9–306 and therefore that the secured party, having a prior perfected interest, prevails over the lienor under Section 9–301(1)(b). Nevertheless, some courts have held under the 1962 Code that the secured party's claim to proceeds does not extend to insurance funds on the basis that loss or destruction does not constitute a voluntary "disposition" of the collateral within Section 9–306(1). The 1972 version of Section 9–306(1) resolves the controversy by explicitly providing that insurance payable by reason of loss of, or damage to, the collateral constitutes "proceeds" unless the casualty policy names someone other than the debtor or secured party as loss payee.[147]

(b) Cash Versus Non-Cash Proceeds; Deposit Accounts

The last two sentences of 1972 Section 9–306(1), quoted pre-

---

[147] Consistent with this change, the language of 1962 Section 9–104(g)—"This Article does not apply . . . to a transfer of an interest in or claim in or under any policy of insurance"—has been modified in the 1972 Code by the addition of the words "except as provided with respect to proceeds (Section 9–306)."

viously, provide that "[m]oney, checks, deposit accounts, and the like are 'cash proceeds.' All other proceeds are 'non-cash proceeds.' " Assume the secured party has a security interest in a debtor-dealer's inventory of automobiles. The dealer sells a car to a buyer, who trades in his old automobile, gives $200 in cash, pays $1,000 by check, and executes a conditional sale contract (chattel paper)[148] for the balance of the purchase price. Section 9–306(1) makes it clear that the security interest extends to all such items received by the debtor-seller. The cash ("money") and check would be classified as cash proceeds, whereas the trade-in and chattel paper would be non-cash proceeds. If the car had been sold on open account, that is, on an unsecured credit basis, the account receivable generated thereby would fall within the category of non-cash proceeds; and when the debtor collected on the account, the funds paid by the buyer would constitute cash proceeds (proceeds of proceeds). If the buyer gave an instrument other than a check, such as a promissory note, the instrument would be non-cash proceeds. As will be seen, the difference between cash and non-cash proceeds is important, since a number of other provisions are geared to the distinction.

It is necessary to distinguish between situations in which a particular item is original collateral and those in which the same item is merely proceeds from disposition of something else that was the original collateral. Several types of Article 9 collateral, notably accounts and chattel paper, may be original collateral in one transaction but only proceeds from original collateral in another. Thus a financer might take a security interest directly in a merchant's accounts or chattel paper, whereupon these items would be original collateral (the funds received when the debtor collected on them would constitute proceeds). On the other hand, in the previous illustration involving the auto dealer's sale of a car, the only original collateral was inventory; all of the items received by the dealer

---

[148] "Chattel paper" is defined in Section 9–105(1)(b).

from the buyer, including the chattel paper and account, were merely proceeds arising from disposition of that original collateral. The distinction between original-collateral status and proceeds status may bear on the outcome in a priority dispute governed by provisions such as Section 9–308, as will be discussed subsequently.[149]

Suppose a buyer from a debtor-dealer pays cash for an automobile from the dealer's secured inventory, whereupon the dealer deposits the funds in his bank account. Does the secured party's interest extend to these funds? Under the 1962 Code there is some question whether deposit in a bank account cuts off the security interest because of Section 9–104(k), which provides that Article 9 does not apply to a transfer with respect to a deposit account maintained with a bank. The 1972 Code makes it clear that the security interest survives by adding "except as provided with respect to proceeds" to the foregoing language [150] and by adding "deposit accounts" to the definition of proceeds in Section 9–306(1).

(3) Identifiability

One of the key requirements of Section 9–306 is that of identifiability; that is, under both the 1962 and 1972 versions of Section 9–306(2), the secured party's interest extends only to those proceeds from disposition of the original collateral that are "identifiable" as such. Little difficulty arises when the debtor is careful to keep proceeds separated from his other non-proceeds property, as by depositing proceeds funds in a special, segregated bank account devoted solely to this purpose and labelled as such. But suppose the debtor carelessly commingles proceeds by depositing them in its general account, which also contains non-proceeds funds. Is identifiability lost? There is good authority that it is not.

---

[149] § 4–3 B (5)(b) infra.
[150] 1972 U.C.C. § 9–104(1).

Universal C.I.T. Credit Corp. v. Farmers Bank [151] is illustrative. In that case the secured party took a security interest in the debtor-dealer's automobile inventory and proceeds. As buyers paid for the automobiles by check, the debtor would deposit the checks, along with other non-proceeds funds, in its general account with defendant bank. The debtor owed the bank $12,000 on a loan it had made in a separate transaction. Upon learning that the secured party had decided to terminate the financing arrangement, the debtor attempted to exact vengeance by urging the bank to debit his account to satisfy the debt owed to the bank, so that the secured party would "come out last." This the bank did, depleting the account to the extent that checks issued by the debtor to the secured party were dishonored. When the secured party sued, asserting priority regarding the funds in the account by virtue of its security interest in proceeds, the bank defended on the ground that commingling of the proceeds funds in the account violated the identifiability requirement of Section 9–306. The court rejected this defense, stating that identifiability could be preserved by analogical application of the "lowest intermediate balance" rule for tracing trust funds commingled by a trustee with his own funds. This fictional method of tracing is simplistically explained in the Restatement of Trusts Second: [152]

> A is trustee [debtor] for B [secured party] of $1,000 [proceeds]. He deposits this money with $1,000 of his own in a bank. He draws out $1,500 and dissipates it. He later deposits $1,000 of his own in the account. [B] is entitled to a lien on the account for $500, the lowest intermediate balance.[153]

---

[151] 358 F. Supp. 317, 13 U.C.C. Rep. Serv. 109 (1972).

[152] Restatement (Second) of Trusts § 202, Illus. 20 to Comment j.

[153] To illustrate further, if another $700 of proceeds funds were deposited, the lowest intermediate balance would rise to $1200 (the total balance being $2200). Under this method, it can be said that the proceeds funds "sink to the bottom."

Other fictional methods of tracing, such as first-in, first-out, may also be permitted.

It should be noted that the use of a fictional tracing method like the

The court also pointed out that under the non-UCC law governing bank set-offs, although a depositary bank ordinarily has a common law lien (often called the "banker's lien" or "right of set-off") allowing it to apply funds in a depositor's account to satisfy the depositor's unpaid indebtedness to it, an exception arises when the bank has knowledge or reason to know of a third party's interest in the account (such as the claim of an Article 9 creditor to proceeds). This points up the fact that one type of competitor the secured party must be concerned with in connection with its claim to proceeds is a bank with a right of set-off [154] and that the major form of protection in this regard is to require the debtor to deposit all proceeds in a special account reserved solely for that purpose and labeled as such, thereby ensuring knowledge on the bank's part. This will, of course, also preserve identifiability as against other types of competitors, such as a bankruptcy trustee or a lienor who has obtained a lien against the debtor's assets.

To ensure compliance with the identifiability requirement, careful financers of merchants often insert a clause in the security agreement requiring the debtor to keep the collateral and its proceeds separate from other property of the debtor, to maintain accurate and complete records in this regard, to either remit the proceeds directly to the secured party or else deposit them in a special account labeled as such, and to allow the secured party to periodically enter the debtor's premises to inspect the collateral and proceeds and the books pertaining to them. It is also commonly provided that non-compliance with these requirements will constitute an event of default.

"lowest intermediate balance" rule is disallowed in insolvency situations by Section 9–306(4), which sets forth its own rule (Section 9–306(4)(d)) on the extent to which the secured party can reach commingled funds. See § 6–9 B *infra*.

[154] When a bank that has taken a security interest in the debtor's collateral also has the debtor's checking account, the bank may have two alternative bases for realizing on the debt; namely, (a) its Article 9 claim to proceeds, and (b) its common law right of set-off.

(4) Perfection

In a conflict with competing claimants the secured party will usually lose unless its security interest in the proceeds is properly perfected (although, as will be seen under Section 9–308, for instance, perfection does not necessarily *guarantee* priority). The rules governing perfection with respect to proceeds are set forth in Section 9–306(3).[155] These rules can generally be subdivided into two categories: (a) perfection during the ten-day period after the debtor receives the proceeds; and (b) perfection thereafter.

(a) Perfection During the Ten-Day Grace Period

Both the 1962 and 1972 versions of Section 9–306(3) provide in essence that the secured party's interest in all types of proceeds is automatically,[156] continuously perfected during the ten-day period following the debtor's receipt of the proceeds, on the sole condition that the interest in the original collateral was perfected (whether by filing or otherwise). To illustrate, assume that under the 1962 Code a financing statement covering the original collateral was filed, but the secured party neglected to check the "proceeds" box—a situation in which, as will be seen,[157] the secured party is required to file a new financing statement covering the proceeds themselves in order to have continuous perfection *beyond* the ten-day period. Or, under the 1972 Code, assume that the secured party files on inventory as original collateral. The debtor sells the inventory for cash proceeds, which are, in turn, used to purchase equipment (second-generation proceeds). Since the original financing statement does not refer to equipment, the secured party will be required

---

[155] Special rules governing perfection when the debtor is involved in insolvency proceedings are found in Section 9–306(4), as discussed in § 6–9 *infra*.

[156] The term "automatically" is used in this context by the author to mean that the secured party need not take special steps to perfect with respect to proceeds themselves (as by filing a new financing statement).

[157] § 4–3 B (4)(b)(i) *infra*.

under 1972 Section 9–306(3)(a) to file a new financing statement covering the equipment itself in order to have continuous perfection *beyond* the ten-day period.[158] In either of the foregoing situations, even though the secured party does not file the new financing statement until the ninth day after the debtor receives the proceeds, he will prevail over a lien arising on the fifth day [159] because, irrespective of the situation beyond the ten-day period, he is continuously perfected *during* the ten-day period by virtue of the original perfection. The ten-day provision gives the secured party a grace period in which to discover that the debtor has disposed of the collateral.

(b) Perfection Beyond the Ten-Day Period

(i) The 1962 Code. Section 9–306(3) of the 1962 Code provides that a security interest in proceeds ceases to be perfected beyond the ten-day period unless "(a) a filed financing statement covering the original collateral also covers proceeds; or (b) the security interest in the proceeds is perfected before the expiration of the ten day period." Thus unless the secured party filed a financing statement on the original collateral and included a reference to proceeds therein (that is, checked the "proceeds box"),[160] he must take steps to perfect separately concerning the proceeds themselves (as by taking possession or filing) during the ten-day period in order to have continuous perfection beyond that period. (As noted, such steps are not necessary for continuous perfection *during* the ten-day period).

---

[158] See § 4–3 B (4)(b)(ii) *infra.*

[159] U.C.C. § 9–301(1)(b). The lien arose after the security interest was perfected because perfection ran continuously from the date of original filing through the ten-day period. Of course, had the security interest not been perfected originally, the secured party would lose, since perfection with respect to the proceeds would not begin until the ninth day.

[160] *See* 1962 U.C.C. § 9–402(3). As discussed in § 4–3 B (4)(b)(ii) *infra,* the 1972 Code eliminates the need for checking the proceeds box but establishes other situations in which perfecting separately with respect to the proceeds themselves may be necessary for perfection beyond the ten-day period.

One should note the significance of the term "continuously perfected," found in 1962 Section 9–306(3) (as well as the 1972 version). Assume in a situation covered by the 1962 Code that the secured party properly files a financing statement covering inventory but neglects to check the proceeds box. On the twelfth day after the debtor sells the inventory and receives the proceeds, the secured party learns of the sale and files a new financing statement covering the proceeds themselves. The security interest in the proceeds will be deemed continuously perfected from the time of the original filing to the tenth day, unperfected on the eleventh day, and reperfected on the twelfth day, with the new perfection dating only from the twelfth day onward. This means that a competing lien arising on the thirteenth day would be subordinate under Section 9–301(1)(b), but a lien arising on the eleventh day would prevail.

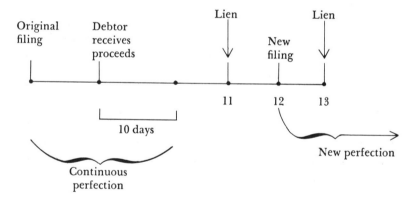

Had the secured party satisfied the requirements for continuous perfection beyond the ten-day period (as by filing a new financing statement covering the proceeds themselves during that period), both lienors would lose.[161]

---

[161] As to whether a lien arising on the ninth day would "rise to the top" and prevail or remain permanently subordinate, upon the secured party's failure to reperfect by the end of the ten-day period, see the discussion of the analogous situations under Section 9–103(3), at § 5–2 C (2) *infra,* and Section 9–403(2), at § 3–3 F *supra.*

Further aspects of perfection beyond the ten-day period under the 1962 Code are discussed below in conjunction with the changes made in the 1972 Code.

(ii) The 1972 Code. The rules under the 1962 Code concerning perfection with respect to proceeds beyond the ten-day period after the debtor's receipt thereof have been changed somewhat in the 1972 Code.

As noted, the 1972 Code eliminates the necessity for claiming proceeds on the original financing statement [162] as a prerequisite for continuous perfection beyond the ten-day period, on the theory that file searchers who find a financing statement should assume that a party claiming a security interest in original collateral will also claim an interest in the proceeds thereof. The requirement of checking the proceeds box has primarily served as a trap for the unwary.[163]

Since 1962 Section 9-306(3) places no restriction on the type of proceeds with respect to which automatic,[164] continuous perfection may be had beyond the ten-day period, it is arguably possible to have such perfection concerning all forms of proceeds. This is not so under 1972 Section 9-306(3), which provides that beyond the ten-day period the security interest in proceeds becomes unperfected unless:

(a) a filed financing statement covers the original collateral and the proceeds are collateral in which a security interest may be perfected by filing in the office or offices where the financing statement has been filed and, if the proceeds are acquired with cash proceeds, the description of collateral in the financing statement indicates the types of property constituting the proceeds; or

---

[162] The requirement has been omitted from 1972 Sections 9-306(3) and 9-402(3).

[163] Similarly, 1972 Section 9-203(3) adds language making it clear that a reference to proceeds need not be included in the security agreement. See § 3-3 B (7) *supra*.

[164] The term "automatic" is used here by the author to mean the lack of any need to take steps to perfect separately with respect to the proceeds themselves, such as filing a new financing statement during the ten-day period.

(b) a filed financing statement covers the original collateral and the proceeds are identifiable cash proceeds; or

(c) the security interest in the proceeds is perfected before the expiration of the ten day period.

It should first be noted that under subsection (3)(b), quoted above, a security interest in the most common form of proceeds—cash proceeds—will be automatically, continuously perfected both during the ten-day period and beyond, without the secured party's having to take any special steps, on the sole condition that a financing statement was filed covering the original collateral.[165]

The first portion of subsection (3)(a), quoted above, was designed to change the fact that under the 1962 Code it is arguably possible for the secured party to obtain a perfected interest in property constituting proceeds by virtue of a filing on the original collateral that would have been inappropriate (regarding either filing itself or the place of filing) had the proceeds themselves been original collateral. In a multi-state situation, for instance, the 1962 Code may require filing on inventory as original collateral in a different place than filing on accounts as original collateral; for example, on inventory, in State *A*, where the inventory is located,[166] but on accounts, in State *B*, where the assignor-debtor keeps his records concerning the accounts.[167] If the secured party were to file on accounts as *original* collateral in State *A*, when the assignor kept its records thereof in State *B*, the security interest in the accounts would be unperfected. But if filing were made on *inventory* in State *A* and the accounts arose as *proceeds* thereof, the lack of limitation

---

[165] This is one reason why a retailer-conditional seller might wish to file a financing statement covering its purchase money security interest in consumer goods despite the exemption from filing afforded by Section 9–302(1)(d). See § 3–2 A *supra*. Another reason is discussed in § 4–3 A (2)(b) *supra*.

[166] 1962 U.C.C. § 9–102(1).

[167] 1962 U.C.C. § 9–103(1). The place for filing on accounts may also be different under the 1972 Code. See § 5–4 *infra*.

concerning types of proceeds in 1962 Section 9–306(3) arguably would give the secured party an automatically, continuously perfected security interest in the accounts beyond the ten-day period, even though the assignor-debtor kept his records concerning the accounts in State *B*. This would disadvantage a competitor, such as a prospective accounts financer, who searched the files only in State *B*.

The first portion of 1972 Section 9–306(3)(a) remedies the foregoing problem by providing, in essence, that there is an automatically, continuously perfected interest in proceeds beyond the ten-day period by virtue of a filing on the original collateral only if that filing would have been proper with respect to the proceeds themselves had they been original collateral. Thus when filing is made on inventory as original collateral in State *A* and filing on accounts as original collateral would be required in State *B*, the secured party will have to make a new filing (during the ten-day period) in State *B* [168] on the accounts proceeds arising from sale of the inventory, in order to have continuous perfection with respect to those proceeds beyond the ten-day period.[169]

The first portion of 1972 Section 9–306(3)(a) would also apply to the following situation: The secured party initially files a financing statement covering inventory. Later, the debtor sells the inventory and receives proceeds in the form of an instrument. Under the 1962 Code the secured party would arguably have a continuously perfected interest during the ten-day period and beyond, simply by virtue of the original filing on the inventory, despite the fact that filing would not have been

---

[168] The new filing is required by subsection (3)(c) of 1972 Section 9–306, since subsection (3)(a) thereof is not satisfied. Under the 1972 Code, State B would be the state where the debtor is located (1972 Section 9–103(3)), whereas State A would generally be the state where the inventory is kept (1972 Section 9–103(1)(b). See §§ 5–4 A and 5–2 B (1), respectively, *infra*.

[169] As noted in § 4–3 B (4)(a) *supra*, perfection continues *through* the ten-day period solely by virtue of the filing with respect to the original collateral.

appropriate had the instrument itself been original collateral (since a security interest in an instrument as original collateral can generally be perfected only by the secured party's taking possession).[170] Under the 1972 Code, since the proceeds are not "collateral in which a security interest may be perfected by filing" within Section 9-306(3)(a), the secured party would be required under Section 9-306(3)(c) to perfect with respect to the instrument itself by taking possession during the ten-day period, in order to have a continuously perfected interest thereafter.[171] This situation also illustrates the operation of the new language in the last sentence of 1972 Section 9-306(3), to the effect that "[e]xcept as provided in this section, a security interest in proceeds can be perfected only by the methods . . . permitted in this Article for original collateral of the same type." [172]

The second portion of 1972 Section 9-306(3)(a), which provides that "if the proceeds are acquired with cash proceeds, the description of collateral in the financing statement [must indicate] the types of property constituting the proceeds," refers to the following type of situation: The secured party takes a security interest in inventory and properly files. Thereafter, the debtor sells the inventory for cash proceeds (first-generation proceeds), which it then uses to purchase a compressor for its plant (second-generation proceeds). Since the collateral description on the financing statement filed on the original collateral refers only to "inventory," whereas the second-generation proceeds in question—the compressor—constitute "equipment," [173] the interest in the compressor will remain automatically, con-

---

[170] U.C.C. § 9-304(1). Temporary perfection without possession is sometimes available under Sections 9-304(4) and (5).

[171] The situation would not come within 1972 Section 9-306(3)(b) because an instrument is not "cash proceeds" as defined in 1972 Section 9-306(1).

[172] The words "except as provided in this section" refer to the opening language of subsection (3)(a) and mean that perfection would obtain *during* the ten-day period by virtue of filing on the original inventory. See § 4-3 B (4)(a) *supra*.

[173] U.C.C. § 9-109(2).

tinuously perfected only for the ten-day period after acquisition by the debtor; in order to continue perfection thereafter, the secured party must take steps to perfect with respect to the compressor itself, pursuant to 1972 subsection (3)(c), by either filing a new financing statement or taking possession before the end of the ten-day period.[174]

The foregoing situation can be used to illustrate the operation of "continuous perfection" during the ten-day period and beyond under 1972 Section 9–306(3).[175] If the secured party did not file on, or take possession of, the compressor until the twelfth day after its acquisition by the debtor, continuous perfection dating from the original filing on inventory would stop at the end of the ten-day period, and the new perfection would date only from the twelfth day on, with the result that under Section 9–301(1)(b) a lien arising on the thirteenth day would lose to the secured party, but a lien arising on the eleventh day would prevail.

Generally speaking, the changes in 1972 Section 9–306(3) will have no substantial impact. The majority of proceeds will arise either in the form of money or checks (cash proceeds) or else accounts or chattel paper. Insofar as cash proceeds are concerned, as long as the interest in the original collateral is perfected by filing, perfection will be automatic and continuous both during the ten-day period and beyond.[176] Apart from an occasional multi-state or second-generation-proceeds situation of

---

[174] Presumably, under the 1962 Code, the interest in the compressor would remain automatically, continuously perfected both during the ten-day period and beyond, solely on the strength of the original filing covering inventory. This would disadvantage a subsequent prospective creditor who searched the files, found no record of a security interest against the debtor's equipment, and lent against the compressor on the assumption that it was unencumbered.

[175] For a discussion of "continuous perfection" under the 1962 version, see § 4–3 B (4)(b)(i) *supra*.

[176] 1972 U.C.C. § 9–306(3) (first clause), (3)(b).

the sort discussed above, the same will be true with regard to accounts and chattel paper proceeds.[177]

(5) Priority Conflicts

The preceding discussion has focussed on identifiability and perfection of a security interest in proceeds. It should be noted that satisfaction of these requirements does not necessarily guarantee priority; these are simply two essential elements. In order to determine the outcome in a conflict involving proceeds, one must consult the relevant priority rule—usually found in Section 9–312, 9–308, 9–309, or 9–301(1)(b). Which of these provisions applies depends partly on the status of the parties and partly on the type of proceeds involved, as discussed in the following sections.

(a) Priority Rules Under Section 9–312

One of the major flaws in the 1962 Code is its failure to provide explicit guidelines about which party prevails in a priority conflict between two competing secured parties concerning proceeds. The 1972 version states clear rules in this regard, which should prove persuasive with respect to the meaning of the 1962 Text in jurisdictions that have not yet enacted the 1972 Code.

(i) Conflicts with Purchase-Money Security Interests—Sections 9–312(3) and 9–312(4). Section 9–312(3) governs conflicts involving a prior perfected security interest in inventory and a subsequent purchase-money security interest in the same inventory. When rights in the original collateral itself are in dispute,[178] both the 1962 and 1972 versions of Section 9–312(3) clearly provide that the subsequent purchase-money creditor

---

[177] Accounts and chattel paper proceeds will generally satisfy the requirement of 1972 subsection (3)(a) that the proceeds be "collateral in which a security interest may be perfected by a filing in the office or offices where the financing statement [covering the original collateral] has been filed. . . ."

[178] That is, when the inventory in question has not yet been sold at the time of the debtor's default.

takes priority, as long as he has satisfied the requirements stated therein.[179] But suppose the inventory has been sold prior to the debtor's default; does the purchase-money creditor's pre-emptive priority extend to the resultant proceeds? The answer is unclear under the 1962 Code.

Assume the following situation: On Day 1, an accounts financer loans directly against the debtor-dealer's accounts receivable, takes a security interest in present and after-acquired accounts, and properly perfects by filing. On Day 2, an inventory financer loans money to enable the debtor to purchase inventory, takes a purchase-money security interest in inventory and proceeds, and properly perfects by filing. On Day 3, a customer of the debtor purchases an item of inventory on unsecured credit, thereby generating an account. Which secured party prevails with respect to the account?

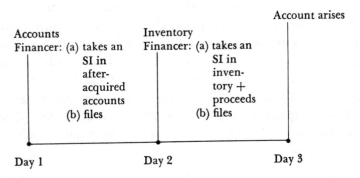

Under the 1962 Code, which contains no language specifically bearing on this issue, it can be argued on behalf of the inventory financer that since Section 9–306(2) states that a security interest in original collateral "continues" in proceeds therefrom, the pre-emptive priority given by Section 9–312(3) in the original collateral also extends to its proceeds; namely, the account in question. On the other hand, it can be argued in favor of the initial accounts financer that Section 9–306(2) is not a priority provision and that since 1962 Section 9–312(3) says nothing

---

[179] These requirements are discussed at § 4–2 B (2) *supra*.

about priority as to proceeds, the situation falls within the "catch-all" provision of Section 9–312(5)—whereunder the first to file (accounts financer) prevails.

The 1972 version of Section 9–312(3) resolves the issue by providing that the pre-emptive priority of the purchase-money financer of inventory extends only to "cash proceeds received on or before the delivery of the inventory to a buyer." [180] Since, as previously noted,[181] the definition of "cash proceeds" in Section 9–306(1) does not include accounts, the conflict over accounts proceeds is excluded from 1972 Section 9–312(3), so that it falls within the catch-all language of Section 9–312(5), whereunder the accounts financer, being the first to file, prevails.[182]

Section 9–312(3) is not confined to conflicts involving a prior *accounts* financer; it applies equally to a dispute between a prior *inventory* security interest and a subsequent purchase-money security interest in inventory.[183] If the inventory was sold for cash proceeds received by the debtor on or before delivery to the buyer, the purchase-money creditor would prevail; but if the proceeds consisted of an account, 1972 Section 9–312(5) would apply, giving priority to the initial inventory secured party. Likewise, if the sale generated proceeds in the form of goods, such as a trade-in auto, Section 9–312(5) would govern. If the proceeds consisted of chattel paper or an instrument such as a promissory note, Section 9–308 or Section 9–309 [184] would deter-

---

[180] As is always true (unless Section 9–306(4)(d) applies, as discussed in § 6–9 B *infra*), the proceeds must be "identifiable." See the discussion of this requirement in § 4–3 B (3) *supra*.

[181] § 4–3 B (2)(b) *supra*.

[182] Since collection on the account would rarely occur before delivery of the goods to the buyer, the "received on or before delivery" language extends the accounts financer's priority to cash proceeds (proceeds of proceeds) received when the account is collected.

The 1972 Code favors the accounts financer in the dispute under discussion on the theory that he is a more fruitful source of working capital than the inventory financer.

[183] The types of conflicts governed by Section 9–312(3) are discussed in § 4–2 B (2) *supra*.

[184] Discussed in §§ 4–3 B (5)(b) and 4–3 B (5)(c) *infra*.

mine the outcome unless the requirements under those sections were not met, in which case Section 9–312(5) would apply.

It should be noted that even when the proceeds in question *are* "cash proceeds received on or before delivery of the inventory to a buyer," if the purchase-money financer of inventory fails to satisfy one of the other requirements of 1972 Section 9–312(3),[185] such as giving notification to the prior creditor,[186] the conflict will fall within Section 9–312(5), whereunder the purchase-money creditor will usually lose by virtue of being second to file. Moreover, a purchase-money financer who has failed to comply with the Section 9–306 requirements concerning identifiability [187] and perfection [188] of his interest in proceeds will lose to a prior secured creditor who has complied with those requirements.

Section 9–312(4) governs conflicts between a prior perfected security interest in collateral *other* than inventory and a subsequent purchase-money interest in the same collateral. Both the 1962 and 1972 versions of Section 9–312(4) clearly give the subsequent purchase-money creditor priority with respect to the original collateral,[189] but the 1962 Code makes no mention of whether that pre-emptive priority extends to proceeds. The 1972 version of Section 9–312(4) (reflecting the general assumption under the 1962 Code) states that it does and, unlike 1972 Section 9–312(3), places no limitation on the type of proceeds. To illustrate, assume that on Day 1, an accounts financer takes a security interest in, and files against, the debtor's present and future accounts. On Day 2, a second secured party loans money enabling the debtor to purchase equipment, takes a purchase-money security interest, and files. On Day 3, the debtor sells the equipment on account. Since the pre-emptive priority of a purchase-money financer of collateral other than inventory extends to all types of proceeds (whether cash or non-cash) under

---

185 § 4–2 B (2) *supra.*
186 § 4–2 B (2)(d) *supra.*
187 § 4–3 B (3) *supra.*
188 § 4–3 B (4) *supra.*
189 § 4–2 B (3) *supra.*

1972 Section 9–312(4), the purchase-money financer wins with respect to the account.[190]

It should be noted that if the purchase-money secured party does not satisfy the requirements set forth in Section 9–312(4),[191] the conflict will be governed by Section 9–312(5), whereunder the prior secured party will win as the first to file. Moreover, a purchase-money creditor who has failed to comply with the Section 9–306 requirements concerning identifiability [192] and perfection [193] of his interest in proceeds will lose to a prior secured party who has satisfied those requirements.

(ii) The General, Catch-All Rule—Section 9–312(5). As previously discussed,[194] when conflicts between secured parties with respect to original collateral are not covered by Section 9–312(3) or 9–312(4) (or, in the case of chattel paper or instruments, Section 9–308 or 9–309), the "catch-all" provision in Section 9–312(5) applies. The same is true of conflicts involving proceeds. Although 1962 Section 9–312(5) does not mention proceeds, 1972 Section 9–312(6) makes explicit what is generally assumed under the 1962 version; namely, that for purposes of the first-to-file-or-perfect rule of Section 9–312(5) the date of filing or perfection with respect to the original collateral will also be deemed the date of filing or perfection with respect to proceeds. In other words, the secured party has the same priority with respect to proceeds as he had with respect to the original collateral.[195] To illustrate,[196] assume that the debtor, an

---

[190] The rationale for not imposing a "cash proceeds" limitation like that found in 1972 Section 9–312(3) is that noninventory collateral like equipment is not expected to be sold and therefore does not ordinarily generate proceeds that would have been relied upon by a prior secured party like an accounts financer; that is, the illustration given in the text would be an unusual occurrence.

[191] § 4–2 B (3) *supra.*

[192] § 4–3 B (3) *supra.*

[193] § 4–3 B (4) *supra.*

[194] § 4–2 A (1) *supra.*

[195] This assumes that the proceeds are identifiable (§ 4–3 B (3) *supra*) and that the requirements for perfection under Section 9–306(3) (§ 4–3 B

auto dealer, gives a non-purchase-money security interest in his inventory to two different secured parties—SP_1, who files on Day 1, and SP_2, who files on Day 2. On Day 3, the debtor sells an automobile to a buyer who pays cash and trades in his old auto. Since SP_2 does not have a purchase money security interest as required by Section 9–312(3), the situation will be governed by 1972 Sections 9–312(5) and 9–312(6), whereunder SP_1, as the first to file on the original collateral, will prevail with respect to the cash and trade-in auto. The same would be true under 1962 Section 9–312(5).[197]

(b) Chattel Paper Proceeds

Priority disputes between secured parties with respect to chattel paper proceeds will be governed by Section 9–308 or Section 9–312.[198] The general provision is the first-in-time rule of Sec-

---

(4) *supra*) have been satisfied. Insofar as the latter requirement is concerned, a secured party who filed first on the original collateral might nevertheless lose with respect to proceeds when, for instance, under the 1972 Code the debtor used first-generation cash proceeds to purchase second-generation proceeds of a type not described on the original financing statement and a new filing describing the second-generation proceeds was not made within ten days after the debtor received them. See § 4–3 B (4)(b)(ii) *supra*.

[196] Another illustration of the operation of 1972 Sections 9–312(5) and (6) is the situation involving a dispute between an initial accounts financer and a later purchase-money financer of inventory with regard to accounts proceeds arising from sale of the debtor's inventory. Since accounts proceeds are excluded from 1972 Section 9–312(3) by the "cash proceeds" limitation, the situation comes within 1972 Sections 9–312(5) and (6), as discussed in § 4–3 B (5)(a)(i) *supra*.

[197] Section 9–312(5) would likewise apply under the 1962 or 1972 Code if the proceeds were in the form of chattel paper or an instrument when the prerequisites for application of Sections 9–308 or 9–309 (§§ 4–3 B (5)(b) and 4–3 B (5)(c), respectively, *infra*) were not satisfied; for example, in the case of chattel paper, where SP_2 did not give new value as required by Section 9–308.

[198] Conflicts between a secured party and a lien creditor will be governed by Section 9–301(1)(b), under which a secured party whose interest in chattel paper proceeds is perfected within the meaning of Section 9–306(3)

tion 9–312(5). Assume, for instance, that the debtor gives a non-purchase-money security interest in its inventory to two secured parties—SP_1, who files on Day 1, and SP_2, who files on Day 2. On Day 3, the debtor sells an item of inventory on secured credit to a buyer, who gives the debtor a security agreement and a note. (The two together constitute "chattel paper," as previously discussed.)[199] Assuming SP_2 fails to satisfy the requirements of Section 9–308 (as by failing to give "new value," which would ordinarily be true here),[200] SP_1 has priority under Section 9–312(5) as the first to file.[201] The first-in-time rule is, however, subject to a major exception set forth in Section 9–308(b)[202] (second sentence of 1962 Section 9–308).[203] This

---

(see § 4–3 B (4) *supra*) before the lien arises will prevail. A lien creditor cannot invoke Section 9–308, since his interest is excluded from the definition of "purchaser" by the "voluntary transaction" language in Section 1–201(32).

[199] § 1–5 B (3) *supra*.

[200] SP_2 is claiming the chattel paper merely as proceeds of another form of collateral (inventory) in which the original security interest was taken. See § 4–3 A (3) *supra*.

[201] For a discussion of Section 9–312(5) as it relates to proceeds, see § 4–3 B (5)(a)(ii) *supra*.

[202] Another exception is found in Section 9–312(4), which, as previously discussed (§ 4–3 B (5)(a)(i) *supra*), gives a purchase-money financer of non-inventory collateral priority over a prior financer of the same collateral with respect to all forms of proceeds, including chattel paper, even though he filed second. (Since the purchase-money financer would be claiming the chattel paper merely as proceeds of another form of collateral (inventory) in which the original security interest was taken, he would not give "new value" and thus would not come within Section 9–308.) At least under the 1972 Code, conflicts with respect to chattel paper proceeds between a purchase-money security interest in inventory and a prior security interest in the same collateral will fall within Section 9–312(5) rather than Section 9–312(3), since the "cash proceeds" limitation in the latter excludes chattel paper. (Again, the purchase-money financer's failure to give "new value" by virtue of asserting nothing more than a proceeds claim would render Section 9–308 inapplicable.) With respect to the "cash proceeds" limitation, see § 4–3 B (5)(a)(i) *supra*.

[203] Although no substantive changes have been made with respect to chattel paper in the 1972 version of Section 9–308 (the change relating to

section provides that as between a party with a security interest in chattel paper "claimed merely as proceeds of inventory" and a subsequent "purchaser" of the chattel paper (meaning a second Article 9 secured party),[204] the subsequent purchaser prevails, even though the initial secured party perfected first [205] if certain requirements are satisfied.

---

instruments is discussed in § 4–3 B (5)(c) *infra*), the section has been subdivided so that the first and second sentences of the 1962 version have become subsections (a) and (b), respectively, of the 1972 version. For the sake of convenience, the present discussion will be phrased in terms of the subdivisions in the 1972 version.

[204] The term "purchaser" includes an Article 9 secured party (Sections 1–201(32) and (33), although not explicit on this, are universally deemed to so provide). Moreover, a person is an Article 9 secured party regardless of whether he takes chattel paper by outright sale or by assignment as security (see the definition of "secured party" in Section 9–105 and the discussion in § 1–4 D *supra*). Thus Section 9–308, in essence, governs conflicts between two Article 9 secured parties.

The language in Section 9–301(1)(c) referring to a "buyer" of chattel paper "who is not a secured party" relates to special parties of the sort listed in Section 9–104(f), such as one who buys chattel paper as part of the business out of which it arose or one who takes an assignment of chattel paper for purposes of collection only (See § 1–4 F (6) *supra*). Interests of this type, although not Article 9 security interests themselves because of the Section 9–104(f) exclusion (and therefore not subject to the rules on creation, perfection, and default), are nevertheless subject to Article 9 priority rules like Section 9–301(1)(c) when they come into conflict with an Article 9 security interest.

[205] The prior security interest referred to in Section 9–308 is often spoken of as a "non-possessory" one, that is, one perfected by filing (as permitted by Section 9–304(1)). If the initial secured party relies on perfection by possession (as permitted by Section 9–305) rather than filing, his perfection will end when the subsequent purchaser takes possession, meaning that the latter party will prevail under Section 9–312(5) by virtue of having the only perfected interest, without needing to invoke Section 9–308. It will be noted that the reference to "temporary perfection" in subsection (a) of 1972 Section 9–308 relates not to chattel paper but to instruments, which can be temporarily perfected without either filing or possession under Sections 9–304(4) and (5), as discussed in §§ 3–2 B and 4–2 B (2)(d)(iv) *supra*.

The requirements imposed by Section 9–308(b) are, with one difference, the same as those applied under Section 9–308(a) (first sentence of 1962 Section 9–308) when a purchaser is in conflict with a party who took a security interest in chattel paper as original collateral; namely, that the purchaser give new value and take possession of the chattel paper in the ordinary course of his business.[206] The difference is that the purchaser can take chattel paper claimed by a secured party "merely as proceeds of inventory" with *knowledge* of the security interest and not lose priority. Thus, like the secured party who claims chattel paper as original collateral,[207] the "mere proceeds" claimant can protect himself by requiring that the debtor deliver the chattel paper to him (as is often done in "direct collection" arrangements, when the secured party collects from account debtors), thereby preventing the subsequent purchaser from taking possession; but unlike the original-collateral claimant, the "mere proceeds" claimant cannot guard against subordination by stamping a notice of the security interest on paper left in the hands of the debtor for collection (the "indirect collection" system), since the knowledge obtained by the purchaser from the stamp will be irrelevant.

It is not entirely clear whether the type of secured party most likely to come in conflict with a subsequent purchaser of chattel paper—the "floor plan" financer of inventory [208]—will be deemed to have a claim to the chattel paper as original collateral, in which case the subsequent purchaser will be subject to the lack of knowledge requirement under subsection (a) of Section 9–308 (first sentence of 1962 Section 9–308), or will be deemed to have a "mere proceeds" claim, in which case the subsequent purchaser can prevail under subsection (b) (second sentence of 1962 Section 9–308), even though he takes with knowledge of the security interest. In view of the important

---

[206] These requirements are discussed in detail in § 4–3 A (3) *supra*.

[207] See § 4–3 A (3) *supra*.

[208] "Floor plan" financing is discussed in § 1–5 B (3) *supra*.

role played by chattel paper in "floor plan" financing,[209] it might be argued that the floor-planner should be allowed to invoke subsection (a); but litigation to date suggests that secured parties who finance inventory will be deemed to come within subsection (b).

(c) Instruments Proceeds

A majority of disputes concerning proceeds in the form of an instrument, such as a check or promissory note, will be resolved by Section 9–309 of the 1962 Code or by Section 9–308(b) of the 1972 Code. As previously noted in the context of disputes concerning instruments as original collateral,[210] Section 9–309 (unchanged in the 1972 Code) provides that the taker of a negotiable instrument who qualifies under Section 3–302 as a holder in due course has priority over a prior perfected security interest in the instrument.[211] Section 3–302 requires that the subsequent party have taken possession of the instrument [212] for value, in good faith, and without notice that someone else (like a prior secured party) has a claim to it.

Assume that a secured party takes a properly perfected security interest in a debtor-retailer's inventory. When an item of inventory is sold, the debtor receives a promissory note from the buyer. The inventory financer's interest in the instrument

---

[209] See § 1–5 B (3) *supra.*

[210] § 4–3 A (4) *supra.*

[211] Section 9–309 similarly subordinates the interest of a prior secured party to good faith purchasers for value of investment securities and negotiable documents.

[212] "Holder" status, a prerequisite under Section 3–302, requires possession, pursuant to Section 1–201(20). The prior security interest addressed by Section 9–309 is a nonpossessory one temporarily perfected under Sections 9–304(4) or 9–304(5) or Section 9–306(3). If the secured party relied on perfection by *possession,* his perfection would have ended when the subsequent holder in due course, by definition, took possession, whereupon the holder would prevail by virtue of having the only perfected interest, without any need for invoking Section 9–309. *See* U.C.C. § 9–301, Comment 2.

is automatically perfected without taking possession for ten days under Section 9–306(3).[213] If during that time an adverse claimant takes the instrument from the debtor under circumstances satisfying Section 3–302, he will prevail, despite the secured party's prior perfection.

Suppose, however, that the subsequent taker in the preceding example had knowledge of the security interest. Since this would deprive him of holder-in-due-course status under Section 3–302, he would lose under 1962 Section 9–309 to the prior inventory financer, even though the latter's interest was a "mere claim to proceeds of inventory." This outcome was deemed anomalous by the drafters of Revised Article 9, since, under the same circumstances, a subsequent taker of *chattel paper* with knowledge would prevail pursuant to the second sentence of 1962 Section 9–308 [214]—a result that elevates chattel paper to a higher level of negotiability than instruments. Section 9–308 of the 1972 Code changes this result by providing that one who takes either chattel paper *or an instrument* and who otherwise satisfies the requirements set forth therein [215] prevails over a prior security interest, even though possession is taken with knowledge of that interest.

(d) Conflicts with Lien Creditors and Bankruptcy Trustees

Conflicts between a secured party and a lien creditor with respect to proceeds are governed by Section 9–301(1)(b), whereunder the secured party will prevail if his interest in the proceeds is perfected [216] before the lien arises.[217]

---

[213] Automatic perfection under Section 9–306(3) is discussed in § 4–3 B (4)(a) *supra*. The interest might also be temporarily perfected for 21 days under Section 9–304(5), as when the secured party took possession of the instrument but then returned it to the debtor for collection from the buyer.

[214] See § 4–3 B (5)(b) *supra*.

[215] The requirements are similar to those imposed by Section 3–302 as a prerequisite to holder-in-due-course status.

[216] § 4–3 B (4) *supra*.

[217] This assumes that the proceeds are identifiable, as discussed in § 4–3 B (3) *supra*.

Section 9-306(4) sets forth special rules governing the secured party's rights to proceeds when the debtor is in bankruptcy. These rules are discussed in a subsequent chapter.[218]

(e) Third-Party Takers of Cash or Goods Proceeds

Occasionally the secured party will come in conflict with a taker of proceeds who cannot be characterized as either a lienor or an Article 9 secured creditor and therefore will not be covered by the priority rules previously discussed under Section 9-301(1)(b), 9-312, 9-308, or 9-309. This will be true in the case of one who takes cash from the debtor or one who purchases goods that the debtor received upon sale of the original collateral.[219]

Suppose the secured party takes a perfected security interest in a debtor-dealer's inventory of automobiles. The debtor sells an automobile to a customer who pays cash and trades in his old auto. The debtor then pays the cash to X for services rendered and sells the trade-in to Y. Generally speaking, the secured party will not be able to follow the cash into the hands of X or the trade-in into the hands of Y. Concerning the cash,[220] the general rule under property law is that a good faith taker for value receives money free from the claims of prior parties.[221] Goods proceeds, such as trade-in autos, will go into the debtor's inventory and, as such, will be subject to the usual Article 9 rules concerning buyers—notably, Section 9-307, whereunder a

---

[218] § 6-9 *infra*.

[219] It would not be true with respect to a buyer of chattel paper or accounts proceeds, since a party is deemed to have an Article 9 security interest in these items irrespective of whether the technical form of his transaction is an outright purchase or a loan against the security of an assignment. Nor would it be true of a taker of a negotiable instrument, whose interest would fall under Section 9-309.

[220] Checks would generally fall under the Article 9 rules pertaining to instruments, discussed in § 4-3 B (5)(c) *supra*.

[221] *See* U.C.C. § 9-306, Comment 2(c). The rationale is to protect the free circulation of money, just as the rules of negotiability under Article 3 protect the free circulation of commercial paper. The same result would generally occur with respect to checks under Section 9-309.

buyer in ordinary course of business will take free of the secured party's proceeds claim.[222]

C. Returned or Repossessed Goods

It sometimes occurs that a merchant seller reacquires goods after they have been sold, either because the buyer returns them (perhaps because of a defect) or because the seller repossesses them upon the buyer's default in payment. In these cases a secured party may have taken a security interest in the goods as inventory prior to the sale,[223] or a financer may have purchased or loaned against the account or chattel paper obtained by the seller at the time of the sale or both may have occurred.[224]

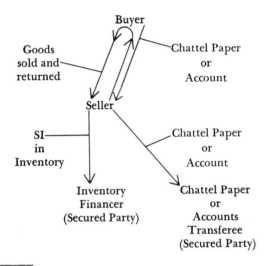

---

[222] See § 4–3 A (2)(a) *supra*.

[223] Section 9–306(5) is not limited in terms to inventory; it could also apply to other categories of collateral, such as equipment. From a practical standpoint, however, disputes in this area will arise almost exclusively in connection with inventory.

[224] The author will use the generic term "receivables financer" or "receivables transferee" to refer both to accounts financers and chattel paper financers.

Regardless of whether the seller assigns the chattel paper or account as security for a loan or makes an outright sale thereof, the receivables trans-

Section 9–306(5) addresses the rights of these three types of secured parties (original inventory financer, accounts transferee, chattel paper transferee) with respect to the returned or repossessed goods (a) against the seller, (b) against each other, and (c) against other claimants.

(1) Inventory or Receivables Financer Versus Seller

The essential problem with returned or repossessed goods is that the return or repossession removes the form of realization anticipated by the secured party. The inventory financer, whose security interest in the goods themselves is cut off at the time of sale to a buyer in ordinary course of business,[225] anticipates repayment from the proceeds paid to the debtor-seller by the buyer. But a buyer who has rightfully rescinded the sale (as for breach of warranty) is entitled to return of the purchase price.[226] Likewise, the chattel paper or accounts transferee expects to collect on the receivable from the buyer. But a buyer who has rightfully returned the goods is no longer obligated on the account or chattel paper. At this point the only basis for realization remaining to the inventory financer or receivables transferee is against the returned goods themselves. Section 9–306(5) provides the basis for such realization. Insofar as the inventory financer is concerned, the first sentence of subsection (5)(a) provides that the original security interest reattaches to the goods when they are returned or repossessed, foreclosing any claim by the seller (or a competing claimant) that the sale permanently cut off the security interest. Insofar as the receivables transferee is concerned, the first sentence of subsection (5)(b) provides that the security interest in chattel paper shifts to the returned goods; and the first sentence of subsection (5)(c) provides likewise with respect to the security interest in the account. These provisions are relevant as between the secured party and the

---

feree is an Article 9 secured party. U.C.C. § 9–102(1)(b), 1962 U.C.C. § 9–105(1)(i), and 1972 U.C.C. § 9–105(1)(m).

[225] U.C.C. § 9–307(1). See § 4–3 A (2)(a) *supra*.

[226] U.C.C. § 2–711(1).

debtor-seller even when there is no conflict with a competing claimant; that is, when the inventory financer, accounts transferee, or chattel paper transferee is the only secured party on the scene.[227]

(2) Inventory Financer Versus Receivables Financer

When both an original inventory financer and a receivables transferee assert a claim to the returned or repossessed goods, the conflict will be resolved under the second sentence of subsection (5)(b) or (5)(c) of Section 9–306.[228] In a dispute between the inventory financer and a chattel paper transferee, the second sentence of subsection (5)(b) provides that the latter party will prevail with respect to the returned goods to the same extent he would have prevailed in a dispute over the chattel paper. Thus a transferee of chattel paper who gives new value and takes possession in the ordinary course of his business will win with respect to the returned goods, since he would have won with respect to the chattel paper under Section 9–308.[229] When the conflict is between the inventory financer and an accounts transferee, the second sentence of subsection (5)(c) states simply that the inventory financer will win with respect to the returned goods.[230]

---

[227] The cited provisions are also relevant when one of the three parties is in conflict with some other claimant. See § 4–3 C (3) *infra*.

[228] The language of Section 9–306(5) restricts its application to "unpaid" secured parties. If the seller has paid his indebtedness to one of the creditors before the goods are returned, that creditor will have no claim, and no conflict will arise.

[229] 1962 U.C.C. § 9–308, second sentence; 1972 U.C.C. § 9–308(b). See § 4–3 B (5)(b) *supra*. This simply effectuates the expectations of the parties, in that the priority that obtained with respect to the chattel paper is carried over to the goods themselves after the chattel paper has been rendered valueless by the return.

[230] Again, this effectuates the expectation of the parties, by applying to the returned goods the priority that obtained with respect to the account. Section 9–312(5) would generally give the inventory financer priority with respect to the account, since his interest in it as proceeds would be perfected (assuming perfection with respect to the original inventory collateral

(3) Inventory   or   Receivables   Financer   Versus   Other Claimants

Portions of paragraphs (a) and (d) of Section 9–306(5) refer to perfection of the secured party's interest in the returned goods. This language apparently applies not to a conflict between the original inventory financer and a receivables transferee [231] but rather to a conflict between one of these parties and a third party (for example, secured party, lienor, or buyer), whose interest in the goods arises after their return or repossession. Assume, for instance, that SP_1 perfects a security interest in the goods as original inventory by filing. After the goods are sold and returned, SP_2 (a second inventory financer)[232] takes a security interest and perfects by filing. Since Section 9–306(5)(a) provides that SP_1's original perfection "continues" with respect to the returned goods, SP_1 will prevail under Section 9–312(5) as the first to perfect,[233] without having to take steps to reperfect after the return.[234]

When the conflict over the returned or repossessed goods is between a receivables transferee [235] and a subsequent claimant (for example, lienor, subsequent buyer,[236] or subsequent inventory financer), Section 9–306(5)(d) provides in essence that it is

---

prior to the sale) before the account transferee's interest. The latter could not be perfected until transfer of the account after the sale.

[231] This type of conflict is discussed in § 4–3 C (2) *supra*.

[232] Once returned, the goods again become part of the debtor-seller's inventory (assuming they are held for sale).

[233] Just as the statement that the original security interest "attaches again to the goods" forecloses any claim that the sale cuts off SP_1's security interest altogether (§ 4–3 C (1) *supra*), the "continues" language precludes a claim that the sale cuts off the original perfection.

[234] The rule that the secured party need not take steps to reperfect applies only if the original perfection was by filing and the filing has not lapsed (Section 9–403(2)) at the time of the return.

[235] The receivables transferee purchases or lends against the account or chattel paper arising at the time of the sale.

[236] The term "subsequent buyer" is used here to mean one who buys the goods after they have been returned or repossessed.

not enough for the receivables transferee to perfect his interest in the account or chattel paper;[237] he must perfect with respect to the returned goods themselves, either by taking possession or by filing.[238]

§4–4. FIXTURES

A. *Applicability of Section 9–313; When Are Goods Fixtures?*

Before delving into the intricacies of Section 9–313, counsel must ask two threshold questions in order to determine whether the section even applies to the dispute in question: (1) Are the goods *fixtures?*; and (2) Is the adverse party a *real estate claimant?*

Concerning the first question, "fixtures" may be defined in the broadest sense as goods that have become so related to real estate that parties who have an interest in the realty have a claim to them under real property law. This definition is reflected in the language of 1972 Section 9–313(1)(a), which was purposely left vague in recognition that the determination of whether goods have become fixtures is a matter of *non-UCC state property law,* as will be discussed subsequently.[239] The same is true under the 1962 Code. If the goods, even though located on, or attached to, realty are not fixtures under state property law, parties with interests in the real estate (such as owners and mortgagees) have no claim to them, and Section 9–313 need not even be consulted.

Concerning the second question, even if the goods *are* fix-

---

[237] However, a financing statement filed against accounts or chattel paper that refers to underlying goods that may be returned or repossessed should suffice.

[238] Even perfection with respect to the returned goods will not avail the receivables financer when the relevant priority rule allows the competing claimant to prevail over a prior perfected security interest. Under Section 9–307(1), for instance, a buyer in ordinary course of business will prevail anyway. See § 4–3 A (2)(a) *supra.*

[239] The purpose behind insertion of this definition, which is not found in the 1962 Code, is further discussed in § 4–4 A (2) *infra.*

tures, Section 9–313 governs only disputes between an Article 9 secured party (commonly referred to in this context as the "fixture financer") and real estate claimants, that is, parties who have a claim to the realty on which the fixture is located by virtue of ownership thereof or a mortgage or judgment lien thereon.[240] Conflicts with adverse chattel claimants, such as other Article 9 secured creditors or creditors with a judgment lien only on the goods themselves, are governed by other Article 9 priority rules.[241]

(1) Tests for Determining Fixture Status

Tests for determining whether goods have become fixtures are, as noted above, a matter of non-UCC property law and vary somewhat from one jurisdiction to another. The following tests, however, are typical.[242] In most jurisdictions the ultimate test for determining whether goods have become fixtures is the objective intent of the parties, particularly that of the party who affixed the goods to the realty. One formulation is "whether under all the facts and circumstances the ordinary reasonable man of the community would consider the article in question as a part of the real estate." In turn, two sub-tests are often applied to ascertain whether this requisite intent is present— the "annexation" test and the "appropriation to use" test.

(a) Annexation Test

Under the "annexation" test it is said that if an article is so permanently affixed ("annexed") to the realty that its removal

---

[240] Section 9–313 also governs disputes between the secured party and a bankruptcy trustee (subject to the rules of the federal Bankruptcy Act) when the realty is part of the bankrupt's estate.

[241] E.g., U.C.C. § 9–312 or 9–301.

[242] The author's discussion of these tests is offered as nothing more than a simplistic overview. Counsel should carefully check the law of the relevant state in this regard.

would be difficult and cause material harm to the realty, it will be treated as a fixture.[243]

(b) Appropriation-To-Use (Institutional) Test

Under the "appropriation-to-use" test (sometimes called the "institutional" test) it is said that if the building in question was constructed for a special purpose and is not easily modified to serve another and if removal of the goods would render the building unsuitable for the purpose for which constructed, the goods will be deemed fixtures. The classic example is that of seats in a movie theatre. In a commercial context this test may be used to characterize as fixtures machinery not technically attached to the realty if the machinery is "necessary or convenient to efficient operation of the enterprise" on the rationale that the building derives its principal value from operation of the equipment therein.[244] The test can even be extended to include such items as beds and television sets in motels.

(2) Goods Incorporated into the Real Estate

Both 1962 Section 9–313(1) and 1972 Section 9–313(2) recognize that certain types of chattels, in the nature of building materials like glass, bricks, and lumber, become such an integral part of the real estate that no security interest in them can survive their incorporation into a structure unless the building itself is not part of the realty (which might be true, for instance, in the case of a mobile home or movable prefabricated steel building).[245]

---

[243] The converse is not necessarily true, however. Under the law of some states, even though the item is held in place only by its own weight and removal would not injure the realty, it may still be deemed a fixture, particularly in the case of machinery in an industrial building. This result is sometimes reached by applying the "institutional" test, discussed in § 4–4 A (1)(b) *infra*.

[244] This test is rarely used in a noncommercial context. Unattached chattels in residential dwellings, for instance, are usually not deemed to be fixtures.

[245] *See* 1972 U.C.C. § 9–313, Comments 2 and 3. In order to resolve some largely academic confusion, the drafters of the 1972 Code removed a

B. *The Secured Party's Right To Remove Fixtures*

Under pre-UCC law it was held in some states that a secured party could not remove a fixture if injury to the realty would result. The UCC rejects this rule, providing in 1962 Section 9–313(5) and 1972 Section 9–313(8) that when the secured party has priority over owners and encumbrancers of the real estate under the rules discussed below, he may, upon default by the debtor, remove the fixture.[246] He must, however, reimburse the encumbrancer or owner (other than the debtor himself) for the cost of repair of any physical injury to the realty.[247]

C. *Secured Party Versus Real Estate Claimant—Priority Rules*

(1) Fixture Hypothetical

The following three-part hypothetical will be used to illustrate various aspects of the priority rules of Section 9–313.

Question (1)

On January 1, X Co. gives a real estate mortgage on its factory to Bank. Bank duly records the mortgage in accordance with non-UCC state property law.

On February 1, X Co. purchases a machine for its factory on credit from Machine Co., which takes a purchase-money security

---

statement in 1962 Section 9–313(1) which might have been interpreted to mean that materials incorporated into a structure could not be called "fixtures" and inserted a definition of the term "fixtures" in 1972 Section 9–313(1) which indicates the contrary (goods which "become so related to particular real estate that an interest in them arises under real estate law"); but the change has no practical significance, since 1972 Section 9–313(2), like 1962 Section 9–313(1), precludes the existence of an Article 9 security interest in these materials. The upshot is that a supplier who sells materials like lumber, bricks, and so forth on credit cannot expect to invoke rights under Article 9 after the materials have been incorporated into a building.

[246] This right is subject to the rules of Part 5 of Article 9.

[247] The secured party need not, however, reimburse for any diminution in value of the real estate caused by the absence of the goods or by any necessity for replacing them.

interest. The security interest attaches (pursuant to 1962 Section 9–204(1) or 1972 Section 9–203(1), whichever is appropriate) on the date of purchase, February 1.

On February 10, the machine is installed as a fixture in the factory.

On March 1, X Co. sells the factory to Buyer Co., who purchases without knowledge of Machine Co.'s security interest. Buyer Co. records its deed, in accordance with non-UCC state property law, on the date of purchase, March 1.

On September 1, X Co. defaults on all of its debts and files a petition in bankruptcy.

Bank, Buyer Co., and Bankruptcy Trustee claim the machine. Ignoring the rights of these three parties among themselves, what is Machine Co.'s priority against each of them under 1962 Section 9–313 if, alternatively:

(a) Machine Co. filed a proper financing statement on February 15 in the office where a mortgage covering the real estate would be filed; or

(b) Machine Co. never filed a financing statement?

Question (2)

What results if the 1972 Code is applied in the foregoing situation (assuming the machine is not "readily removable")?

Question (3)

Assume that the machine was purchased for cash and installed as a fixture on January 15 and that the loan on February 1 was made by Finance Co. (rather than Machine Co.), which took a *non*-purchase-money security interest. Assuming the other facts remain the same, what priority would Finance Co. have against Bank, Buyer Co., and Bankruptcy Trustee in Question (1) and Question (2)?

(2) Purchase-Money Security Interests

Since a large majority of fixture financing arrangements are conditional sales, the rules in Section 9–313 pertaining to purchase-money security interests are the most important of the fixture provisions.

(a) The 1962 Code

(i) Against Prior Realty Interests. Subsection (2) of 1962 Section 9–313, which states that "[a] security interest which attaches to goods before they become fixtures takes priority . . . over the claims of all persons who have an interest in the real estate except as stated in subsection (4)," largely governs the priority of purchase-money security interests, since in most conditional sale situations the security interest will attach before the debtor installs the fixture. Subsection (2) can be analyzed as follows.

1. The word "attaches" refers to the requirements of 1962 Section 9–204(1); namely, that there be a security agreement, that "value" have been given, and that the debtor have acquired "rights in the collateral." [248]

2. The phrase "before they become fixtures" means that in order for subsection (2) to apply, the security interest must attach (pursuant to Section 9–204(1)) before the goods are annexed to the realty (or otherwise become fixtures).[249]

3. The words "except as stated in subsection (4)" mean es-

---

[248] For a discussion of the requirements for attachment, see Chapter 2 *supra.*

[249] As noted in § 4–4 A (1)(a) and (b) *supra,* it is possible for some goods to become fixtures without being technically affixed to the realty. For the sake of simplicity, in the remainder of the discussion of fixtures it will be assumed that the goods in question become fixtures by actual annexation unless otherwise indicated. The author will also use the terms "affixation" or "annexation" to refer to physical attachment to the realty, in order to avoid confusion with the term "attachment," which refers to the requirements of 1962 Section 9–204(1) and 1972 Section 9–203(1).

sentially that priority conflicts between a purchase-money fixture financer and a real estate claimant whose interest arises *after* the security interest attaches (referred to herein as a "subsequent real estate interest") are governed by Section 9–313(4), as discussed *infra*.[250]

4. Since the "except" clause refers to real estate claims arising after attachment of the security interest, real estate interests arising *prior* thereto (referred to herein as "prior real estate interests") are encompassed within the language "all persons who have an interest in the real estate."

5. Since subsection (2) makes no mention of perfection, to the extent that subsection (2) alone (without reference to subsection (4)) governs a particular situation, it awards priority to the secured party even though the security interest is not perfected.

The end result of the foregoing analysis is that usually a purchase money security interest (assuming that it attaches pursuant to Section 9–204(1) before annexation of the goods to the realty) takes priority over a prior real estate interest (buyer, lien creditor, or mortgagee), even though the security interest has not been perfected. Thus, under either Question (1)(a) (security interest perfected) or Question (1)(b) (security interest not perfected) of the Fixture Hypothetical previously posed,[251] Machine Co. will prevail over Bank, the prior mortgagee.

The reason for giving the purchase-money fixture financer priority over prior real estate interests is that the lending of "new money" will be encouraged thereby—the rationale behind the preemptive priority given purchase-money financers under Sections 9–312(3) and 9–312(4)[252]—and the notion that the real estate claimant cannot be heard to complain, since the value of the real estate in which he has an interest is increased by the addition of the fixture. The drafters of the 1962 Code

---

[250] § 4–4 C (2)(a)(ii) *infra*.
[251] § 4–4 C (1) *supra*.
[252] See § 4–2 B (1) *supra*.

gave the purchase-money financer priority over parties like a prior mortgagee even in the absence of filing on the theory that since the fixture was not on the premises at the time the mortgage was taken, the mortgagee could hardly have relied on the presence of the fixture in making his loan.

(ii) Against Subsequent Realty Interests. By virtue of the language in 1962 Section 9–313(2), "except as stated in subsection (4)," 1962 Section 9–313(4) governs conflicts between purchase-money fixture financers and subsequent real estate interests. Subsection (4) can be analyzed as follows.

1. The term "subsequent" means subsequent to the time the security interest attaches pursuant to 1962 Section 9–204(1).[253]

2. The language "subsequent purchaser for value of any interest in the real estate" in subsection (4)(a) refers not only to subsequent buyers of the real estate but also to subsequent real estate mortgagees.[254]

3. The language "a creditor with a lien on the real estate subsequently obtained by judicial proceedings" in subsection (4)(b) refers both to persons who obtain a judgment lien covering the real estate and to bankruptcy trustees.[255]

4. The language "a creditor with a prior encumbrance of record on the real estate to the extent that he makes subsequent advances" in subsection (4)(c) refers to a construction mortgagee, as discussed *infra*.[256]

5. The language following subsection (4)(c), beginning with "if the subsequent purchase is made," applies equally to subsections (4)(a), (4)(b), and (4)(c).

The upshot of the foregoing analysis is that subsection (4), taken together with subsection (2), gives priority to a purchase

---

[253] Attachment is discussed in Chapter 2 *supra*.
[254] See the definition of "purchaser" in Sections 1–201(32) and (33).
[255] U.C.C. § 9–301(3).
[256] § 4–4 C (5)(a) *infra*.

money fixture security interest over the interests listed in subsections (4)(a), (b), and (c) if either (1) the security interest was
perfected before the subsequent real estate interest arose or
(2) even though the security interest was not perfected before
the subsequent real estate interest arose, the real estate claimant
took its its interest with knowledge of the prior security interest.

Under the foregoing analysis, in Question (1)(a) of the Fixture Hypothetical previously posed,[257] Machine Co., having
filed before the later interests arose, prevails over both Buyer
Co. and (subject to the rules of the Bankruptcy Act)[258] Bankruptcy Trustee. In Question (1)(b) Machine Co., not having
filed, loses to both parties.

(b) The 1972 Code

(i) Against the Interest of an Owner or Mortgagee Arising Prior to Affixation. When the 1962 Code was first promul-
gated, many real estate lawyers assumed that it pertained solely
to disputes between chattel financers. With the passage of time,
however, it became apparent that Section 9–313 affected realty
interests. Critics pointed to, among other things, the rule in
subsection (2) giving unfiled purchase money security interests
priority over prior real estate interests,[259] arguing that although
a real estate mortgagee does not make its initial loan in reliance
on the presence of a fixture subsequently installed,[260] it may
indeed rely later, after installation, in deciding whether to foreclose on, or grant an extension to, a defaulting debtor (the addition of the fixture having given the appearance of an increase
in the value of the realty collateral).[261] It was urged, therefore,

---

[257] § 4-4 C (1) *supra.*

[258] Chapter 6 *infra.*

[259] § 4-4 C (2)(a)(i) *supra.*

[260] See § 4-4 C (2)(a)(i) *supra* for a discussion of the rationale for the
1962 provision.

[261] In the context of the Fixture Hypothetical, § 4-4 C (1) *supra,* this
would be illustrated by the Bank's observing the addition of the fixture
to the realty and then granting an extension on the mortgage to X Co. on
February 20.

that the fixture financer should be required to give warning of his security interest by filing or else be subordinated to the mortgagee. That this argument prevailed is indicated in 1972 Section 9–313(4)(a), which provides that a purchase money secured party takes priority over the interest of an encumbrancer or owner of the real estate arising before the goods become fixtures only if he perfects (via a "fixture filing," as explained *infra*)[262] before affixation of the goods or within a ten-day grace period thereafter.[263]

Subsection (4)(a) of the 1972 Code (as well as subsection (4)(b), discussed *infra*)[264] limits the priority afforded fixture financers thereunder to security interests given by a debtor who "has an interest of record in the real estate or is in possession of the real estate." The "interest of record" requirement protects against the type of situation in which a contractor engaged by the real estate owner to make improvements buys a fixture from a supplier on secured credit rather than for cash as anticipated by the owner. Even if the supplier makes a fixture filing, his security interest surprises the owner, who would not think to check for a UCC filing before paying the contractor. The owner becomes aware of the security interest only upon subsequent default by the debtor-contractor, who, by then, may have disappeared or become insolvent. The words "or is in possession of the real estate" create an exception to the "interest of record" requirement to allow debtors such as tenants under short-term leases (which are not generally recorded) to give security interests carrying the benefits of 1972 Section 9–313(4)(a) (or 9–313(4)(b), as the case may be). Contractors of the type just referred to do not fall within this exception because, being in the nature of licensees or invitees, they have no possessory interest in the real estate.

---

[262] § 4–4 F *infra*.

[263] Failure to file by the deadline will subordinate the secured party under subsection (7) unless the real estate interest has not yet been recorded (a rare situation), in which case the secured party can still win under subsection (4)(b).

[264] § 4–4 C (2)(b)(ii) *infra*.

In light of the foregoing, the answer to Question (2) of the Fixture Hypothetical previously posed [265] is that Machine Co. will prevail over Bank under 1972 Section 9–313(4)(a) if it made a fixture filing on February 15, since this was within the ten-day period after the goods became fixtures; whereas it will lose if it failed to file.[266]

(ii) Against the Interest of an Owner or Mortgagee Arising Subsequent to Affixation. Conflicts between purchase money fixture financers and buyers or mortgagees whose interests arise after the goods are affixed (as well as conflicts between non-purchase-money fixture financers and buyers or mortgagees whose interests arise either before *or* after affixation) are governed by 1972 Section 9–313(4)(b),[267] which provides that the secured party prevails only if he makes a fixture filing before the real estate interest is recorded.[268] Section 9–313(4)(b) of the 1972 Code differs from the provision in the 1962 Code which is roughly analogous to it—Section 9–313(4)—in that knowledge of the security interest on the realty claimant's part has no bearing on priority and in that the security interest must be perfected before the realty interest is recorded rather than before it arises. Both changes were made in the interest of greater evidentiary certainty.

Section 9–313(4)(b) of the 1972 Code also requires that the debtor have an interest of record in the real estate or be in possession thereof and that the security interest have "priority over any conflicting interest of a predecessor in title of the encumbrancer or owner." The "interest of record" require-

---

[265] § 4–4 C (1) *supra.*

[266] Machine Co. would win or lose under the same circumstances if the adverse party were an earlier buyer of the realty who purchased before the goods were affixed.

[267] Subsection (4)(a) is expressly limited to conflicts between purchase-money security interests and realty interests that arise before the goods become fixtures.

[268] Subsection (4)(b) differs from subsection (4)(a) in that it keys the time for perfection to the time of recording of the real estate interest rather than the time the goods become fixtures.

ment has previously been discussed.[269] The "priority over a predecessor in title" language was aimed at the following type of situation: Mortgagee$_1$ records its real estate mortgage on January 1. On February 1, a fixture financer makes a fixture filing. On March 1, Mortgagee$_1$ assigns its mortgage to Mortgagee$_2$, who then records the assignment. The language in question prevents the secured party, who is subordinate to Mortgagee$_1$ under subsection (4)(b), from claiming priority over Mortgagee$_2$ on the basis that the security interest was perfected before Mortgagee$_2$'s interest was recorded. As stated in Comment 4(b) to 1972 Section 9–313, this is simply an expression of "the usual rule that a person [Mortgagee$_1$] must be entitled to transfer what he has."

In Question (2) of the Fixture Hypothetical just posed,[270] Machine Co. prevails over Buyer Co. under 1972 Section 9–313 (4)(b) if a fixture filing was made prior to recordation of the buyer's deed; otherwise, Machine Co. loses.[271]

    (iii) Against Lien Creditors. Conflicts between a purchase-money (or non-purchase-money) secured party and a lienor, including both a party with a judgment lien on the realty and (subject to the rules of the Bankruptcy Act)[272] a bankruptcy trustee, are governed under the 1972 Code by Section 9–313(4)(d), which institutes essentially the same change as 1972 subsection (4)(a);[273] namely, the purchase-money or non-purchase-money secured party will now be required to perfect before the lienor's interest arises in order to prevail.

Subsection (4)(d) differs from subsections (4)(a) and (4)(b) in that as against a lien creditor the fixture financer need not make a "fixture filing"[274] but rather can perfect "by any method per-

---

[269] § 4–4 C (2)(b)(i) *supra.*

[270] § 4–4 C (1) *supra.*

[271] The same would be true if a mortgagee were substituted for Buyer Co.

[272] Chapter 6 *infra.*

[273] § 4–4 C (2)(b)(i) *supra.*

[274] § 4–4 F *infra.*

mitted by this Article" (that is, by any method that would be permissible under non-fixture circumstances)—on the theory that "generally a judgment creditor is not a reliance creditor who would have searched the records." [275] The "by any method" language means, for instance, that when the fixture would be classifiable as equipment in non-fixture circumstances, a central filing (instead of the local filing ordinarily required for fixtures) will suffice to subordinate a subsequent lien creditor. It also means that a purchase-money secured party who makes no filing at all on an item classifiable as consumer goods (aside from its fixture status) will prevail, since 1972 Section 9–302 (1)(d) requires a fixture filing on purchase-money security interests in consumer goods which are fixtures only "to the extent provided in Section 9–313."

In light of the foregoing, under Question (2) of the Fixture Hypothetical previously posed,[276] Machine Co. will (subject to the rules of the Bankruptcy Act) prevail over Bankruptcy Trustee [277] under 1972 Section 9–313(4)(d) if perfection was accomplished on February 15, before filing of the bankruptcy petition; whereas it will lose if a filing was never made.

(3) Non-Purchase-Money Security Interests

(a) The 1962 Code

Since non-purchase-money security interests will generally attach only after installation of the goods as fixtures, conflicts involving such interests are usually governed by Subsection (3) of 1962 Section 9–313, which provides that "[a] security interest which attaches to goods after they become fixtures is valid against all persons subsequently acquiring interests in the real estate except as stated in subsection (4)." Because subsection (3) provides only that the security interest is valid against "subsequent" realty interests, the secured party will lose to prior real

---

[275] 1972 U.C.C. § 9–313, Comment 4(c).

[276] § 4–4 C (1) *supra*.

[277] A bankruptcy trustee is included within the Article 9 definition of "lien creditor" in Section 9–301(3).

estate claimants, regardless of whether or when the security interest is perfected. Thus in Question (3) of the Fixture Hypothetical,[278] Finance Co., whose security interest was taken after Bank's mortgage, will lose to Bank under 1962 Section 9–313(3) either with or without perfection.

Subsection (3) of 1962 Section 9–313 refers conflicts between a non-purchase-money secured party and a subsequent realty interest to subsection (4), whereunder the non-purchase-money party will win or lose under the same circumstances as a purchase-money party, as discussed above.[279]

(b) The 1972 Code

Subsection (4)(b) of 1972 Section 9–313 governs conflicts between a non-purchase-money security interest and the interest of a buyer or mortgagee that arises either before or after affixation of the goods.[280] Subsection (4)(b) (together with subsection (7)) gives priority to the non-purchase-money financer only if he makes a fixture filing [281] before the adverse claimant has recorded his realty interest.[282]

Conflicts between a non-purchase-money secured party and a lienor are governed by 1972 Section 9–313(4)(d), as previously discussed.[283]

(4) "Readily Removable" Items—1972 Section 9–313(4)(c)

Subsection (4)(c) of 1972 Section 9–313 states a special rule with respect to conflicts involving fixtures that are "readily

---

[278] § 4–4 C (1) *supra.*

[279] § 4–4 C (2)(a)(ii) *supra.*

[280] Subsection (4)(a) is limited to conflicts between a purchase-money security interest and the interest of a buyer or mortgagee that arises before the goods are affixed.

[281] § 4–4 F *infra.*

[282] The requirements in subsection (4)(b) that the debtor have "an interest of record" and that the secured party have "priority over a predecessor in title" are discussed in §§ 4–4 C (2)(b)(i) and 4–4 C (2)(b)(ii), respectively, *supra.*

[283] § 4–4 C (2)(b)(iii) *supra.*

removable factory or office machines or readily removable replacements of domestic appliances which are consumer goods." In these situations the secured party need not make a "fixture filing" in the real estate records, as would ordinarily be required under subsections (4)(a) and (4)(b), but need only perfect "by any method permitted by this Article" before the goods become fixtures.[284] This means that in the case of readily removable factory or office machines, a central filing on the goods as equipment will suffice as against adverse real estate interests; [285] and in the case of purchase-money security interests in replacements of domestic appliances that are consumer goods, no filing at all need be made.[286]

It should be noted that subsection (4)(c) will be academic in many situations, since the "readily removable" items referred to therein will not be deemed fixtures under the law of many states.

(5) Secured Party versus Construction Mortgagee

A construction mortgagee may be defined as one who advances money (usually in periodic "progress payments") to finance the construction of buildings or other improvements on realty, taking a mortgage on the realty to secure repayment of the loan.[287]

---

[284] The special priority given construction mortgagees (§ 4–4 C (5)(b) *infra*) does not extend to the items specified in subsection (4)(c).

[285] This alleviates the confusion in some states about whether items of this sort are fixtures, as previously discussed in §§ 4–4 A (1)(a) and (b) *supra*); under the "perfection by any method" language, the secured party does not run the risk of guessing wrongly about fixtures status and thereby filing in the wrong place.

[286] 1972 U.C.C. § 9–302(1)(d). Subsection (4)(c) is limited to "replacements" of domestic appliances so as to facilitate financing of original appliances in new dwellings as part of the real estate financing of the dwelling; and it has no application to appliances in a commercial context, such as an apartment building. 1972 U.C.C. § 9–313, Comment 4(d).

[287] This definition is essentially reflected in 1972 Section 9–313(1)(c).

(a) The 1962 Code

Conflicts between Article 9 fixture financers and construction mortgagees are governed under the 1962 Code primarily by subsections (2)[288] and (4)(c) of Section 9–313, as illustrated by the following situation: On January 1, Construction Mortgagee (perhaps a bank or savings and loan company) enters into an agreement with the owner of the real estate to finance construction of a building thereon. The loan is to be made in four installments of $10,000 each, on February 1, March 1, April 1, and May 1. On March 15, Secured Party, a supply company, installs an air-conditioning unit in the building and takes a purchase-money security interest. Assuming that all four payments are made by Construction Mortgagee without knowledge of the security interest and further assuming that the item is deemed to be a fixture with a value of $40,000, who has priority if (a) the security interest was not perfected, or (b) it was perfected by a fixture filing on March 15?

(a) If Secured Party did not perfect, it nevertheless will win with respect to the initial $20,000 advanced prior to installation of the fixture under subsection (2) of Section 9–313, since subsection (4)(c) applies only to "subsequent advances." But under the latter provision Secured Party will lose with respect to the $20,000 advanced after installation.

(b) If Secured Party did perfect on March 15, it will again prevail with respect to the initial two advances under subsection (2). A controversy exists, however, with respect to the last two advances, arising from the language "made or contracted for" in subsection (4)(c). Under one line of reasoning Construction Mortgagee should prevail, since even though the last two advances were *made* after the secured party perfected, they were *contracted for* prior thereto. The opposing school of thought holds that the words "contracted for" should be ignored, with the result that Construction Mort-

---

[288] In a large majority of situations, the secured party will have a purchase-money security interest in the fixture.

gagee would lose with respect to the last two advances as well as the first two.[289]

The foregoing result, which partially or totally subordinates the construction mortgagee under the 1962 Code, was criticized by real estate interests, who argued that the ordinary policy of preferring purchase-money creditors in other Article 9 situations so as to encourage the lending of "new money" [290] does not dictate favoring the purchase-money fixture financer in this situation, since the construction mortgagee is itself a "new money" party who finances improvements on the real estate.

(b) The 1972 Code

That the foregoing argument prevailed in the drafting of the 1972 Code is manifest in 1972 Section 9-313(6), which gives the construction mortgagee priority with respect to all of its advances as long as the mortgage is recorded before the goods are installed as fixtures (which is virtually always true) and the goods are installed before completion of construction (which they almost always are). Thus in the immediately preceding hypothetical [291] Construction Mortgagee will win under 1972 Section 9-313(6) with respect to all four progress payments, regardless of whether the security interest was perfected and regardless of whether it was a purchase money or non-purchase-money interest.[292]

---

[289] This result has been defended on the ground that it is more consistent with the pre-UCC Uniform Conditional Sales Act.

[290] *E.g.,* under Section 9-312(3) and (4), as discussed in § 4-2 B (1) *supra.*

[291] § 4-4 C (5)(a) *supra.*

[292] The words "notwithstanding paragraph (a) of subsection (4)" at the beginning of subsection (6) mean that the secured party's purchase-money status gives him no advantage here. The words "but otherwise subject to subsections (4) and (5)" mean essentially that the construction mortgagee's special priority does not extend to the readily removable factory or office machines or replacements of domestic appliances referred to in subsection (4)(c) (discussed in § 4-4 C (4) *supra*) and that under subsection (5)(a) the construction mortgagee can relinquish its priority by executing a subordination agreement (as discussed in § 4-4 D *infra.*)

D. Subordination Agreements—1972 Section 9–313(5)(a)

Subsection (5)(a) of 1972 Section 9–313 adds a new provision making it clear that a security interest, even though unperfected, prevails over a real estate claimant who has consented in writing to the security interest or disclaimed an interest in the fixture. The subsection creates an exception to the other priority rules of 1972 Section 9–313; when the fixture financer can persuade the real estate claimant to make such an agreement, the fixture financer will prevail under all circumstances. Obviously this is the safest procedure for the secured party to follow, whenever possible.

E. Tenant Debtors—1972 Section 9–313(5)(b)

(1) Purpose and Effect

Subsection (5)(b) of 1972 Section 9–313 is a new provision not found in the 1962 Code, which provides that a security interest in fixtures, *whether or not perfected,* has priority over the conflicting interest of an encumbrancer or owner of the real estate "where the debtor has a right to remove the fixture as against the encumbrancer or owner." This provision was aimed at the following type of situation: The secured party sells an item, such as an air-conditioning unit, on secured credit to a debtor who leases the premises on which his business is located. The secured party never files on the security interest. The debtor's lease (or the real property law of the debtor's state, as discussed below) permits the debtor to remove items of the type in question when he vacates the premises. The lessor gives a mortgage on the realty to a real estate financer. Who has priority with respect to the item, the secured party or the real estate mortgagee?

Ordinarily, under both the 1962 and 1972 versions of Section 9–313(4), a secured party who makes no filing is subordinated to a subsequent encumbrancer or owner of the real estate. The question here is whether the debtor-tenant's right of removal gives the secured party an alternative basis on which to claim the goods. Subsection (5)(b) of 1972 Section 9–313 indicates that it does.

(2) When a Tenant-Debtor Has a "Right To Remove"

Under the law of many states a tenant-debtor has a "right to remove" fixtures within the meaning of 1972 Section 9–313 (5)(b) primarily in two situations:

1. The landlord and tenant (merchant or nonmerchant) may expressly agree in the lease that the tenant shall have the right to remove certain goods affixed to the premises.

2. Regardless of whether the lease contains a removal clause, goods annexed to the realty to serve the convenience of a *merchant*-tenant's trade—termed "trade fixtures"—are removable by the tenant.

In either of the foregoing situations the rule of 1972 Section 9–313(5)(b) giving priority to the unfiled fixture financer is defensible on the ground that mortgagees or buyers of the realty should be sufficiently alerted to the possibility that the goods will not be subject to their claims either by the status of the tenant (merchant) and the nature of the goods (trade-type fixtures) or by the removal clause in the lease.

F. The "Fixture Filing"

The 1972 Code introduces the term "fixture filing," defined in Section 9–313(1)(b) as the filing of a financing statement complying with the requirements of Section 9–402(5)[293] in the office where a mortgage on the real estate would be filed or recorded.[294] The crux of the fixture filing concept is the notion

---

[293] For a discussion of the requirements of 1972 Section 9–402(5) and the reasons for them, see § 3–3 B (6) *supra*.

[294] The 1962 Code also requires filing with respect to fixtures in the office where a real estate mortgage would be filed or recorded, but, unlike 1972 Section 9–402(7), it does not compel the filing officer to *index* the filing in the real estate records. Consequently, under the 1962 Code, when real estate mortgage records and chattel filing records are kept in the same

that the secured party who is not concerned about priority against mortgagees or owners of the realty can protect himself against other interests, such as judgment lienors, bankruptcy trustees,[295] or other Article 9 secured parties, by a filing that would be appropriate in nonfixture circumstances. Thus a central filing on an item properly classifiable as equipment [296] (aside from its fixture status), rather than a local fixture filing, will suffice against the latter parties. This is not true under the 1962 Code, which, in the same situation, leaves the secured party unperfected as against all adverse claimants.[297] Only if the secured party wishes protection against real estate owners and encumbrancers must he make a fixture filing under the 1972 Code.[298]

G.   The Real Estate Mortgagee as an Article 9 Secured Party— 1972 Code Provisions

The drafters of the 1972 Code recognized that a real estate mortgagee can take a valid Article 9 security interest in a fixture by virtue of an appropriate clause to that effect in the mortgage

---

office, filings with respect to fixtures may end up indexed in the chattel records. The purpose of the new indexing requirement is to aid prospective real estate buyers or mortgagees, who will always search the real estate records for encumbrances against the realty but may not think to check the chattel records.

[295] As noted in § 4-4 C (2)(b)(iii) *supra,* 1972 Section 9-313(4)(d) provides that perfection "by any method permitted by this Article" protects the fixture financer against bankruptcy trustees and other lienors.

[296] U.C.C. § 9-109.

[297] Thus the advice often given under the 1962 Code, "When in doubt as to whether it is a fixture, file everywhere." The situation specified in the text (central, rather than local, filing) illustrates the application of 1972 Section 11-104, a transition provision which states, in essence, that when a financing statement filed in the wrong place under the 1962 Code is in the proper place under the 1972 Code, the security interest automatically becomes properly perfected upon enactment of the new UCC.

[298] Reasons for Change following 1972 Section 9-401. A fixture filing under the 1972 Code protects the secured creditor (to the extent that filing gives protection) against *all* adverse claimants.

document without the need for a separate Article 9 security agreement [299] and provided in 1972 Section 9–402(6) that recordation of a mortgage satisfying the usual requirements of Sections 9–402(1) and 9–402(5) for a filing covering fixtures serves as a fixture filing, without the need for filing a separate financing statement.[300] Moreover, 1972 Section 9–403(6) exempts such mortgages from the usual five-year limitation on the life of financing statements; that is, the fixture filing will be deemed effective for the duration of recordation of the mortgage, with no need for a continuation statement to be filed.

§ 4–5. ACCESSIONS

Just as goods are sometimes attached to realty as fixtures, they may also be installed in, or attached to, other goods (as in the case of a radio or cassette tape player installed in an automobile), in which case they are called "accessions." Seeing the analogy between these two situations, the drafters of the original UCC applied virtually the same rules to accessions under Section 9–314 as to fixtures under Section 9–313. Since no change was made in Section 9–314 in the 1972 Code, the rules

---

[299] 1972 U.C.C. § 9–402, Comment 6. It is questionable, however, whether the typical reference to "all fixtures and other appurtenances to the realty" would satisfy the security agreement requirement in Section 9–203 in the absence of a more precise description of the fixture. See the discussion of specificity of collateral description in § 2–2 C *supra.*

In a dispute with a fixture financer, the real estate mortgagee with a valid Article 9 security interest could claim both his rights as a realty claimant under Section 9–313 and his rights as a competing secured party under Section 9–312. In many cases, however, the outcome would be the same under either provision.

[300] The requirement in 1972 Section 9–402(6)(a) that the goods be "described in the mortgage by item or type" raises the question of the specificity with which the fixture must be described. See the preceding footnote and the discussion of specificity in § 3–3 B (5) *supra.*

One of the transition provisions in the new Code, 1972 Section 11–105 (4), retroactively validates as a fixture filing a mortgage complying with 1972 Section 9–402(7) that was recorded before enactment of the 1972 Code.

governing accessions in both the 1962 and 1972 Codes are essentially those governing fixtures under the 1962 Code.[301]

Assume, for instance, that the debtor purchases an automobile on secured credit from Dealer and then buys a cassette tape player to be installed in the auto on secured credit from Department Store. The latter security interest attaches (as is usually the case) at the moment of purchase and before affixation to the auto. If the debtor defaults on both loans, may Dealer repossess both the automobile and the tape player installed therein? As a general rule, under Section 9–314(1) a security interest in an accession that attaches [302] before affixation of the goods (usually a purchase-money interest) will take priority over the interest of the party who financed purchase of the item to which the goods are affixed; whereas under Section 9–314(2) a security interest that attaches after affixation (usually a non-purchase-money interest) will be subordinate thereto. Thus in the hypothetical, Dealer would not be allowed to repossess the tape player, regardless of whether or when Department Store perfected its security interest.[303]

It should be noted that a financer who claims a security interest in a part which has been manufactured, processed, or assembled into a finished product [304] may not also claim a separate security interest in the part as an accession.[305]

---

[301] Section 9–314(1) is analogous to 1962 Section 9–313(2) (discussed in §§ 4–4 C (2)(a)(i) and (ii) *supra*); Section 9–314(2) is analogous to 1962 Section 9–313(3) (discussed in §§ 4–4 C (3)(a) and 4–4 C (2)(a)(ii) *supra*); and Section 9–314(3) is analogous to 1962 Section 9–313(4) (discussed in § 4–4 C (2)(a)(ii) *supra*).

[302] 1962 U.C.C. § 9–204(1); 1972 U.C.C. § 9–203(1).

[303] U.C.C. § 9–314(1). This situation is analogous to the conflict between a purchase-money security interest in a fixture and the interest of a party with a prior mortgage on the real estate, as discussed in § 4–4 C (2)(a)(i) *supra*.

[304] See § 4–6 *infra*.

[305] U.C.C. §§ 9–314(1), 9–315(1).

§4-6. COMMINGLED OR PROCESSED GOODS

A secured party who finances goods that are to be manufactured, processed, assembled, or commingled with other goods to form a finished product will usually wish to claim an interest in the product, in which case the situation comes under Section 9-315. Subsection (1) of Section 9-315 provides that a security interest in the original goods carries over into the product only if the interest is perfected [306] before the goods are converted. In addition, when the goods will not lose their identity (as in the case of components assembled into a machine), the secured party must check the "products" box on the financing statement.[307] When the goods will lose their identity (as in the case of flour, sugar, and eggs commingled into cake mix), filing is sufficient, without the need for claiming products on the financing statement.[308]

Subsection (2) of Section 9-315 provides that when more than one financer has a security interest in the product by virtue of compliance with subsection (1), the interests "rank equally according to the ratio that the cost of the goods to which each interest originally attached bears to the cost of the total product or mass."

§4-7. CROPS

Section 9-312(2) (unchanged in the 1972 Code) applies a special rule in certain circumstances to priority disputes between secured creditors concerning crops.[309] To the extent that a dispute involving crops does not fall within the narrow confines of Section 9-312(2), the outcome will be determined under

---

[306] In this situation filing will be the only available means of perfection.

[307] U.C.C. § 9-315(1)(b). The "products" box is provided for in Section 9-402(3).

[308] U.C.C. § 9-315(1)(a).

[309] For a listing of other special provisions pertaining to crops, see § 1-5 A (4) *supra*.

the other, more general priority rules discussed earlier in this chapter.[310]

The basic purpose of Section 9–312(2) is to enable the farmer to obtain from a secured party the financing needed to plant current crops, despite the presence of an earlier security interest. If all of the following requirements are satisfied, the "new money" security interest will enjoy preemptive priority under Section 9–312(2): [311]

1. The new secured party must give "new value." [312]

2. The new value must be given to "enable the debtor to produce the crop during the production season." The "enabling" requirement is similar to that imposed by Section 9–107, as previously discussed,[313] but there is no requirement

---

[310] Growing crops are expressly included within the definition of "goods" in 1962 Section 9–105(1)(f) and 1972 Section 9–105(1)(h). Already-severed crops are, of course, also "goods" under the same sections by virtue of the more general language therein "all things movable at the time the security interest attaches." In sections that mention "farm products," crops are included, by virtue of the definition in Section 9–109(3) (see, for instance, Sections 9–307(1) and 9–401(1)(a)).

Conflicts between secured creditors that do not fall within Section 9–312(2) will be governed by Section 9–312(5), as discussed below. Conflicts between a secured creditor and a lien creditor will be resolved under Section 9–301(1)(b). Conflicts between a secured creditor and a buyer from the debtor will be governed by Sections 9–306 and 9–307, as discussed in § 4–3 A *supra*.

There has been virtually no litigation under Section 9–312(2), probably because it is a common practice among crop lenders to obtain subordination agreements from all holders of earlier interests.

[311] Section 9–312(2) is analogous to the rules in Sections 9–312(3) and 9–312(4) giving purchase-money creditors preemptive priority over earlier secured parties (§ 4–2 B (1) *supra*), but, as will be seen, the scope of the protection is much narrower.

[312] For a discussion of "new value" see § 4–2 B (4)(b) *supra*. The term is broad enough to encompass arrangements in which a seed company furnishes seed for the crop or a service company assists in harvesting it.

[313] § 4–2 B (4)(b) *supra*.

that the credit have been "in fact so used." The "production season" will vary with the crop—from a few months for wheat to several years for establishment of fruit trees.

3. The new security interest must be perfected.[314]

4. The secured party must have given the new value not more than three months prior to the time the crops became growing crops by planting or otherwise.

5. The debt owed the earlier secured party must have been in default and unpaid for a period of more than six months before the crops became growing crops.[315]

If all of the foregoing requirements are satisfied, the new secured party will enjoy preemptive priority, even though he had knowledge of the earlier security interest. If one or more of the requirements are not met, however, the situation falls within the catch-all provision of Section 9–312, subsection (5)—whereunder the earlier creditor will usually win as the first to file.[316]

At present it is uncertain whether an earlier interest in crops asserted by a real estate mortgagee or lessor (for example, for unpaid rent) is a security interest within the meaning of Section 9–312(2)[317] or is a non-Article 9 interest.[318]

---

[314] But there is no requirement that it be perfected by a particular time.

[315] This requirement makes the scope of Section 9–312(2) extremely narrow and has caused more than one commentator to call the section "essentially useless."

[316] Section 9–312(5) is discussed in § 4–2 A (1) *supra.* Any argument that the new secured party could invoke the priority of a purchase-money financer of noninventory collateral under Section 9–312(4) would seem to be foreclosed by the presence of the preemptive priority rule expressly aimed at crops in Section 9–312(2), which indicates that the drafters intended the latter section to be the exclusive source of preemptive priority.

[317] If so, it would be subordinated to the later security interest of the crop financer under the circumstances specified in Section 9–312(2).

[318] If so, it would usually prevail over the later security interest under non-UCC common law by virtue of being the first interest recorded.

5

Multiple-State Transactions

Previous discussions of Aricle 9 rules have assumed that all the incidents of the secured transaction in question are confined to one state. However, many secured financing arrangements touch on two or more states. In these cases a question often arises about which state's law will govern—particularly with respect to the proper place for perfection. In most situations the answer will be found in Section 9–103. Because of the numerous problems that have arisen from the language of the 1962 version, Section 9–103 has been completely rewritten in the 1972 Code. For purposes of organizational convenience, the headings in the remainder of this chapter are keyed to the 1972 Code, but the discussions thereunder include an examination of both the 1962 and 1972 rules.

§ 5-1. THE BASIC CHOICE OF LAW RULES: SECTION 1–105 VERSUS SECTION 9–103

The general choice of law rule applicable to all articles of the UCC is found in Section 1–105, which provides, in essence, that (a) when the parties have not contractually stipulated which state's law will govern, the controlling law will be that of the state to which the transaction bears an "appropriate relation," [1] or, if the parties have stipulated choice of law, that stipulation will control; *unless* (b) their rights and duties are governed by one of the UCC sections listed in Section 1–105(2), in which case the law of the state specified in the listed provision will control. Under the 1962 Code essentially *all* Article 9 multi-

---

[1] This is simply a lead-in to non-UCC conflict of laws rules.

state questions fall within category (b), since the 1962 version of Section 1–105(2) includes within its listing both Sections 9–102 and 9–103, and 1962 Section 9–102(1) lays down a choice of law rule applying all of the forum state's Article 9 rules when the collateral is located in the state except as otherwise provided in Section 9–103. The drafters of the 1972 Code have deleted the location-of-the-collateral choice of law rule in Section 9–102(1) and omitted the reference in Section 1–105(2) to Section 9–102, with the result that matters other than the proper place of perfection, such as requirements for the security agreement and rules on default (that is, matters affecting the relationship between the secured creditor and the debtor) will be thrown under the general rule of Section 1–105(1), leaving only the place of perfection (a matter affecting conflicts between the secured creditor and competing claimants) mandatory under 1972 Section 9–103.[2] These changes will have very little practical impact, since a majority of multi-state questions under either the 1962 or 1972 Code come within Section 9–103.

§5–2. ORDINARY GOODS, DOCUMENTS, AND INSTRUMENTS

Subsection (1) of 1972 Section 9–103 lays down rules for ordinary goods, instruments, and documents with respect to the

---

[2] The reasoning behind this change was as follows:

Section 9–103 was drafted in the light of the uncertainty whether the Code would be widely adopted, and the emphasis was on conflicting rules of law and a desire to make the Code rules applicable when such a result was justified under general principles. Today, when 51 jurisdictions have adopted the Code, situations of actual conflict in rules of law within the ambit of the Code will be few, and the emphasis may shift to the question of certainty as to where to file in order to perfect security interests.

Review Committee for Article 9, Final Report 229–30, at ¶ F-2 (April 25, 1971). The main point made in this statement is that since every state (except Louisiana) has now adopted UCC Article 9, there will be very few *conflicts* of laws problems. Counsel should remain alert, however, to the fact that many states have made at least a few nonuniform changes in the Official Text.

place for initial perfection and with respect to reperfection
when collateral already subject to a perfected security interest
in one state is moved to another.

A. Applicability of Section 9–103 to Documents and Instruments

Uncertainty exists under the 1962 Code concerning whether
documents and instruments are covered by Section 9–103 since
these items are not specifically referred to either in the heading
of the section or the language thereof.[3] Subsections (1) and (2)
clearly do not apply; and whereas the term "personal property"
in subsection (3) would seem broad enough to cover documents
and instruments, the heading of Section 9–103 refers to "incoming *goods.*" The problem arises when one of these items is subject to a perfected security interest in State A and is then moved
to State B, where a conflicting claim, such as a judicial lien,
arises. If Section 9–103(3) applies, the secured party has a four-
month grace period within which to reperfect,[4] but if not, the
security interest will be deemed unperfected from the day the
item enters State B. The drafters of the 1972 Code have clarified this situation by making 1972 Section 9–103(1) expressly
applicable to instruments and documents.[5]

B. Rules Dictating the Place for Initial Perfection

(1) The "Last Event" Rule

Subsection (1)(b) of 1972 Section 9–103 provides that the law
governing perfection of a security interest in documents, instruments, and ordinary goods,[6] and thus the place for filing (or,

---

[3] The same uncertainty exists with respect to chattel paper, discussed in
§ 5–5 *infra.*

[4] The four-month period is discussed in § 5–2 C *infra.*

[5] The similar ambiguity with respect to chattel paper has been resolved
by making 1972 Section 9–103(4) expressly applicable thereto.

[6] Special rules apply to goods covered by a certificate of title (Section
9–103(2), discussed in § 5–3 *infra*), mobile goods (Section 9–103(3), discussed
in § 5–4 *infra*), and minerals, including oil and gas (Section 1–103(5), discussed in § 5–6 *infra*).

when appropriate, perfecting by taking possession[7] or perfecting temporarily under Sections 9–304(4) and 9–304(5)), is that of the state where the collateral is located at the time the last event leading to perfection occurs.[8]

Under Section 9–303, the "events leading to perfection" consist in (a) the steps required for attachment of the security interest, plus (b) the additional steps, if any,[9] required for perfection. Pursuant to 1972 Section 9–203(1) the steps for attachment[10] are (1) execution of the security agreement or the secured party's taking possession of the collateral; (2) the giving of value by the secured party;[11] and (3) the debtor's acquisition of rights in the collateral.[12] The additional step for perfection consists in the secured party's taking possession or, more frequently, filing. In a majority of situations the "last event" will be filing, so that the state where the collateral is located at the time of filing will be the proper state in which to file.

To illustrate: Assume that the debtor, whose main office is located in Georgia, wishes to borrow on the security of equipment located in the debtor's plant in Mississippi from a secured creditor located in New York. When the debtor executes the security agreement and receives the loan in New York, the first two steps for attachment—security agreement and value—are

---

[7] Taking possession is the only permissible means of perfecting a security interest in instruments. U.C.C. § 9–304(1).

[8] The equivalent provision in the 1962 Code is Section 9–102(1), which also imposes a rule based on the location of the collateral.

[9] No additional steps are required for perfection when the security interest is automatically perfected upon attachment under Section 9–302 (for example, a purchase-money security interest in consumer goods).

[10] For further discussion of the prerequisites for attachment, see Chapter 2.

[11] Under Section 1–201(44), this can consist in the secured party's actually extending credit or else entering into a binding commitment to do so in the future. See § 2–3 *supra*.

[12] The debtor is deemed to have "rights" in the collateral as soon as he has a contractual right to receive goods and they are "identified to the contract" within the meaning of Section 2–501, even though the seller has not yet shipped them. See § 2–4 *supra*.

satisfied. The third step—debtor's rights in the collateral—is also satisfied, since the debtor already owns the collateral. Thus the "last event" leading to perfection will be filing. And since the collateral will be located in Mississippi when this last event occurs, Mississippi's law governing perfection controls, and filing must be made in Mississippi. If the secured party files in New York or Georgia, he will be unperfected in the state where the collateral is located when the "last event" occurs and will thus be vulnerable to conflicting interests arising in any of the three states. If, on the other hand, filing were to precede execution of the security agreement or the secured party's extending credit,[13] then execution of the security agreement or the extension of credit would be the "last event"; but, since the collateral remains in Mississippi during occurrence of all of the "events" leading to perfection, Mississippi will still be the proper place to file.[14]

Although the "last event" rule may occasionally lead to strange results, as when the "last event" is the debtor's acquisition of "rights" when the seller identifies goods to the contract in a state otherwise unrelated to the transaction,[15] the rule will, in the large majority of cases, be relatively easy to apply. In the ordinary *non-purchase-money* transaction the collateral will remain in one state while all the "events" leading to perfection occur, so that the secured party will have no difficulty in knowing to file in that state. In the ordinary *purchase-money* transaction, when the collateral consists in goods that will be shipped from the seller's state to another jurisdiction, the secured party will require the debtor at the time of contracting to name the state in which the collateral will ultimately be kept, will there-

---

[13] This is permissible under Section 9–402(1).

[14] If the collateral were moved to Florida before the "last event" occurred, Florida would be the proper place to file.

[15] For example, the debtor is located in Mississippi, the creditor is located in New York, and the seller identifies the goods to the contract at the time of marking them for shipment (per Section 2–501) at its plant in Oregon.

fore know to file in that state, and will be protected by the 30-day rule of Section 9–103(1)(c), discussed below,[16] while the goods are in transit. Moreover, the secured party who is in doubt about which state's law applies can protect himself by filing in both states.

(2) The 30-Day Rule

Assume that a debtor wishes to purchase from a conditional seller located in New York equipment to be installed in his plant in Mississippi. The debtor executes a security agreement giving the secured party a purchase money security interest, receives credit, and enters into a purchase agreement giving him a contractual "right" to receive shipment of the goods. At this point attachment has occurred under 1972 Section 9–203(1), the goods are located in New York (destined for Mississippi), and the remaining "last event" leading to perfection is filing. Were it not for the 30-day rule of subsection (1)(c) of 1972 Section 9–103, the "last event" rule of subsection (1)(b) would compel the secured creditor to file in New York, as previously discussed.[17] But if the secured party did so, a hardship would be imposed on a prospective Mississippi creditor (or buyer) who, seeing the goods in Mississippi after they arrived, might well search only the Mississippi records and, finding no filing, would assume that the goods were unencumbered. The 30-day rule of subsection (1)(c)[18] partially relieves this hardship. Under subsection (1)(c), if the interest is a *purchase-money* security inter-

---

[16] § 5–2 B (2) *infra*.

[17] § 5–2 B (1).

[18] Although the 30-day rule set forth in 1962 Section 9–103(3) contains language similar to that of 1972 Section 9–103(1)(c), it is questionable whether the two provisions are parallel, since the latter concerns perfection, whereas the former speaks to "validity" of the security interest. It is felt by many that the references to "validity" in 1962 Section 9–103 pertain to such things as "formal requisites," including the need for, and contents of, the security agreement under Section 9–203 but not to perfection. Because of its vagueness, the term "validity" is nowhere used in 1972 Section 9–103.

est in *goods*[19] and the secured party is aware at the time of attachment that the goods are to be transported, say, from New York to Mississippi, the proper place for filing is Mississippi rather than New York. Mississippi remains the proper place for filing for 30 days after the debtor receives possession of the goods and thereafter if the goods are actually brought to the state within the 30-day period.

It should be noted that the 30-day period is not a "grace period" like the four-month period discussed next in connection with *reperfection;*[20] it simply dictates the place where *initial* filing must be made as quickly as possible. If in the immediately preceding hypothetical the secured party were to file in Mississippi, say, only 13 days after the goods arrived, but a competing creditor obtained a judicial lien on the twelfth day, the latter would prevail.[21]   *INITIAL PERFECTION VS. ALREADY PERFECTED.*

C. *Reperfection When Collateral Already Subject to a Perfected Security Interest in One State Is Moved to Another*

(1) *The Four-Month Rule*

The "last event" rule of subsection (1)(b) of 1972 Section 9–103 and the 30-day rule of subsection (1)(c), as previously discussed,[22] are aimed at determining the place where *initial* perfection must be made. By contrast, the four-month grace period of subsection (1)(d) operates only when collateral is brought into the forum state subject to a security interest that has *already* been perfected elsewhere. To illustrate, assume the same sort of situation previously discussed[23] in which the debtor purchases from a conditional seller residing in New York equipment to be

---

[19] Non-purchase-money interests in goods and interests in collateral other than goods do not fall within the 30-day rule and will therefore be governed solely by the "last event" rule.

[20] § 5–2 C (1) *infra.*

[21] U.C.C. § 9–301(1)(b).

[22] §§ 5–2 B (1) and (2), respectively, *supra.*

[23] 5–2 B (2) *supra.*

installed in the debtor's plant in Mississippi. While the goods are still located in New York, the debtor executes a security agreement giving the seller a purchase money security interest, receives credit, and obtains a contractual right to the goods. If the seller-creditor is unaware that the goods are to be moved out of New York, the 30-day rule does not apply, whereupon the "last event" rule dictates perfection by filing in New York. Assuming a filing is in fact made in New York and the goods are then moved to Mississippi, 1972 subsection (1)(d) gives the secured creditor a four-month grace period in which to discover the move and to reperfect in Mississippi. The same four-month period is provided for in 1962 Section 9–103(3), but the 1972 Code has made a number of clarifications, as discussed next.

(2) Failure To Reperfect Within the Four-Month Period

Both 1962 Section 9–103(3) and 1972 Section 9–103(1)(d) clearly provide that when a secured party whose interest was perfected in State A files (or otherwise reperfects) in State B within four months after removal of the collateral to the latter state, the security interest remains continuously perfected beyond the four-month period, with priority relating back to the time of initial filing (or other perfection) in State A.[24] But what of the secured party who neglects to reperfect within the four-month period? Assume the following situation: SP_1 perfects a security interest in an item of equipment [25] in State A. Thereafter, on January 1, the debtor moves the collateral to State B. On May 15, SP_1 learns of the removal and reperfects by filing in

---

[24] It should be noted that when reperfection is by filing, both the 1962 and 1972 versions of Section 9–402(2)(a) permit the new financing statement to be signed by the secured party rather than by the debtor. This allows circumvention of a debtor who, having already received the desired credit, may have no inducement to be cooperative about signing the new financing statement.

[25] This hypothetical assumes that the goods are not "mobile," within the meaning of 1972 Section 9–103(3) (as discussed in § 5–4 infra), and are not covered by a certificate of title (as discussed in § 5–3 infra).

State B. Suppose a second secured party, SP_2, obtains a security interest in the goods and perfects in State B, in the alternative, (a) on May 17, (b) on May 13, or (c) on April 15. Which party prevails under Section 9–312(5)?

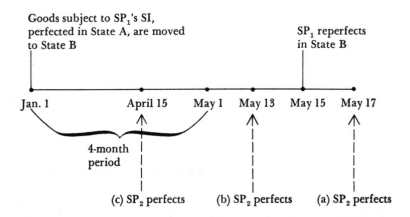

The answers to alternatives (a) and (b) are clear under both the 1962 and 1972 Code. In alternative (a) SP_1 reperfected, albeit outside the four-month period, prior to SP_2's perfection and therefore prevails. In alternative (b) SP_1's interest became unperfected on May 1 and remained so until May 15. Since the reperfection on May 15 was outside the four-month period, it does not relate back to the earlier time of perfection, with the result that SP_2, who perfected in the "gap," prevails. The answer to alternative (c), wherein SP_2 perfected *within* the four-month period, has caused considerable difficulty under the 1962 Code.[26] On the one hand, it can be argued that since SP_2's interest was subordinate *at the time it arose* [27] it should remain permanently subordinate even after the four-month period ends and SP_1's interest becomes unperfected. On the other hand, it

---

[26] There would be no difficulty, of course, if SP_1 had reperfected within the four-month period (on April 20, for instance). In that case Sp_1 would prevail under alternatives (a), (b), and (c).

[27] During the four-month grace period, SP_1's priority relates back to the time of his earlier perfection in State *A*.

can be argued that the formerly junior interest should "rise to the top" and prevail at the end of the four-month period. Despite language in Comment 7 to 1962 Section 9–103 seemingly dictating the latter result, a majority of courts have held under the 1962 Code that the junior interest remains permanently subordinate. Subsection (1)(d)(i) of 1972 Section 9–103 changes this outcome, indicating the drafters' intent that the junior interest "rise to the top," by stating that if reperfection is not accomplished within the four-month period, the interest becomes unperfected "and is thereafter deemed to have *been* unperfected as against a person who became a purchaser after removal." [28] Thus, under the 1972 Code, SP_2 would prevail in alternative (c).[29]

(3) Reperfection of Automatically Perfected Security Interests

The language of the third sentence of 1962 Section 9–103(3) states that a security interest perfected in State A in collateral brought into State B continues perfected in the latter state only "if within the four month period it is perfected" in State B. Since this language is unqualified, an inference might be drawn that reperfection always requires affirmative action by way of

---

[28] Emphasis added. Under the 1962 Code, the same controversy exists, whether the party in SP_2's position in alternative (c) is an Article 9 secured party whose interest was perfected on April 15, a judicial lien creditor whose lien arose on April 15, or a buyer who purchased the collateral from the debtor on April 15. The relevant priority provisions are found in Sections 9–312(5), 9–301(b), and 9–301(1)(c) (a buyer in ordinary course of business would win anyway, since Section 9–307(1) would give him priority even over a *prior* perfected security interest—see § 4–3 A (2)(a) *supra*), respectively. Under 1972 Section 9–103(1)(d)(i), however, the term "purchaser" (which is confined to "voluntary transactions" under the definition in Section 1–201(32)) excludes judicial lien creditors from the "rising to the top" formulation, with the result that this type of competitor (unlike competing secured parties and buyers) will remain permanently subordinate, as under the 1962 Code.

[29] Even in states that have not yet enacted the 1972 Code, the language of 1972 Section 9–103(1)(d)(i) should prove persuasive concerning the meaning of 1962 Section 9–103(3) and may suffice to overturn what has previously been the majority rule under the latter section.

filing, even with respect to security interests that would be automatically perfected if the situation were not a multi-state one
(for example, purchase-money security interests in consumer
goods under Section 9–302(1)(d)). The "if action is required"
language of 1972 Section 9–103(1)(d) negates any such inference
and makes it clear that affirmative action is not required to
reperfect when the transaction falls within one of the exclusions
from filing in State B's Section 9–302.[30]

(4) Lapse of Filing in the State from Which the Collateral Was Removed

Since the third sentence of 1962 Section 9–103(3) states un-
qualifiedly that a security interest perfected in State A "continues perfected for four months" in State B, it is arguable
under the 1962 Code that even though perfection in State A
would have lapsed under Section 9–403(2) had the collateral
been left in that state for one more day, it nevertheless continues for an additional four months by virtue of removal to
State B. Under this reasoning the effectiveness of an otherwise
expired financing statement might be prolonged indefinitely by
successive removals from one state to another every four months.
To foreclose any such inference, language has been added to
1972 Section 9–103(1)(d)(i) to the effect that perfection continues in State B only if reperfection is accomplished there within
four months after removal or before expiration of perfection in
State A, whichever period first expires.

§ 5–3. GOODS COVERED BY A CERTIFICATE OF TITLE

Subsection (2) of 1972 Section 9–103 sets forth special rules
with respect to perfection of security interests in goods covered
by a certificate of title when the goods are moved from one state

---

[30] 1972 Section 9–103(1)(d)(iii) also makes it clear, however, that a secured party with a purchase-money security interest in consumer goods is
not protected against an unauthorized sale by the consumer-debtor to a
subsequent consumer-buyer (a situation falling within Section 9–307(2), as
discussed in § 4–3 A (2)(b) *supra*) unless filing is accomplished in the new
state within the four-month period.

to another. Basically, a certificate of title is a document issued by a state agency (frequently the department of motor vehicles) that shows on its face ownership of, and encumbrances against, motor vehicles that are covered by the state certificate of title act.[31] Typically, such acts provide that when a vehicle is brought into the state under circumstances that require registration (that is, obtaining license plates), the owner must apply for a certificate of title, and, in so doing, surrender any outstanding certificate previously issued by another state. When a creditor takes a security interest in the vehicle, perfection is accomplished by sending the certificate back to the issuing agency, which then issues a new copy of the certificate showing the existence of the security interest.[32] The purpose of the certificate is to protect prospective creditors and buyers who, prior to lending against or purchasing the vehicle, will ask to see the certificate and will thereby be alerted to prior encumbrances.

It should be noted that in a large majority of jurisdictions an Article 9 security interest in a vehicle covered by the state's certificate of title act can be perfected *only* by complying with the procedure specified in that act, as discussed above; in other words, as indicated in UCC Sections 9–302(3) and 9–302(4), the filing of a UCC financing statement is neither necessary *nor effective* to perfect an interest in such a vehicle.[33] This does not

---

[31] Only some ten states have enacted the Uniform Motor Vehicle Certificate of Title and Anti-Theft Act [hereinafter UMVCTA], the language of which can be found in 11 Uniform Laws Annotated 421 *et seq.* (1974). But a number of other states have provisions quite similar to the UMVCTA, at least insofar as Article 9 security interests are affected.

[32] UMVCTA Section 20(b) provides, "A security interest is perfected by the delivery to the Department [of motor vehicles] of the existing certificate of title, if any, an application for a [new] certificate of title containing the name and address of the lienholder and the date of his security agreement and the required fee." In many states the agency then sends the amended certificate to the creditor (rather than the owner), who keeps it until the debt is paid.

[33] It is important to note that most certificate of title acts exempt from their coverage security interests created by vehicle dealers or manufacturers, which means that a UCC filing *is* the proper means of perfecting with respect to vehicles which are inventory in the hands of the debtor.

mean that a certificate of title act pre-empts UCC Article 9 in its entirety; on the contrary, Article 9 rules other than the filing provisions—such as the priority rules—will still be applicable.[34]

Heretofore, problems have resulted from the fact that some states, referred to as "title" states, had certificate of title acts, whereas others, called "non-title" states, did not. Instead of requiring notation of the security interest on a certificate, the latter states permitted perfection by UCC filing. As a result, prior encumbrances were often concealed, and difficulties in resolving priority disputes arose when a vehicle subject to a security interest perfected by filing in a "non-title" state was moved to a "title" state that issued a "clean" certificate or when a vehicle subject to a security interest noted on a certificate in a "title" state was moved to a "non-title" state. Subsection (2) of 1972 Section 9–103 was drafted with an eye to resolving such problems, which were not adequately dealt with by the 1962 Code. Irrespective of the 1972 changes, however, the incidence of these problems should now be greatly reduced, since almost all "non-title" states have enacted certificate of title acts within recent years.[35]

------

[34] Thus, for instance, a conflict between two non-purchase-money creditors, each of whom has a security interest in a vehicle covered by the certificate of title act, will still be governed by UCC Section 9–312(5); but the outcome under the "first to perfect" rule will hinge on who first complied with the certificate of title act rather than who filed first.

[35] As a result, in the ordinary course of events, a security interest taken in State *A* will be noted on that state's certificate of title. When the vehicle is moved to State *B* and application is made for registration, the owner will also be required to apply for a certificate, whereupon the old certificate must be surrendered and the security-interest notation thereon will be transferred to State *B*'s certificate. If the owner cannot (or will not) produce a certificate from State *A*, officials will become suspicious and investigate the vehicle's past history; or, at the least, the owner will not obtain a "clean" certificate and will therefore have nothing to show prospective lenders or buyers, who will know that no matter what state the vehicle came from, there should be a certificate. Some problems remain, however, as evidenced by the fact that there have been a numbr of thefts of blank certificate-of-title forms from state agencies.

The basic rule imposed by 1972 Section 9–103(2) is found in subsections (2)(a) and (2)(b), which essentially provide that when a security interest is perfected in State *A* by notation on a certificate of title and the vehicle is then moved to State *B*, the security interest remains perfected indefinitely as long as the vehicle is not registered in State *B* and the certificate is not surrendered.[36] If, on the other hand, the vehicle is registered in State *B*, the security interest remains perfected only for four months after removal from State *A* plus the additional period, if any, preceding registration; but, in any event, perfection terminates whenever the certificate from State *A* is surrendered.[37] This gives the secured party a grace period in which to discover that the vehicle has been moved and to take steps to perfect in State *B*. As long as the creditor does perfect in State *B* within the prescribed period,[38] the interest remains continuously perfected.

---

[36] Essentially the same rule obtains under 1962 Section 9–103(4). The significance of surrender of the certificate is that since it is the creditor who usually has possession thereof, as previously noted, a request from the owner or officials in State *B* that he relinquish possession is tantamount to notice that the vehicle has been moved and that the creditor should take steps to ensure that he is perfected in the new state.

[37] To illustrate: (a) If registration (that is, application for license plates) in State *B* occurs at the end of the third month after removal from State *A*, perfection continues for one more month. (b) If registration occurs at the end of the fifth month after removal from State *A*, perfection ends at the time of registration. But if the certificate were surrendered before the end of either of these periods, the period would be cut down to the time of surrender; that is, in either (a) or (b), if the certificate were surrendered on the third day after removal, perfection would end then.

Since many states require that a certificate from a previous state be surrendered and a new certificate be applied for at the time the vehicle is registered, "registration" and "surrender" will often coincide, at which time (whether two days or six months after removal) protection would cease were it not for the fact that perfection is continued thereafter in the *new state* by application for, and notation of, the security interest on the certificate issued by the new state.

[38] In a majority of cases this will require making application for issuance of a new certificate by State *B* showing the existence of the security interest.

Subsection (2)(c) of 1972 Section 9–103 applies to the rapidly vanishing situation in which a vehicle subject to a security interest perfected by filing in a "non-title" state is brought into a "title" state and thereafter covered by a certificate of title. Such cases are relegated to the rule of subsection (1)(d),[39] which means that the secured party is protected only if he perfects in the new state within four months after removal.

Subsection (2)(d) of 1972 Section 9–103 applies to the rare situation in which a vehicle subject to a security interest perfected either by filing in a "non-title" state or by notation on a certificate in a "title" state is brought into a new state that issues a certificate failing to show the pre-existing security interest.[40] In such a case the secured party is subordinate to a buyer who is not in the business of selling vehicles if the buyer gives value and receives delivery after issuance of the "clean" certificate without knowledge of the security interest.[41] Protection is limited to consumer buyers.[42]

It should be noted that some state certificate of title acts themselves set forth multi-state perfection rules of the sort found in 1972 UCC Section 9–103(2).[43] Upon enactment of the 1972 Code, Section 9–103(2) will supersede such rules.

§ 5–4. ACCOUNTS, GENERAL INTANGIBLES, AND MOBILE GOODS

A. Initial Place of Perfection

Section 9–103(3) of the 1972 Code provides that the proper

---

[39] See § 5–2 C (1) *supra*.

[40] Such a situation might occur when a vehicle is moved from one "title" state to another and the officials in the new state inadvertently fail to transfer the security-interest notation on the old certificate to the new one.

[41] This rule does not apply, however, if the new state's certificate of title form bears a warning that the certificate may not show all security interests.

[42] That is, merchants, who are in the business of selling vehicles, are not protected.

[43] This is true, for instance, of states that have enacted Section 20(c) of the Uniform Motor Vehicle Certificate of Title and Anti-Theft Act, 11 UNIFORM LAWS ANNOTATED 446–47 (1974).

place for perfection of a security interest in accounts,[44] general intangibles,[45] and mobile goods [46] which are not covered by a certificate of title [47] is the state in which the debtor is "located." [48] The debtor will be deemed "located" at his place of business, or his chief executive office if he has more than one place of business, or his residence if he has no place of business.[49]

The major change made by subsection (3) of 1972 Section 9–103 consists in the inclusion of accounts receivable within the rules governing the place of perfection for general intangibles and mobile goods. Under 1962 Section 9–103(1) the place for perfection with respect to accounts is the state where the debtor-

[44] Accounts arising from the sale of minerals, including oil and gas, are subject to a special rule in 1972 Section 9–103(5), as discussed in § 5–6 *infra*.

[45] "General intangibles" are defined in Section 9–106 and are discussed in § 1–5 C (2) *supra*.

[46] The reference in 1972 Section 9–103(3)(a) is to "goods which are mobile and which are of a type normally used in more than one jurisdiction, such as motor vehicles, trailers, rolling stock, airplanes, shipping containers, road building and construction machinery and commercial harvesting machinery and the like, if the goods are equipment or are inventory leased or held for lease by the debtor to others, and are not covered by a certificate of title."

[47] Goods covered by a certificate of title are discussed in § 5–3 *supra*.

[48] 1972 U.C.C. § 9–103(3)(a), (b).

[49] 1972 U.C.C. § 9–103(3)(d). This is essentially the same rule applied to general intangibles and mobile goods (but not accounts) under 1962 Section 9–103(2) except that "chief place of business" has been changed to "chief executive office" to eliminate any argument that the place referred to is the debtor's principal plant rather than his executive office. A special rule is applied under 1972 Section 9–103(3)(d) when the debtor is a foreign air carrier. In such event, the debtor will be deemed located at the designated office of the agent upon whom service of process may be made. Another special rule, found in 1972 Section 9–103(3)(c), provides that when the debtor is located in a jurisdiction outside the United States which has no provision for perfection by filing or recordation, perfection by filing may be made in the place in the United States where the debtor has its major executive office or, in the alternative, if the collateral is accounts or general intangibles, the security interest may be perfected by notification to the account debtor.

assignor "keeps his records concerning them." Determining the proper place to file and search under this rule has proved difficult when the debtor is a multi-state corporation that keeps records in a number of offices in different states or keeps them in a computer terminal in a state otherwise unrelated to the debtor or the transaction. The 1972 Code applies a more certain rule by requiring filing in the state where the debtor is located.

B. Change in the Debtor's Location

Subsections (a), (b), and (d) of 1972 Section 9–103(3), previously discussed, dictate the debtor's "location" as the proper place for initial perfection of a security interest in accounts, general intangibles, or mobile goods. Suppose the debtor subsequently changes his location to another state, however. In that event subsection (e) imposes a four-month rule similar to that previously discussed under 1972 Section 9–103(1)(d)(i); [50] namely, the secured party has four months in which to discover the change and reperfect in the new state. If reperfection is accomplished within that time, the secured party is protected; if not, the security interest becomes unperfected and is deemed to have *been* unperfected as against a person who became a purchaser after the change.[51]

§ 5–5. CHATTEL PAPER

Under the 1962 Code it is unclear whether Section 9–103 applies to security interests in chattel paper.[52] Subsection (4) of 1972 Section 9–103 lays down specific rules in this regard. Since a possessory security interest in chattel paper is regarded as localizable personal property, subsection (4) prescribes that the rules of subsection (1)[53] shall be applied to this type of interest.

---

[50] § 5–2 C *supra.*

[51] The significance of the reference to "purchasers" is discussed in § 5–2 C (2) *supra.*

[52] For a discussion of the similar ambiguity with respect to documents and instruments, see § 5–2 A *supra.*

[53] Discussed in § 5–2 *supra.*

A nonpossessory interest, on the other hand, being more in the nature of an intangible, is subjected to the rules of subsection (3) pertaining to general intangibles.[54]

§ 5–6. MINERALS

Subsection (5) of 1972 Section 9–103 states that the proper place for perfection of a security interest taken in minerals, including oil and gas, before extraction (assuming the interest attaches upon extraction)[55] is the state where the wellhead or minehead is located.[56] This is also the place designated for filing on accounts that arise from the sale of minerals at the wellhead or minehead.[57]

---

[54] Discussed in § 5–4 *supra*.

[55] A security interest taken *after* extraction would be an interest in ordinary goods, covered by 1972 Section 9–103(1), as discussed in § 5–2 *supra*.

[56] Under 1972 Section 9–401(1), the place for perfection *within* the state is the office where a mortgage on the real estate would be filed or recorded. A financing statement covering minerals must contain the recitals prescribed by 1972 Section 9–402(5).

[57] Filing is the only permissible means of perfecting an interest in an account. U.C.C. § 9–304, Comment 1. Since account debtors in transactions of this sort may be scattered across many states, the drafters deemed it impracticable to apply the ordinary rule in 1972 Section 9–103(3) that perfection be accomplished in the state of the debtor's location. Apparently the place where the debtor keeps his records is the appropriate place under the 1962 Code (1962 Section 9–103(1)).

6

The Article 9 Creditor Versus the Bankruptcy Trustee

§ 6–1. INTRODUCTION

Heretofore, the rights of an Article 9 secured party vis-à-vis the bankruptcy trustee have been governed by a combination of UCC Article 9 and the federal Bankruptcy Act of 1898 [1] (hereinafter referred to as the "old Bankruptcy Act"). Recently, however, Congress enacted a substantial revision of the bankruptcy law in the form of the Bankruptcy Reform Act of 1978 (hereinafter, "BRA").[2] Whereas, with a few exceptions, the BRA makes only modest changes in the status of Article 9 creditors, it does answer a number of unresolved questions existing under the old Act.

On the eve of bankruptcy the financially failing debtor is frequently encircled by a ring of hungry creditors, each of whom would like to dash in and tear off as large a chunk of the debtor's remaining assets as possible, irrespective of whether anything is left for the others. It is the function of the bankruptcy proceeding to ensure that each creditor obtains a fair share of the bankrupt's assets (collectively called the "bankrupt's estate"). This is accomplished by the bankruptcy trustee who, upon commencement of the proceedings by the filing of

---

[1] Bankruptcy Act of 1898, ch. 541, 30 Stat. 544, 11 U.S.C.A. § 1 *et. seq.*

[2] 92 Stat. 2549, 11 U.S.C.A. § 1 *et. seq.* The BRA governs cases filed on and after October 1, 1979.

a petition (either by the debtor himself or by his creditors against him) in federal bankruptcy court, is appointed by the creditors to take charge of the estate. One of the major duties of the trustee is to contest what, in the trustee's view, are improper claims of creditors to a disproportionate share of the assets. The Article 9 secured party's claim potentially falls in this category, since, if enforced, the security interest permits the secured party to satisfy all of the debt owed him by realizing against the specific collateral covered by the security interest (at least to the extent of the value of the collateral). By contrast, other, unsecured creditors have no claim to specific assets and will usually recoup only a tiny fraction, if anything, on their debts. If the trustee can successfully challenge the security interest on one of the bases discussed below, however, the Article 9 secured party is then reduced to the status of an unsecured creditor and must share pro-rata with the others. To illustrate simplistically, assume that on the eve of bankruptcy the bankrupt party owes $1,000 to each of three creditors, two unsecured and one claiming an Article 9 security interest in the debtor's sole asset—a piece of equipment worth $1,000. If the security interest is enforceable, the secured party will realize the entire $1,000, leaving nothing for the unsecured creditors. If, on the other hand, the trustee succeeds in having the security interest struck down, all three parties will share equally in the $1,000 . The Bankruptcy Act affords the trustee several alternative bases for attacking the Article 9 security interest, as discussed in the following sections.

§ 6–2. THE TRUSTEE AS A HYPOTHETICAL LIEN CREDITOR (BRA SECTION 544(a))

Section 544(a) of the BRA gives the bankruptcy trustee whatever priority would be enjoyed under state law by a lien creditor who obtained his lien on the date of the filing of the bankruptcy petition, "without regard to any knowledge of the trustee or of any creditor," [3] and "whether or not such a creditor ex-

---

[3] It should be noted that Section 544(a) explicitly renders irrelevant knowledge of the security interest on the part of the bankruptcy trustee or

ists."[4] The relevant state law is found in UCC Section 9–301 (1)(b), which provides that a lien creditor whose lien is obtained before the security interest is perfected takes priority. Section 544(a) will be the most frequent basis for attack against Article 9 security interests. Generally speaking, it means that a secured party who has not perfected before the date of filing of the bankruptcy petition will lose to the bankruptcy trustee.[5] To illustrate: Assume that on Day 1 the security interest is taken. On Day 2, the petition in bankruptcy is filed. And on Day 3, the secured party perfects. Under the combination of UCC Section 9–301(1)(b) and BRA Section 544(a), the trustee will prevail (unless the situation falls within section 9–301(2) as discussed *infra*).

It should be noted that Section 544(a), unlike Section 544(b) discussed *infra*,[6] does not require the trustee to find an *actual* lien creditor with rights against the secured party he can subrogate to; it gives the trustee whatever rights a *hypothetical* lien creditor would have had.

One exception to the general rule that a security interest not perfected by the date of filing of the petition is subordinated to the trustee arises from UCC Section 9–301(2), which provides that a secured party who files with respect to a purchase money security interest within ten days after the debtor receives possession of the collateral takes priority over the rights of a lien

---

the creditors he represents. This coincides with elimination in the 1972 Code of the requirement in 1962 Section 9–301(1)(b) that the lien creditor obtain his lien without knowledge of the security interest and with removal of the reference in 1962 Section 9–301(3) to knowledge on the part of the bankruptcy trustee. Thus under both the 1972 Code and the BRA, knowledge of the security interest has no bearing on the outcome.

[4] The concept of giving the trustee the rights of a hypothetical lien creditor was carried forward, essentially unchanged, from Section 70c of the old Bankruptcy Act.

[5] U.C.C. Section 9–301(3) includes a bankruptcy trustee within the definition of "lien creditor" and provides that the trustee's "lien" will be deemed to arise for purposes of Section 9–301(1)(b) at the time of filing of the bankruptcy petition.

[6] § 6–4 *infra*.

creditor arising between the time the security interest attaches and the time of filing.[7] Assume, for instance, that on Day 1 the Article 9 secured party takes a purchase money security interest in an item of equipment. On Day 2, the debtor obtains possession when the equipment is delivered. On Day 3, the debtor files a petition in bankruptcy. On Day 4, the secured party files. Under UCC Section 9–301(2) and Section 544(a) of the Bankruptcy Act, the security interest is enforceable against the bankruptcy trustee.

Note that even though the bankruptcy trustee is unable to achieve priority over the secured party by virtue of hypothetical-lienor status under Section 544(a), he may still be able to subordinate the security interest on one of the other bases discussed below.

§ 6–3. THE TRUSTEE'S POWER TO SUBORDINATE THE SECURITY INTEREST AS A VOIDABLE PREFERENCE (BRA SECTION 547)

A. The Elements of a Preference

Section 547 of the BRA continues the policy of Section 60a of the old Act in permitting the trustee to avoid certain transfers made by the debtor prior to the filing of the petition that "prefer" one creditor over others. In order to prevail, however, the trustee must establish all of the following elements required by Section 547(b):

1. A transfer was made, "to or for the benefit of a creditor"

2. The transfer was "for or on account of an antecedent debt owed by the debtor"

3. The transfer was made at the time the debtor was insolvent

4. The transfer was made on or within 90 days of the filing of the petition; or was made between 90 days and one year before the date of the filing of the petition if the transferee

---

[7] Note that this exception applies only to purchase-money security interests. For a discussion of what constitutes a purchase-money interest, see § 4–2 B (4) *supra*.

creditor (i) was an "insider" and (ii) had reasonable cause to believe the debtor was insolvent at the time of the transfer; and

5. The transfer would increase the amount the creditor would receive if the transfer had not been made and the estate were liquidated and distributed under chapter 7.

Section 547(c) also sets out several exceptions; that is, situations in which even though all of the elements listed are satisfied the trustee will still be unable to avoid the transfer. The exceptions that are relevant to the Article 9 creditor include (1) transfers intended to be, and which are in fact, "contemporaneous exchanges" (Section 547(c)(1)); (2) purchase money security interests perfected before ten days after the security interest attaches (Section 547(c)(3)); and (3) a special rule to determine the avoidability of "floating lien" security interests. These exceptions will be discussed below in the context of the particular situations to which they apply.

(1) What Is a "Transfer" and When Does It Occur?

Since the elements of an avoidable preference center around the concept of a "transfer" by the debtor, it is crucial to ascertain the time when a transfer will be deemed to have occurred in the context of an Article 9 secured transaction. This is particularly important in determining (a) whether the transaction falls within the 90-day period preceding filing of the petition and (b) whether the debt was "antecedent," that is, prior to, the transfer. The basic rule under Section 547 is that a "transfer" occurs at the time of perfection of the security interest—in the words of Section 547(e)(1)(B), "when a creditor on a simple contract cannot acquire a judicial lien that is superior to the interest of the transferee"—and not at the possibly earlier time when the interest attaches under 1962 Section 9–204(1) or 1972 Section 9–203(1).[8] An exception is found in Section 547(e)(2)(A),

---

[8] The quoted language in essence refers to U.C.C. Section 9–301(1)(b): An unsecured creditor cannot acquire a judicial lien that is supérior to the Article 9 security interest after the time the security interest is perfected. See § 4–1 A (1) *supra*.

however, which provides that if the security interest is perfected within ten days of attachment, the "transfer" will be deemed to have occurred at the earlier time of attachment.[9]

To illustrate, assume that on January 1, X advances funds to the debtor in what both parties intend to be an unsecured loan. On January 10, X demands security for the loan, whereupon the debtor executes an Article 9 security agreement giving X a security interest in equipment then owned by the debtor. On January 15, the 90-day period prior to filing of the bankruptcy petition commences to run. On January 22, X perfects the security interest by filing. If the "transfer" were deemed to occur on January 10, at the time the security interest attached,[10] it would be outside the 90-day period and the trustee would be unable to avoid the security interest as a preference. If, on the other hand, the "transfer" were deemed to occur on January 22, at the time of perfection, it would be within the 90-day period and the trustee would win. The answer Section 547 gives is that since the security interest was not perfected within ten days after attachment, the transfer will be deemed to have occurred at the time of perfection on January 22, and the trustee will prevail.[11]

---

[9] Section 574(e)(2)(A) refers to "the time such transfer takes effect between the transferor [debtor] and transferee [Article 9 creditor]"; and 1972 Section 9–203(1) provides that the security interest is not enforceable as between the debtor and secured creditor until attachment has occurred. The 10-day period under Section 547(e)(2)(A) of the BRA is analogous to the 21-day period provided for in Section 60a of the old Act.

[10] At this time, in compliance with 1962 Section 9–204(1) or 1972 Section 9–203(1), (a) a security agreement was executed; (b) the secured creditor had given value (on January 1); and (c) the debtor had rights in the collateral.

[11] The result would be otherwise if the secured party had perfected on January 18, within ten days of attachment. In that case, the time of "transfer" would be deemed to coincide with the time of attachment on January 10, so that even though the debt (incurred on January 1) would still be "antecedent" to the transfer, the transfer would be outside the 90-day period, and the trustee would be unable to invoke Section 547. This situation illustrates that a trustee who fails to satisfy *any one* of the elements listed in Section 547(b) cannot succeed on a voidable preference claim.

(2) The Requirement That the Debt Be "Antecedent"

(a) What Is an "Antecedent" Debt?

The second requirement for a preference under Section 547(b) is that the debt have been "antecedent" to the transfer.[12] In the context of an Article 9 transaction, the debt will be incurred at the time the secured creditor extends credit, that is, gives "value" within the meaning of 1962 Section 9–204(1) or 1972 Section 9–203(1). The time the "transfer" will be deemed to occur will be determined under the principles previously discussed.[13] Assume, for instance, that on January 10 the Article 9 creditor loans money against collateral already owned by the debtor and obtains a security agreement. On January 15, the 90-day period preceding filing of the bankruptcy petition begins to run. On January 22, the secured creditor perfects. Since the secured party perfected more than ten days after the security interest attached (January 10), the rule in Section 547 (e)(2)(A) pegging the time of transfer at the time of attachment cannot be invoked. Thus, under Section 547(e)(2)(B), the transfer will be deemed to have occurred at the time of perfection on January 22, within the 90-day period. Moreover, the debt was incurred at the earlier date the secured party gave value, January 10, and is therefore antecedent. Hence the trustee may avoid the security interest as a preferential transfer.

(b) The Effect of the Ten-Day Rule on "Antecedency"

When applicable, the rule in Section 547(e)(2)(A) that the "transfer" will be deemed to occur at the time the security interest attaches if the secured party perfects within ten days thereafter (hereinafter, the "ten-day" rule) will usually deprive the trustee of the power to avoid the security interest under Section 547. To illustrate, assume that the 90-day period preceding filing of the petition commences on January 1. On January 15, the secured creditor loans funds against an item of equipment already owned by the debtor and obtains a security agreement.

---

[12] BRA § 547(b)(2).

[13] § 6–3 A (1) *supra*.

On January 22, the secured party perfects. Since the ten-day rule applies, "transfer" will be deemed to have occurred on the date of attachment, January 15. This is still within the 90-day period, *but* since the debt was incurred *contemporaneously* with the transfer (on January 15), it is not "antecedent," and the trustee will be unable to avoid the security interest as a preference.[14]

(c) The Purchase-Money Exception

One situation in which the ten-day rule of Section 547 (e)(2)(A) will not prevent the debt from being "antecedent" is as follows: On January 1, the 90-day period preceding filing of the petition commences to run. On January 15, the secured creditor loans funds to enable the debtor to acquire an item of equipment and obtains a security agreement. On January 20, the debtor purchases the item. On January 22, the secured party perfects. Here attachment occurred on January 20, when the debtor acquired "rights in the collateral" pursuant to 1962 Section 9–204(1) or 1972 Section 9–203(1).[15] And since perfection was accomplished within ten days thereafter, the ten-day rule of Section 547(e)(2)(A) sets the time of "transfer" on January 20. But the debt, incurred on January 15, is still "antecedent." Thus (the transfer being within the 90-day period) the security interest would be avoidable under Section 547 were it not for the exception in Section 547(c)(3), which provides that even though the criteria for a preference listed in Section 547(b)[16] are satisfied, the trustee may not avoid a security interest given to enable the debtor to acquire property [17] when the

---

[14] If, on the other hand, the security interest had not been perfected until January 28, beyond the 10-day period, the transfer would be deemed to have occurred on that date, whereupon the debt incurred on January 15 would be "antecedent" and, since the transfer would be within the 90-day period prior to filing of the petition, the security interest would be avoidable under Section 547.

[15] The other two requirements for attachment—"agreement" and "value"—were satisfied on January 15.

[16] § 6–3 A *supra.*

[17] The reference is to a purchase money security interest, as defined in U.C.C. Section 9–107. See § 4–2 B (4) *supra.*

interest is "perfected before 10 days after such security interest attaches."

(d) The Exception for "Substantially Contemporaneous Exchanges"

Another situation in which the ten-day rule of Section 547 (e)(2)(A) does not prevent the debt from being "antecedent" is illustrated by the following: On January 1, the 90-day period preceding filing of the bankruptcy petition commences. On January 15, the secured creditor advances funds against collateral already owned by the debtor in what both parties intend to be a secured loan. Execution of the security agreement is delayed, however, until January 16. On January 22, the secured party perfects. Under the ten-day rule of Section 547(e)(2)(A), the "transfer" would be deemed to have taken place on January 16, when the last event for attachment—"agreement"—occurred.[18] But the debt, incurred on January 15, would still be "antecedent." Thus (the transfer having occurred within the 90-day period) the security interest would be avoidable, were it not for the exception in Section 547(c)(1), which provides that the trustee may not avoid a transfer, even though it satisfies the criteria for a preference under Section 547(b), if the transfer was "intended by the debtor and the creditor . . . to be a contemporaneous exchange for new value . . . and [was] in fact a substantially contemporaneous exchange." [19]

(3) The Insolvency Requirement

The third requirement for a preference under Section 547(b) is that the transfer have been made "while the debtor was

---

[18] 1962 U.C.C. § 9–204(1); 1972 U.C.C. § 9–203(1).

[19] This exception also saves from avoidance transactions that necessarily involve a brief extension of credit but are essentially intended by the parties to be for cash, as when a buyer gives his seller a check that is not presented to the bank for several days.

Note that the same result would occur in the hypothetical if the 90-day period commenced on January 16 or January 20 rather than January 1. If it commenced on January 20, however, there would be no need to invoke the "substantially contemporaneous exchange" exception, since the "transfer" would have occurred prior to the 90-day period (January 16).

insolvent." [20] This criterion will usually be easy to satisfy, since Section 547(f) establishes a presumption that the debtor is insolvent during the 90-day period prior to filing of the petition. The only remnant of the requirement under Section 60a of the old Bankruptcy Act that the creditor have "reasonable cause to believe" the debtor was insolvent at the time of the transfer is found in Section 547(b)(4)(B), which applies when the creditor is an "insider" and the transfer occurred between ninety days and one year before the filing of the petition. The term "insider" is defined at length in Section 101(25) to include parties such as a relative, partner, officer, director, or person in control of the debtor.

(4) The 90-Day Period

As previously illustrated,[21] the fourth requirement for a preference under Section 547(b) is that the "transfer" occur "on or within 90 days before the date of the filing of the petition." [22] In addition, a transfer occurring between 90 days and one year before filing of the petition is vulnerable if made to an "insider" who had "reasonable cause to believe the debtor was insolvent at the time of such transfer." [23]

(5) The Requirement That the Transfer Enable the Creditor To Receive More Than He Would Have in a Liquidation

The fifth element of a preference under Section 547 is the requirement in Section 547(b)(5) that the "transfer" enable the creditor to receive more than he would have received if the estate were liquidated and distributed under Chapter 7 and the transfer had not been made. This criterion will virtually always be satisfied when the "transfer" is the giving of an Article 9 security interest, since a security interest, if enforceable, will

---

[20] BRA § 547(b)(3).
[21] §§ 6–3 A (1) through 6–3 A (2)(d) *supra.*
[22] BRA § 547(b)(4).
[23] See § 6–3 A (3) *supra.*

almost always enable the creditor to receive more than he would have as an unsecured creditor. The trustee will lose under this criterion only in a couple of situations; namely, (1) when there are sufficient assets in the estate to permit full payment of all general claims, or (2) when the "transfer" consists in a repayment to a fully secured party whose security interest itself is not subject to attack.

To illustrate: Assume that on January 1, X makes a $100,000 unsecured loan to the debtor. On January 10, the 90-day period prior to filing of the petition commences to run. On January 15, X demands security for the loan, whereupon the debtor executes an Article 9 Security agreement giving X a security interest in equipment that, at all relevant times, has a fair market value of $150,000. On January 16, X perfects the security interest. The assets of the estate are sufficient to pay each general creditor 25 per cent (an unusually large percentage) of its claim. The first four requirements for an avoidable preference under Section 547(b) are satisfied; namely, there was a "transfer" that occurred within the 90-day period and was for an antecedent debt, and the debtor will be presumed insolvent at the time of the transfer.[24] The fifth requirement is also fulfilled, since, if the estate were liquidated and the transfer (security interest) had not occurred, X, as an unsecured general creditor, would receive $25,000 (25 per cent of the debt), whereas if the security interest were enforced, X would receive $100,000. If the facts are changed to assume that the assets are sufficient to pay 100 per cent of general claims (a virtually nonexistent possibility), the fifth element would, of course, not be satisfied; but in that case X would not care whether his security interest was avoidable.

One realistic situation in which the trustee will lose on the fifth criterion is as follows: On January 1, the secured creditor loans $100,000 to the debtor, takes a security interest in equipment worth $100,000, and perfects. On January 15, the 90-day period preceding filing of the petition commences. On Jan-

---

[24] See §§ 6–3 A (1), (2) and (3) *supra*.

uary 20, the debtor makes a $20,000 payment on the loan. Here, since the security interest itself was taken outside the 90-day period, it is not subject to attack. Thus the "transfer" in question is the $20,000 payment (which was made within the 90-day period and was for an "antecedent debt" incurred on January 1). The payment is not avoidable, since, had the payment not been made, the security interest would still have been enforceable upon a liquidation, whereunder the secured party would have received the full $100,000.

B. Avoidability of "Floating Lien" Security Interests

Under the old Bankruptcy Act the extent to which the bankruptcy trustee could avoid security interests in after-acquired property under a "floating lien" arrangement [25] was widely debated. Assume the following situation arising under the old Act: On January 1, the secured creditor lent funds and took a "floating lien" security interest in all of the debtor's existing and after-acquired accounts. On the same day a financing statement was filed. On January 15, the four-month period preceding filing of the bankruptcy petition commenced to run. On January 25, the debtor acquired a new account when Customer Jones purchased an item on credit. The bankruptcy trustee would argue that the security interest in the Jones account was a preferential transfer [26] on the ground that the "transfer" with respect to the account did not occur until the account arose on January 25 because it was not until that time that the debtor acquired "rights" in the collateral and the security interest attached and became perfected.[27] Thus in the trustee's view the

---

[25] For a discussion of "floating liens," see § 2–2 D (2) *supra*.

[26] Had the Jones account arisen on January 10, it would have been outside the four-month period and thus not vulnerable to attack. The same would be true under the BRA if the 90-day period commenced on January 15 (unless the creditor were an "insider").

[27] The acquisition of "rights" is a prerequisite to attachment (1962 Section 9–204(1); 1972 Section 9–203(1)), which is, in turn, a prerequisite to perfection (Section 9–303(1)). The argument was bolstered by the state-

transfer occurred within the preference period and, since it followed the making of the loan, was made "on account of an antecedent debt." This argument was virtually always rejected, however, on one of several theories. For instance, the court might invoke UCC Section 9–108.[28] Or it might hold that under Section 60(a)(2) the "transfer" occurred at the time the security interest became only "so far perfected" that no subsequent lien could become superior under UCC Section 9–301 (1)(b) and that that time was the date of filing, January 1— outside the four-month period.[29] Another theory was the "entity" or "Mississippi River" theory, whereunder it might be held that there was no transfer "on account of an antecedent debt" because all of the accounts together constituted a single entity covered by a single security interest (rather than individual accounts subject to separate security interests)[30] which attached and became perfected at the outset on January 1.[31] Hence the loan made on January 1 was not "antecedent" to the "transfer," which was made at the time of attachment and perfection—also on January 1.

In general, it may be said that the Bankruptcy Reform Act is less protective of "floating liens" than were the courts under

---

ment in Section 9–204(2)(d) of the 1962 Code that a debtor has no rights in an account until the account comes into existence. The statement has been omitted in the 1972 Code, as discussed *supra* § 2–4.

[28] The difficulty with relying upon Section 9–108 was that state law, to the extent that it is deemed to conflict with the federal Bankruptcy Act, must yield to the latter.

[29] That is, the account was not in existence for a lien to attach to until January 25, and when it did come into existence on that date, it was automatically covered by the perfected security interest, so that a lienor appearing on the scene after January 1 could not have had priority under Section 9–301(1)(b). See § 2–4 *supra*.

[30] A comparison was sometimes made to a river or stream: Individual accounts (or items of inventory) in the stream might change, but it was still the same stream.

[31] This assumes that at least one account was in existence on January 1, so that there was *something* for the security interest to attach to on that date.

the old Act. Section 547(c)(5) of the BRA essentially provides that a security interest in after-acquired accounts or inventory (or proceeds thereof) can be invalidated to the extent that the creditor improves his position by becoming better collateralized as of the date of filing of the petition than he was 90 days prior thereto. To apply the test of Section 547(c)(5), one compares two figures—the difference between the amount of the debt and the value of the collateral at the beginning of the 90-day period [32] and the same difference as of the date the petition is filed.[33] To illustrate, assume that on January 1 the secured creditor takes a "floating lien" security interest in the debtor's present and after-acquired inventory and files. On February 1, the date on which the 90-day period commences to run, the debtor owes $100,000, and the value of his inventory is $50,000 (the difference being $50,000). On February 15, the debtor acquires a new item of inventory worth $25,000. On the date the petition is filed the debtor owes $110,000 and the value of his inventory is $75,000 (the difference being $35,000). If one subtracts the $35,000 from the $50,000, it becomes apparent that during the 90-day period the creditor became better collateralized in the amount of $15,000. The trustee may therefore reduce the secured creditor's claim by $15,000.[34]

Since Section 547(c)(5) speaks only in terms of inventory and accounts (and their proceeds), it appears that a creditor with a security interest in other types of after-acquired collateral, such as equipment, cannot invoke whatever benefit the section affords. Thus if the collateral in the preceding illustration were equipment, rather than inventory, the trustee could reduce

---

[32] The test assumes that the value of the collateral will be less than the debt. If the secured party is already 100 per cent secured before the debtor's acquisition of the new item of collateral, the secured party is protected under another provision—Section 547(b)(5). See § 6–3 A (5) *supra*.

[33] Fluctuations in the interim are ignored.

[34] It is not clear whether an increase in value of the collateral by virtue of market appreciation, rather than the debtor's acquiring new property, triggers the trustee's avoidance powers; but it can be argued that such an increase is not the result of a "transfer."

the secured party's claim by the full value of after-acquired property—$25,000.

§ 6–4. THE TRUSTEE'S RIGHT OF SUBROGATION TO THE CLAIMS OF OTHER CREDITORS (BRA SECTION 544(b))

Section 544(b) of the BRA [35] permits the trustee to "avoid any transfer of an interest of the debtor . . . that is voidable under applicable law [that is, state law] by a creditor holding an *unsecured* claim. . . ." [36] At first glance one might assume that since lien holders are commonly referred to as "unsecured creditors" in the Article 9 literature, this provision gives priority to the trustee whenever he can find a lien creditor who would prevail over the secured party under UCC Section 9–301(1)(b). The provision is much narrower than this, however, since the term "unsecured claim" as used in Section 544(b) refers only to a lien that the trustee can avoid as a preferential transfer under Section 547 (or other avoidance provision).[37] To illustrate, assume that on January 1 the secured party takes a security interest. On February 1, an unsecured creditor obtains a judicial lien on the debtor's property. On March 1, the secured party perfects. On July 1, the debtor files a petition in bankruptcy. Even though the lien creditor would prevail over the secured party (in a non-bankruptcy situation) under UCC Section 9–301(1)(b) by virtue of having obtained his lien before the security interest was perfected, the bankruptcy trustee cannot subordinate the secured party by stepping into the lienor's shoes; since the lien was obtained prior to the beginning of the 90-day period prescribed by Section 547, the trustee cannot avoid it as a preferential transfer, and thus the lien is, in the terminology of the Bankruptcy Act, a "secured" rather than

---

[35] The analogous provision under the old Bankruptcy Act was Section 70e.

[36] Emphasis added.

[37] The provisions of Section 547 apply to avoidance of a lien as well as a security interest.

"unsecured" claim.[38] By contrast, if the petition had been filed on May 1, within the 90-day period, and assuming the other requirements for avoidance of the lien as a preferential transfer had been satisfied, the trustee could invalidate the lien, whereupon the lien would be an "unsecured claim" within Section 544(b), and the trustee could step into the lienor's shoes and defeat the secured party by virtue of UCC Section 9–301(1)(b).[39]

It should be noted that Section 544(b), unlike the "hypothetical lien creditor" provision in Section 544(a) discussed above,[40] requires the trustee to find an actual, existing creditor with rights against the secured party to subrogate to.

Section 544(b) answers a widely debated question under the old Bankruptcy Act; namely, whether a trustee subrogated to a party whose claim was less than that of the secured creditor could avoid the security interest in toto or only to the extent of the subrogee's claim. The language "[t]he trustee may avoid any transfer" in Section 544(b) apparently gives the trustee priority over the secured party's claim in its entirety, even if the lien creditor's claim is smaller than the amount owed the secured party.

As noted next,[41] the trustee can use Section 544(b) to invalidate a security interest that constitutes a fraudulent conveyance.

---

[38] Section 551 provides for preservation of liens invalidated by the trustee. The trustee is subrogated only to claims he can invalidate.

[39] If the lien creditor had lent money to the debtor before the secured party's perfection but had either not obtained the lien until thereafter or obtained no lien at all, the trustee would lose, since the lienor to whose rights he would be subrogated would be subordinate to the secured party under Section 9–301(1)(b). In other words, in order for the trustee to prevail under Section 544(b), the lien must be avoidable by the trustee, *and* the lien must be superior to the security interest under Section 9–301(1)(b).

[40] § 6–2 *supra*.

[41] § 6–5 *infra*.

§ 6–5. THE TRUSTEE'S ABILITY TO INVALIDATE FRAUD-ULENT CONVEYANCES (BRA SECTIONS 548 AND 544(b))

The Bankruptcy Reform Act continues the policy of the old Act in allowing the bankruptcy trustee to invalidate a security interest that constitutes a fraudulent conveyance. This can be done either under Section 548 or Section 544(b).[42]

A. Section 548

Section 548 spells out what will be deemed to constitute a fraudulent transfer: [43] Subsection (a) permits invalidation of transfers when the debtor (1) made the transfer with actual intent to defraud or (2) received less than a reasonably equivalent value in exchange for the transfer and (i) was insolvent on the date of the transfer or became insolvent as a result thereof, or (ii) was engaged, or about to engage, in a transaction for which his capital was unreasonably small, or (iii) intended or believed he would incur debts beyond his ability to pay as they matured.[44]

Section 548 applies to transfers made within one year of the filing of the petition. It does not require the trustee to find an actual creditor as against whom the transfer was fraudulent; and it protects transferees who take for value and in good faith.

B. Section 544(b)

The trustee's right to subrogate to the claims of other credi-tors against an Article 9 secured party has previously been dis-cussed.[45] Although not specifically mentioned in the Act, this

---

[42] The analogous provisions under the old Bankruptcy Act were Sections 67d and 70e.

[43] The language is quite similar to that of the Uniform Fraudulent Conveyances Act.

[44] Section 548(b) permits the trustee of a partnership debtor to avoid any transfer to a general partner if the debtor was insolvent on the date of the transfer or became insolvent as a result thereof.

[45] § 6–4 *supra*.

right includes the ability to step into the shoes of a creditor who has a valid claim under state fraudulent conveyance law. In many states, the "applicable [state] law" referred to in Section 544(b) will be the Uniform Fraudulent Conveyances Act.

Under Section 544(b), the time limit for reaching a transfer will be the limitation period under the applicable state statute rather than the one-year period prescribed by Section 548.[46] The trustee will prevail under Section 544(b) (unlike Section 548) only if he can find an actual creditor against whom the security interest was fraudulent; but if he can find such a party, he can avoid the security interest in its entirety rather than being limited to the amount of the defrauded creditor's claim.[47]

§ 6–6. THE TRUSTEE'S ABILITY TO ASSERT DEFENSES OF THE DEBTOR (BRA SECTION 541(e))

In addition to the bases already mentioned,[48] the trustee may be able to subordinate an Article 9 security interest on the ground that it is invalid as against the debtor, either under the UCC or other law. BRA Section 541(e) provides that the trustee shall have "the benefit of any defense available to the debtor . . . including statutes of limitation, statutes of frauds, usury, and other personal defenses." One basis for invalidation under the UCC would be failure of the security agreement to contain the items prescribed in Section 9–203, such as the debtor's signature and an adequate description of the collateral. In addition to the bases specified in the foregoing quotation, non-UCC law might permit invalidation for things such as fraud, mistake, duress, and unconscionability.

§ 6–7. RULES TO WHICH AN ARTICLE 9 CREDITOR IS SUBJECT EVEN THOUGH HIS SECURITY INTEREST IS NOT SUBORDINATED

Even though the bankruptcy trustee is unsuccessful in sub-

---

[46] Typically, under state law, the period is longer than a year.

[47] See § 6–4 *supra*.

[48] §§ 6–1 through 6–5 *supra*.

ordinating the Article 9 security interest,[49] there are a number of rules in the Bankruptcy Reform Act that can have a considerable impact on the secured creditor's rights. These rules are found primarily in Sections 361 through 364.

A. *The Stay (BRA Section 362)*

Under Section 362, the filing of the bankruptcy petition acts as an automatic stay preventing the secured creditor from commencing, or continuing with, actions aimed at perfecting or enforcing his security interest. Thus after the petition is filed, the secured party may not exercise the right of self-help repossession under UCC Section 9–503, nor, if he has already taken possession of the collateral, may he dispose of it under UCC Section 9–504. Nor may he perfect the security interest after filing of the petition, with the exception of purchase money security interests entitled to the ten-day "grace period" under UCC Section 9–301(2).[50] Nor may he begin, or continue with, judicial proceedings for realization upon the collateral, as permitted under UCC Section 9–501(1).

Subsection (d) of Section 362 does, however, provide that "[o]n request of a party in interest and after notice and a hearing, the court shall grant relief from the stay . . . for cause, including the lack of adequate protection. . . ." The term "adequate protection" (which is also relevant under Sections 363 and 364 discussed *infra*) is not defined, but examples are given in Section 361, as follows:

> (1) requiring the trustee to make periodic cash payments to such entity, to the extent that the stay under section 362 of this title, use, sale, or lease under section 363 of this title, or any grant of a lien under section 364 of this title results in a decrease in the value of such entity's [that is, secured party's] interest in such property.
>
> (2) providing to such entity an additional or replacement lien to the extent that such stay, use, sale, lease, or grant results in a decrease in the value of such entity's interest in such property; or

---

[49] The methods for doing so are discussed in §§ 6–1 through 6–6 *supra*.
[50] Section 362(b)(3).

(3) granting such other relief, other than entitling such entity to compensation allowable under section 503(b)(1) of this title as an administrative expense, as will result in the realization by such entity of the indubitable equivalent of such entity's interest in such property.

Category (1) might call for periodic payments to be made to the secured creditor when the property is depreciating in value. Category (2) might, in the same situation, require giving the secured creditor a lien on other property of the debtor. Category (3) might call for a guarantee from a solvent third party or a bond covering any losses incurred by the secured creditor.

B. Use, Sale, or Lease of Property Subject to a Security Interest (BRA Section 363)

When the debtor remains in business beyond the filing of the petition under Chapters 7, 11, or 13, Section 363 permits the debtor or trustee to use, sell, or lease property, even though it is subject to a perfected security interest. Depending on the circumstances, however, it may first be necessary that notice be given to the secured party and that a court hearing be held to determine whether the secured party has been given "adequate protection": [51] Prior notice and court approval are required when "cash collateral" [52] is involved (as when the debtor wishes to withdraw funds from its bank account to pay bills) but not for use, sale, or lease in the ordinary course of business of non-cash property (as when a merchant debtor wishes to sell inventory covered by the security interest).[53]

---

[51] For a discussion of "adequate protection," see § 6–7 A *supra*.

[52] Section 363(c)(2). "Cash collateral" is defined in Section 363(a) to include "cash, negotiable instruments, documents of title, securities, deposit accounts, or other cash equivalents."

[53] Section 363(c)(1). In this situation, however, the secured creditor may *request* a hearing to determine whether he is receiving "adequate protection."

C. *The Power To Incur Debts Senior to the Security Interest (BRA Section 364)*

When the debtor remains in business beyond the filing of the petition under Chapters 7, 11, or 13, it may be necessary to obtain credit to finance the operation of the business. BRA Section 364(d) provides that if the trustee is unable to obtain credit otherwise,[54] he may offer post-petition creditors seniority over pre-petition secured parties. This power is subject, however, to prior notice to the secured creditor and a court hearing to determine whether the secured creditor is being given "adequate protection." [55]

§ 6–8. THE TRUSTEE VERSUS A SELLER WITH RECLAMATION RIGHTS UNDER UCC SECTION 2–702 (BRA SECTION 546(c))

Under UCC Section 2–702, a seller who discovers after selling goods on credit that the buyer is insolvent can stop delivery or, if delivery has already been made, reclaim the goods (a) if he makes demand on the buyer within ten days after receipt of the goods or (b) if he makes demand more than ten days after receipt and the buyer misrepresented his solvency in writing within three months before delivery. Under the old Bankruptcy Act there was considerable controversy concerning whether a seller's reclamation rights took priority over the claims of the bankruptcy trustee.[56] Section 546(c) of the BRA resolves the controversy largely in favor of the seller in provid-

---

[54] For instance, the trustee might offer the postpetition creditor administrative-expense priority over prepetition unsecured creditors under Section 364(a).

[55] "Adequate protection" is discussed in § 6–7 A *supra*.

[56] The controversy partially derived from the fact that Section 2–702(3) of the 1962 Code purported to give the seller priority over a "lien creditor." The Permanent Editorial Board removed the "lien creditor" reference in a 1966 amendment, but a number of states did not enact the amendment. *See* 1972 U.C.C. § 2–702, Comment 3.

ing that the trustee's rights under Sections 544(a), 545, 547, and 549 are subject to the seller's reclamation right, as long as the seller demands reclamation in writing within ten days after the debtor receives the goods.[57]

§6–9. THE SECURED CREDITOR'S RIGHT TO PROCEEDS UNDER UCC SECTION 9–306(4) AND THE BANKRUPTCY ACT

Outside the bankruptcy situation the secured creditor's rights with respect to proceeds are governed by subsections (1), (2)), and (3) of UCC Section 9–306 and other provisions of Article 9, as previously discussed.[58] When insolvency proceedings are instituted by or against the debtor, however, Section 9–306(4) comes into play.[59] It should be noted that Section 9–306(4) does not purport to dictate the circumstances under which the secured creditor with a claim to proceeds will *win or lose* as against a bankruptcy trustee; it simply lists situations in which "a secured party with a perfected security interest in proceeds [pursuant to the ordinary rules in subsections (1), (2), and (3) of Section 9–306] has a *perfected security interest*" [60] in the proceeds in an insolvency proceeding. Although the *absence* of a "perfected security interest" will generally cause the secured party to lose to the trustee under Bankruptcy Act sections such as 544(a)[61] or 544(b),[62] the *presence* of a "perfected security interest" under Section 9–306(4) does not necessarily guarantee seniority. This is illustrated, for instance, by the language of

---

[57] Section 546(c) differs from U.C.C. Section 2–702 in that no protection is afforded when the demand is made beyond the ten-day period. Also, under Section 546(c)(2), the court may deny the seller's reclamation right if it gives other protection in the form of a lien on the goods or an administrative-expense priority.

[58] § 4–3 B *supra.*

[59] Section 9–306(4) applies to both state and federal proceedings. The following discussion focuses on the latter.

[60] Emphasis added.

[61] § 6–2 *supra.*

[62] § 6–4 *supra.*

Section 547(c)(5) of the BRA which, in setting forth the "improvement of position" test discussed previously in the context of floating liens,[63] makes it clear that "a perfected security interest in inventory or a receivable or the *proceeds* of either" [64] may well be subject to the trustee's avoidance powers under Section 547. It should also be noted that the seemingly repetitive language at the beginning of Section 9–306(4)[65] means that in order for the secured party to invoke whatever benefits are to be derived from the section, the proceeds in question must fall within one of the categories listed in subsection (4) *and* the security interest must have been perfected in compliance with the requirements of subsection (3) of Section 9–306.[66]

A. Non-Commingled Proceeds

Paragraphs (a), (b), and (c) of Section 9–306(4) cover proceeds that are "identifiable" in the sense that they have not lost their identity as proceeds of the original secured collateral by being commingled with other property of the debtor.

Assume that the secured creditor has a security interest in an automobile dealer's inventory. The debtor-dealer sells an auto to a buyer, who trades in his used auto and pays part of the remaining purchase price in cash and part by check. Under paragraph (a) of subsection (4), the trade-in would fall within the category of "identifiable non-cash proceeds." If the dealer deposited the check in a segregated bank account used solely for proceeds from this creditor's collateral, the account would fall within the additional category found in 1972 subsection (4)(a)— "separate deposit accounts containing only proceeds." [67] If the

---

[63] § 6–3 B *supra.*

[64] Emphasis added.

[65] "[A] secured party with a perfected security interest in proceeds has a perfected security interest . . . in the following proceeds."

[66] The requirements of Section 9–306(3) are discussed in § 4–3 B (4) *supra.*

[67] This category, added in the 1972 Code, enables the secured party to protect himself by requiring the debtor to deposit cash proceeds in a special

debtor kept the cash segregated in a suitably labelled envelope, it would fall within the category set forth in 1972 subsection (4)(b)—"identifiable cash proceeds in the form of money which is neither commingled with other money nor deposited in a deposit account prior to the insolvency proceedings." [68] If the debtor kept the check in his desk, it would fall within the category of 1972 subsection (4)(c)—"identifiable cash proceeds in the form of checks and the like which are not deposited in a deposit account prior to the insolvency proceedings." [69] If, on the other hand, the debtor deposited the cash or check in his general bank account along with other, non-proceeds funds, they would fall within subsection (4)(d) pertaining to commingled proceeds, as discussed next.

B. Commingled Proceeds

When the debtor has commingled proceeds funds with other funds in a bank account, subsection (4)(d) of Section 9–306 sets forth a special rule for determining the extent to which the secured creditor will have a "perfected security interest" in such funds in insolvency. The 1972 version of subsection (4)(d) provides that there will be a perfected security interest:

> in all cash and deposit accounts of the debtor in which proceeds have been commingled with other funds, but the perfected security interest under this paragraph (d) is
>
> (i) subject to any right to set-off; and
>
> (ii) limited to an amount not greater than the amount of any cash proceeds received by the debtor within ten days before the institution of the insolvency proceedings less the sum of
>
> (I) the payments to the secured party on account of cash proceeds received by the debtor during such period and
>
> (II) the cash proceeds received by the debtor during such period

---

bank account as an alternative to requiring remission of the proceeds directly to the secured party.

[68] The 1962 version was slightly reworded, without substantive change.

[69] The 1962 version was slightly reworded, without substantive change.

to which the secured party is entitled under paragraphs (a) through (c) of this subsection (4).[70]

It should be noted that unlike the situation outside of insolvency, in which the secured party can reach proceeds funds that have been commingled in the debtor's bank account by using fictional tracing methods such as the "lowest intermediate balance" concept,[71] Section 9–306(4) prohibits tracing and gives the secured party the rights specified in subsection (4)(d) in lieu thereof.[72]

At present there is considerable uncertainty about the meaning of the Section 9–306(4)(d) language and the extent to which bankruptcy courts will abide by the section in deciding disputes between secured creditors and trustees. The latter question will be addressed *infra*. Insofar as the meaning of subsection (4)(d) is concerned, the major question centers on the words "any cash proceeds received by the debtor" (within the ten-day period preceding filing of the petition). Assume, for instance, that the debtor (a merchant) has more than one secured creditor, SP being the creditor whose rights are in question. Within the ten-day period the debtor receives a total of $23,000 in proceeds—$9,000 from sale of SP's collateral and the remaining $14,000 from collateral in which other parties have a security interest. The debtor deposits (and commingles) $12,000 of the $23,000 in his general bank account. Of the $12,000, SP can show that $5,000 came from "his" collateral.

---

[70] The change in the language of the 1962 Code with respect to the amounts to be subtracted (subparagraphs (I) and (II) of the 1972 version) was apparently intended to make it clear that the subtraction amount is not limited to proceeds that are *commingled* before being paid over to the secured party but rather includes *all* proceeds funds paid over during the ten-day period, such as checks which the debtor indorses over to the secured party without first depositing them in his general account.

[71] See § 4–3 B (3) *supra*.

[72] This is made clearer in the 1972 Code by the addition of the word "only" in the language at the beginning of subsection (4): "a secured party . . . has a perfected security interest *only* in the following proceeds. . . ."

Assuming the bankruptcy court considers UCC Section 9–306 (4)(d) to be determinative of the outcome as between SP and the trustee, does the "any cash proceeds received by the debtor" language mean (1) any cash proceeds received from whatever source (SP's collateral or the collateral of others) ($23,000); (2) proceeds received from whatever source but only to the extent that such proceeds are deposited ($12,000); (3) the amount of proceeds from SP's collateral only, irrespective of whether deposited ($9,000); or (4) only the amount of proceeds from SP's collateral that SP can show were deposited ($5,000)? Although alternative (3) would seem to represent the better view, the matter is currently the subject of dispute, particularly with respect to whether alternative (4) should obtain.

C. The Impact of the Bankruptcy Reform Act

As noted, UCC Section 9–306(4) does not purport to dictate whether the secured creditor will win or lose as against the bankruptcy trustee; it simply tells when the secured party will be deemed to have a "perfected security interest" in the proceeds. There is very little language in the Bankruptcy Reform Act directly bearing on a secured creditor's rights to proceeds, other than that setting forth the "improvement of position" test in Section 547(c). To the extent that payments of proceeds by the debtor to the secured creditor during the 90-day period preceding filing of the petition improve the secured party's position under the Section 547(c)(5) test,[73] the trustee would seem to have the power of avoidance, notwithstanding anything to the contrary in UCC Section 9–306(4).[74] A clearer understanding of the impact of the BRA on proceeds claim must await judicial development.

---

[73] For a discussion of the Section 547(c)(5) test, see § 6–3 B *supra*.

[74] To the extent that state law in the form of the U.C.C. conflicts (or is deemed to conflict) with the federal act, the latter will, of course, control.

Default

§ 7-1. INTRODUCTION

Part 5 of Article 9 (Sections 9–501 through 9–507) governs the procedures by which a secured party may satisfy his claim by realizing upon the collateral when the debtor defaults on the secured obligation. The availability of these procedures serves as a major reason for creation of the security interest and is what distinguishes the secured from the unsecured credit transaction. The rules of Part 5 attempt to strike a balance between affording the secured party maximum freedom of action in the realization process and protecting the debtor and other creditors against overreaching.

Once a default has occurred, the secured party may either proceed against the collateral under the rules of Part 5[1] or ignore his security rights and proceed outside Article 9 by bringing suit on the debt.[2] Section 9–501(1) makes the point that the secured party's rights are "cumulative," meaning that his pursuit of one of these routes does not foreclose the other; that is,

---

[1] When bankruptcy proceedings have been instituted by or against the debtor, certain Article 9 default rules may be superseded by provisions of the Bankruptcy Act. On the latter, see Chapter 6 *supra*.

[2] U.C.C. § 9–501(1). Another choice between realization within or outside Article 9 is presented when (as is often true of corporate security issues) the security agreement covers both real and personal property. In such cases, Section 9–501(4) allows the secured party to assert his Article 9 rights against the personal property separately or, in the interest of speed and simplicity, to proceed against the realty and personalty together under the law applicable to real estate.

he is not put to an election. If the secured party chooses to proceed against the collateral, further options unfold: When the collateral consists of intangibles (such as instruments, accounts, or chattel paper), the secured party may either sell the items or collect them. When tangible collateral is involved, the secured creditor may generally take possession with or without judicial process and may thereafter choose either to keep the collateral in satisfaction of the obligation or to sell or otherwise dispose of it under a variety of circumstances and with a minimum of formalities. If the disposition brings less than the unpaid balance of the debt, the secured party may generally sue the debtor for the deficiency.

These rights, and the limitations placed on them for the protection of the debtor and other creditors, will be examined in the sections that follow. It is worth noting at the outset, however, that the rights afforded the debtor in Part 5, as outlined in Section 9–501(3), are generally not waivable before default (that is, in the security agreement)[3]—although a number of sections permit post-default waivers.

§7–2. WHEN DOES "DEFAULT" OCCUR?

A. In General; Events of Default

A secured party is not entitled to pursue the various default remedies provided in Part 5 of Article 9 unless and until a "default" has, in fact, occurred; premature attempts to do so may subject him to a claim for conversion or other liability to the debtor under Section 9–507(1).[4] "Default," which is not de-

---

[3] Within the bounds of reasonability the parties may, however, contractually define the standards for measuring fulfillment of the debtor's rights and the correlative duties of the secured party. U.C.C. § 9–501(3). For example, a predefault waiver by the debtor of the right to be notified in advance of resale under Section 9–504(3) (see § 7–4 C (2) infra) would be ineffective, but the parties might validly require in the security agreement that the notice be sent no later than a specified number of days prior to resale.

[4] See § 7–7 infra.

fined in the Code, most commonly occurs upon the debtor's failure to make payments when due. Beyond that, subject to the dictates of good faith, reasonableness, and conscionability, default occurs whenever the parties have contractually agreed that it will occur. Thus the well-drafted security agreement will specify which acts or occurrences are to be events of default.[5] Among the events more commonly listed are insolvency or bankruptcy of the debtor; sale or removal of the collateral without the secured party's consent; [6] the creation of other encumbrances on the collateral including liens or security interests; [7] loss of, damage to, or failure properly to care for, the collateral; misrepresentations by the debtor to the secured party; breach of the debtor's obligation to pay taxes and insurance on the collateral; death or dissolution of the debtor; and, more generally speaking, nonperformance of any of the debtor's obligations under the security agreement.[8]

B. Acceleration Clauses

Virtually all security agreements contain an "acceleration clause" providing that under prescribed conditions the entire remaining balance of the loan shall become due and payable immediately rather than in installments or on the maturity date originally agreed to. One form of acceleration clause matures the debt upon the occurrence of one or more of the events of

---

[5] In the absence of contractual stipulation, a court may well find that an occurrence other than nonpayment—for instance, the death of the debtor—is not an event of default.

[6] Although a clause in the security agreement prohibiting the debtor from transferring his rights in the collateral by way of sale or creation of encumbrances does not deprive the third-party transferee of title or of priority against the secured creditor, it will create a valid basis for declaring a default against the debtor. See Section 9–311 and the discussion thereof *supra* § 4–3 A (1)(a).

[7] *Id.*

[8] The security agreement will, of course, also provide that default occurs upon the debtor's failure to make timely payments of principal or interest.

default specified in the security agreement.[9] Such clauses are widely enforced. Another version—the so-called "insecurity clause"—purports to empower the creditor to call the loan "at will" or whenever he "deems himself insecure" or the like. Although acceleration clauses of this sort are also frequently enforced, there has been some confusion in the case law concerning the proper standard for enforcement: May the secured party assert insecurity on a purely arbitrary basis; or must he have reasonable grounds for so doing?[10] Section 1–208, which permits a party to invoke an insecurity clause as long as he "in *good faith* believes that the prospect of payment or performance is impaired," seems to point toward the former standard;[11] but some courts and a number of commentators have favored the latter. One thing is clear: "Good faith" is the antithesis of dishonesty; the secured party who can be shown to have feigned insecurity in contemplation of a more profitable investment of his funds elsewhere will receive short shrift in the courts. It will be noted, however, that the last sentence of Section 1–208 imposes on the debtor the often difficult burden of proving bad faith.

Acceleration clauses in consumer agreements are effectively negated in states that have adopted non-Code consumer protection legislation permitting the debtor to cure default by paying delinquent installments.[12]

C. Waiver

Because of the expense and effort involved in repossessing and reselling collateral, the low likelihood of fully satisfying the

---

[9] See § 7–2 A *supra*.

[10] An accurate awareness that one of the events of default specified in the security agreement (for example, the death or bankruptcy of the debtor) has occurred will, of course, satisfy the "reasonableness" test; but reliance on an unverified and, as it turns out, unfounded rumor of a deterioration in the debtor's financial condition is another matter.

[11] Section 1–201(19) defines "good faith" as requiring only "honesty in fact."

[12] *See, e.g.,* Uniform Consumer Credit Code §§ 5.110 and 5.111.

claim thereby, and the consequent necessity of suing for a deficiency, creditors often tend toward leniency in accepting late payments, partial payments, and the like. Such conduct, particularly if repeated on numerous occasions, may support an argument that the debtor's reliance on past practices estops the secured party from now insisting on strict compliance with the terms of the security agreement—in other words, the creditor may be deemed to have waived what would otherwise be an event of default. The secured party who repossesses under such circumstances may be guilty of conversion or otherwise actionable misconduct,[13] and he may or may not be protected by a clause in the security agreement to the effect that "waiver of one or more defaults shall not constitute waiver of subsequent defaults."

§ 7-3. BRINGING SUIT ON THE DEBT

Once default has occurred, Section 9–501(1) authorizes the secured party either (a) to proceed against the secured collateral under the rules of Article 9 (as discussed in the sections that follow), or (b) to disregard his security rights and proceed, like an unsecured creditor, on the underlying debt. The latter option, governed by non-Code state law, is usually exercised by bringing suit on the debt, obtaining a judgment, and having the court issue a writ of execution ordering the sheriff to seize (that is, "levy" on) the debtor's property.[14] After seizure, the sheriff sells the property at public auction and remits whatever proceeds are required to satisfy the debt to the secured party. Although the delays involved in judicial action make this a much less frequently used route than repossession and resale, it has certain advantages. For one thing, since both seizure and sale are carried out under the auspices of the court, the secured party avoids the potential pitfalls attendant upon repossession and resale of the collateral himself—including, for instance, the possi-

---

[13] See § 7-7 infra.

[14] Depending on non-Code law, which varies from state to state, the creditor will be deemed to acquire a lien on the debtor's property at some point during this process—most commonly at the time of levy.

bility of committing a breach of the peace in the course of repossession, of failing to give proper notice of the sale, or of conducting the sale in a "commercially unreasonable" manner. Moreover, if for some reason the value of the collateral is substantially less than the outstanding amount of the debt, pursuit of the Article 9 remedies will eventuate in a lawsuit for a deficiency anyway, and the lien of a post-judgment levy reaches *all* of the debtor's property, not just the collateral subject to the security interest.

A priority question may arise when a secured party reduces his claim to judgment and a competing claimant (lienor, bankruptcy trustee, second secured party) acquires an interest in the collateral between the time of perfection of the security interest and the time the secured party obtains his lien by levy. Assuming that the secured party has priority (by virtue of prior perfection) before acquiring his lien, does he retain that priority afterward, or is his claim subordinated to the intervening interest? In other words, may the secured party still assert his security rights once he has become a lienor? [15] Section 9-501(5) answers the latter question in the affirmative, stating that "[w]hen a secured party has reduced his claim to judgment the lien of any levy [16] . . . shall relate back to the date of perfection of the security interest." [17]

---

[15] If the secured party's claim were regarded as merely that of a lienor, an intervening security interest perfected before attachment of the lien would take priority under Section 9-301(1)(b). The same result would occur vis-à-vis an intervening lienor under non-Code law.

[16] Although explicit reference is made only to "levy," liens arising upon judgment, attachment, or garnishment are no doubt included.

[17] Thus when the 90-day period preceding the institution of bankruptcy proceedings by or against the debtor commences in the interim between perfection and acquisition of the lien, the bankruptcy trustee will be unsuccessful in avoiding the secured party's interest as a preferential transfer. See § 6-3 *supra*. Insofar as other conflicting interests are concerned, an intervening lienor will be subordinate (Section 9-301(1)(b), discussed *supra* § 4-1 A (1)), as will an intervening security interest in situations in which priority goes to the first to perfect (Section 9-312(5), discussed *supra* § 4-2 A).

§ 7–4. REALIZING ON TANGIBLE COLLATERAL

A. Repossession

Once the secured party has decided to assert his Article 9 security rights against tangible collateral—whether by retaining it in satisfaction of the obligation under Section 9–505 or reselling under Section 9–504—his first step will generally be to obtain possession.[18] This he may do either by "self-help" or by judicial proceedings, as provided in the first two sentences of Section 9–503: "Unless otherwise agreed a secured party has on default the right to take possession of the collateral. In taking possession a secured party may proceed without judicial process if this can be done without breach of the peace or may proceed by action."

(1) Self-Help Repossession: Constitutionality; the "Breach of the Peace" Limitation

In the early 1970s there was considerable controversy about whether self-help repossession violated the Fourteenth Amendment by depriving the debtor of property without due process of law. Subsequent state and federal decisions have apparently laid the issue to rest, however, upholding Section 9–503 on the ground that seizure by private action of the secured party does not entail "state action."

The major focus of litigation involving self-help repossession

---

[18] Taking possession is not, however, a *prerequisite* to resale, as indicated in the last sentence of Section 9–503: "Without removal a secured party may render equipment unusable, and may dispose of collateral on the debtor's premises under Section 9–504." From the comment to Section 9–503, it appears that the drafters primarily had in mind saving the parties (ultimately the debtor, under Section 9–504(1)(a)) the expense of removal and storage of bulky equipment pending resale. The latter part of the quoted sentence is not in terms confined to equipment, however.

It will be noted that the third sentence of Section 9–503 validates a clause in the security agreement requiring the debtor to assemble the collateral in one place for the secured party (the place to be designated by the latter, as long as it is convenient for both). This provision will prove helpful, for instance, when the collateral is scattered across several states.

has been on what constitutes a "breach of the peace" within the prohibition in the second sentence of Section 9–503. The question is a significant one, since a secured party who is guilty of misconduct in repossession may incur liability for damages [19] under Section 9–507(1)[20] as well as civil or criminal liability on grounds such as assault, battery, trespass, infliction of emotional suffering, invasion of privacy, or conversion.[21] And courts routinely ignore clauses in security agreements purporting to authorize in advance repossession by conduct that would otherwise invoke such sanctions. Hence in a situation that poses a risk of breach of the peace, the secured party will be well-advised to forego self-help and to rely on judicial process.

Although what constitutes a "breach of the peace" is not susceptible of precise definition, some rough guidelines have emerged from the cases. Conduct most likely to fall within the prohibition includes acts of violence or threats thereof and unauthorized entry into the debtor's dwelling or garage. On the other hand, removal from the debtor's driveway, a public street, or a parking lot is usually unobjectionable. But retaking in the face of oral protests from the debtor will likely (though not inevitably) constitute misconduct in any of the situations just mentioned.[22] Conversely, the debtor's consent, freely given, will legitimize otherwise impermissible conduct,[23] although even a hint of intimidation by the repossessor may suffice to negate the

---

[19] In particularly outrageous cases punitive, as well as compensatory, damages may be awarded.

[20] See § 7–7 *infra*.

[21] Irrespective of whether there is a breach of the peace and conversion of the collateral itself, the secured party may be found guilty of converting property located *within* the repossessed item—as in the case of jewelry locked in the glove compartment of a repossessed automobile.

[22] Oral protests from a third party, such as the debtor's spouse, sister, or child, are more questionable. Obviously, a repossession carried out in the face of violent resistance or threats thereof from the debtor or some other person will involve a breach of the peace.

[23] Reference is made to consent at the time of repossession, as opposed to advance consent in the security agreement.

consent.[24] Finally, a certain amount of trickery, although frowned upon, may be tolerated—as when the secured party repossesses under the pretense of taking an automobile to be repaired.

(2) Repossession by Judicial Process

When self-help repossession entails a risk of "breach of the peace," [25] the only safe method of retaking the collateral is with the aid of the courts via an action in replevin or the like.[26] This generally involves filing a complaint and obtaining from the court a writ ordering the sheriff to seize the property and turn it over to the secured party pending adjudication of the latter's right to possession. Once a judgment has been obtained, the creditor is free to realize on the collateral by resale or retention.

At present, the constitutional validity of state statutes allowing replevin prior to judgment is in doubt. Such statutes—particularly those providing for issuance of a writ without affording the debtor prior notice and an adequate opportunity to be heard [27]—may violate the "due process" clause of the Fourteenth Amendment.[28]

B. Retention of Collateral in Satisfaction of the Debt ("Strict Foreclosure")

In lieu of reselling under Section 9–504, the secured party may be permitted to keep the collateral as his own (a method of realization often referred to as "strict foreclosure") pursuant

---

[24] The effectiveness of consent given by a member of the debtor's family is questionable, and that given by an unrelated third party such as a landlord is even more questionable.

[25] § 7–4 A (1) *supra*.

[26] Depending on the jurisdiction, the action may be for sequestration or for claim and delivery.

[27] Statutory provisions allowing issuance of a writ by the clerk of the court, as opposed to a judge, have been outlawed.

[28] In contrast to self-help repossession (see § 7–4 A (1) *supra*), replevin clearly involves "state action."

to Section 9–505, whereupon the debt is discharged and the debtor is neither liable for a deficiency nor entitled to any surplus if the creditor later sells. Although less often used than resale, retention in satisfaction of the debt is sometimes the more desirable option because it is simpler, cheaper, and avoids the risk that the secured party will be held answerable for selling in a "commercially unreasonable" manner or otherwise violating Section 9–504.[29] Keeping the collateral is only feasible, however, when the value of the goods approximately equals the unpaid balance of the debt plus the anticipated costs of disposition: When the value is considerably less, the secured party will opt for resale so as to retain the right to recover a deficiency; and when it is substantially more, the debtor or other creditors will (or at least should) demand resale in order to obtain the surplus.

Under the 1972 version of Section 9–505(2), the requirements for strict foreclosure are as follows: The secured party must send written notice of his proposal to retain the collateral to the debtor except when the latter has signed *after default* a statement renouncing his rights under Section 9–505(2).[30] In the case of consumer goods no other notice need be given.[31] When collateral other than consumer goods is involved, notice must also be sent [32] to any other secured party from whom the fore-

---

[29] On the requirements of Section 9–504 and the sanctions for violating them, see § 7–4 C and 7–7, respectively, *infra*. Avoidance of resale may benefit the debtor as much as the secured party, since the debtor is accountable for the costs of disposition under Section 9–504(1).

[30] Thus a waiver in the security agreement will be ineffective. *See* U.C.C. § 9–501(3)(c). Pursuant to Section 9–112(b), when the secured party knows that the collateral is owned by a person other than the debtor (that is, someone who has furnished security for the debtor), that person has the same right as the debtor to receive notice of, and to object to, a strict foreclosure proposal. Notice to a surety or guarantor is also called for by the definition of "debtor" in Section 9–105(1)(d).

[31] On the rationale for this limitation, see the discussion of the similar provision in Section 9–504(3), *infra* § 7–4 C (2).

[32] Registered mail should be used, so that the time of sending can be proved for purposes of establishing the 21-day period discussed below.

closing creditor has received (before notice is sent to the debtor or before the debtor renounces his rights)[33] a written claim of interest. If the secured party receives an objection in writing from a party entitled to notice (that is, the debtor or another secured party) within 21 days after the notice is sent to that party, the collateral must be disposed of under Section 9–504.[34] If no such objection is received, the secured party may keep the collateral.[35]

The foregoing rules make several changes in the 1962 Code— all designed to expedite the strict foreclosure process. First, unlike the 1962 version, 1972 Section 9–505(2) provides for renunciation or modification by the debtor of his right to notice of the strict foreclosure proposal—although only after default.[36]

---

[33] Although Section 9–505(2) does not prescribe the contents of the notice, aside from requiring a statement of intent to retain, it may be assumed that the notice will be ineffective unless it adequately identifies the parties, describes the collateral, and discloses the amount owed. This information is needed by other creditors as a basis for deciding whether to object to the proposal and thereby force a resale, or perhaps whether to redeem under Section 9–506.

[34] On failure to do so, the secured party is subject to liability under Section 9–507(1). See § 7–7 *infra*.

[35] The foreclosure will be complete and title will pass to the secured party 21 days after the last notice is sent (assuming notice is sent to all parties entitled to it), at which time the right to redeem under Section 9–506 ceases.

Although Section 9–505(2) does not address the question, it may be assumed that upon completion of strict foreclosure the same situation will obtain as under Section 9–504(4) after disposition (see § 7–4 C (4) *infra*); namely, that security interests junior to the foreclosing party's interest will be discharged, whereas senior interests (at least those held by parties who were unaware of the situation, did not give notice of a claim of interest, and therefore were not notified of the proposal) will remain viable, entitling the senior to replevy the goods or to sue the junior who has already foreclosed for conversion.

[36] The idea seems to be that the debtor will more fully appreciate the significance of a renunciation made in the face of loss of his property after default than one made beforehand in the security agreement at a time when no default is anticipated.

Second, the 1962 Code requires the secured party to give notice of his strict foreclosure proposal to competing secured parties who have filed a financing statement or whose interests are "known" to him. This compels the foreclosing creditor not only to make a filing search but also to examine his own records for any informal communications (including oral ones) received by him or a member of his organization that might be deemed to have given him "knowledge" of the competing interest. Viewing these requirements as unduly burdensome in light of the fact that junior secured parties seldom have any interest to protect,[37] the drafters of the 1972 Code shifted to competing secured parties the burden of notifying the foreclosing creditor of their claims of interest.

Third, under the 1962 Code a party entitled to notice of a strict foreclosure proposal may object within *30 days* from *receipt* of the notice. Accordingly, the secured party must wait to foreclose for a period consisting of the several days required for the notice to reach the other party (debtor or competing secured party) by mail,[38] plus 30 days thereafter, plus (arguably) the several more days needed for the other party's objection to reach the secured party.[39] The 1972 Code shortens this period substantially by requiring that the foreclosing creditor *receive* the objection within 21 days after sending it.[40]

There is one situation in which retention in satisfaction of the debt is prohibited even in the absence of objection thereto: Under Section 9–505(1), when the collateral is consumer goods

---

[37] Junior interests benefit from an opportunity to object to a strict foreclosure proposal only if the resultant resale produces a surplus—a rare occurrence.

[38] Under both versions of the Code the notice must be in writing.

[39] It is unclear from the wording of 1962 Section 9–505(2) whether the objection must be received by the 30th day or need only be mailed by that date.

[40] The new provision also shifts the risk of the mails to the parties being notified and removes language in the 1962 Code allowing parties other than those entitled to notice to object to the proposal.

and the debtor has paid at least 60 per cent of the cash price (in the case of a purchase money security interest) or 60 per cent of the loan (in the case of a non-purchase-money interest), unless the debtor has signed after default a statement renouncing his rights, the secured party must dispose of the collateral under Section 9–504 within 90 days after taking possession. Failure to do so exposes the creditor to liability in conversion or under Section 9–507(1). The notion is that the debtor may well have built up enough equity in this situation to produce a surplus on resale.[41]

Suppose a secured party retains repossessed collateral for an unreasonable length of time without attempting either to dispose of it or to serve a strict foreclosure proposal. He then belatedly resells and sues the debtor for a deficiency. Some courts have imposed involuntary strict foreclosure on the creditor as a basis for denying the deficiency claim. Others have rejected this approach on the ground that the misconduct consists in a "commercially unreasonable" disposition (or lack thereof) in violation of Section 9–504(3)[42] for which the appropriate remedy is an award of damages under Section 9–507(1).[43]

C. Sale or Other Disposition of Collateral

Most secured creditors choose to realize on tangible collateral by selling (often termed "reselling") under Section 9–504,[44] subsection (1) of which provides: "A secured party after default

---

[41] Consumer debtors who have paid less than 60 per cent of the price or loan are relegated to the ordinary rules of Section 9–505(2). Business debtors, regardless of how much they have paid, are also relegated to Section 9–505(2), presumably on the theory that they (unlike consumer debtors) are sufficiently sophisticated to object to a strict foreclosure proposal when it is in their interest to do so.

[42] See § 7–4 C (3) *infra.*

[43] See § 7–7 *infra.* The monetary outcome under the latter approach may or may not be essentially the same as under the former, depending on the court's interpretation of Section 9–507(1).

[44] Disposition is mandatory in cases when strict foreclosure is prohibited under Section 9–505. See § 7–4 B *supra.*

may sell, lease or otherwise dispose of . . . the collateral." [45] In reselling, the secured party must carefully comply with the rules set forth in Section 9–504 in order to avoid liability for misconduct under Section 9–507(1).

(1) Application of Proceeds; Treatment of Surplus or Deficiency

Section 9–504(1) directs that the proceeds of resale be applied by the secured party in the following order: first, to the reasonable expenses of repossessing and selling, including the costs of storage, refurbishing, completion of manufacture, and (to the extent provided for in the security agreement and not prohibited by law) legal fees and expenses; second, to the satisfaction of the secured obligation (including principal and interest); and third, to the satisfaction of claims asserted by junior security holders [46]—but only if written notice of demand therefor is received before distribution of the proceeds is completed, and only if, upon request, the junior claimant seasonably furnishes reasonable proof (such as a copy of the security agreement) of his interest. The provision for distribution to junior security holders is necessitated by the fact that Section 9–504(4) discharges such interests upon resale.[47]

Any remaining proceeds—"surplus"—must be turned over to the debtor [48] under Section 9–504(2).[49] When the proceeds are

---

[45] Since disposition by lease is rare and "or otherwise" methods are nonexistent, the discussion hereafter will focus on resale alone.

[46] When a priority conflict between junior claimants arises, the secured party may pay the money into court and interplead, leaving the disputants to resolve the conflict.

[47] Curiously, no mention is made of distribution of proceeds to junior lienors, although their interests are likewise discharged under Section 9–504(1).

[48] Under Section 9–112, when the secured party knows that someone other than the debtor owns the collateral (that is, a third party who has furnished security on the debtor's behalf), that person is entitled to any surplus. (Not being obligated on the debt, however, the third party is not liable for a deficiency.)

[49] The debtor's right to surplus is not waivable. See U.C.C. § 9–501(3)(a).

insufficient to cover the unpaid balance of the debt plus expenses (by far the most common situation), the debtor is personally liable for the deficiency unless otherwise agreed.[50] An exception exists, however, when the transaction between the debtor and the secured party was a sale (as distinguished from an assignment for security) of accounts or chattel paper,[51] in which case the debtor is not entitled to any surplus or liable for any deficiency unless the security agreement so provides.[52]

(2) The Notice Requirement

Under the 1972 version of Section 9–504(3), the rules regarding when, and to whom, the secured party must give advance notice of resale are as follows: No one (not even the debtor) need be notified when the collateral (1) is perishable (for example, agricultural products), (2) threatens to decline speedily in value (for example, commodities), or (3) is of a type customarily sold on a recognized market (for example, corporate securities). In the first two instances the benefits of advance notice are outweighed by the need for rapid sale; in the third, the "recognized market" will presumably produce a fair resale price. To date, only commodities and securities have been regarded as items sold in a "recognized market"; used automobiles and other durables have not.

Apart from the three situations just mentioned, notice of resale must be sent to the debtor [53] unless he has renounced the

---

[50] In some states, non-Code statutes like the Uniform Consumer Credit Code preclude recovery of a deficiency against a consumer debtor in certain circumstances—as when the original price of the goods or the size of the loan is below a specified amount (for example, $1,000).

[51] On the distinction, see § 1–4 D *supra.*

[52] This simply effectuates the normal intent of the parties (usually made explicit in the security agreement) that the secured party take "without recourse" in an outright sale transaction. See §§ 1–5 B (3) and 1–5 C (1) *supra.* If the parties wish to deviate from the norm, they must expressly so provide.

[53] In light of the definition of "debtor" in Section 9–105(1)(d), notice should also be given to sureties, guarantors, and third-party owners of the collateral. In regard to the latter category, the absence of a reference to

right in writing after default.[54] In the case of consumer goods only the debtor need be notified.[55] When collateral other than consumer goods is involved, notice must also be sent to any other security holder who asserts a claim of interest in the collateral [56]—but only if written notice of the claim is received by the secured party before he sends his notice to the debtor or before the debtor signs a renunciation, as the case may be.

Since the secured party need only "send" the notice of resale called for in Section 9–504(3), the risk of loss or delay in the mails is on the party being notified.[57] Moreover, although there is some controversy on the question, the better view is that "send" implies a requirement of written notification.[58]

The secured party should give careful attention to both the contents and timing of the notice of resale, bearing in mind that the purpose behind the notification requirement is to give the debtor and other creditors adequate information on which to base a decision whether to redeem the collateral or bid for it at the sale and sufficient time in which to make the necessary arrangements.[59] Insofar as content is concerned, Section 9–504(3) states only that the notice must specify the time and place of public sale or the "time after which" a private sale is to be held;

---

notice of disposition in Section 9–112 is probably the result of a drafting oversight.

[54] The renunciation provision was introduced in the 1972 Code; on the rationale behind it, see the discussion of the similar provision in 1972 Section 9–505(2), *supra* § 7–4 B.

[55] Creditors other than the initial purchase-money lender rarely rely on consumer goods, which depreciate rapidly and seldom produce any surplus.

[56] This provision differs from the requirement in the 1962 Code that notice be given to any other secured party who has filed or whose interest is known to the foreclosing creditor. The reasons for the change are discussed in connection with the similar change in Section 9–505(2), *supra* § 7–4 B.

[57] The secured party will be well advised to use registered mail, however, so as to be able to prove the fact and the time of sending.

[58] See the definition of "send" in Section 1–201(38).

[59] See U.C.C. § 9–504, Comment 5.

however, common sense suggests that it should also contain a description of the collateral, an identification of the security transaction and of the parties thereto, and a specification of the amount of indebtedness and the amount needed for redemption. With respect to timing the notice should be sent in sufficient time for it to arrive in ordinary course a minimum of five business days before the date of resale: Two or three days' notice is likely to be deemed inadequate. It should be noted that failure to give adequate notice of resale in a timely manner is one of the most common grounds for imposition of liability or denial of a deficiency claim under Section 9–507(1).

(3) The Requirement of "Commercial Reasonableness"

Section 9–504 gives the secured party broad discretion in disposing of the collateral—the goal being to encourage resale under optimum conditions, thereby maximizing realization and minimizing deficiency claims. On default, the collateral may be resold "in its then condition or following any commercially reasonable preparation or processing." [60] Disposition may be by public or private proceedings, by way of one or more contracts, as a unit or in parcels, and "at any time and place and on any terms." [61] *However*, "every aspect of the disposition including the method, manner, time, place and terms" must be commercially reasonable; otherwise the sanctions for creditor misconduct under Section 9–507(1) come into play.[62]

Although "commercial reasonableness" is nowhere defined in the Code, Section 9–507(2) provides a list of nonexclusive guidelines for determining whether the standard is met. The fact that the secured party could have obtained a better price by selling at a different time or in a different manner "is not of itself sufficient to establish that the sale was not made in a commercially reasonable manner." But a growing body of case law sug-

---

[60] U.C.C. § 9–504(1).

[61] U.C.C. § 9–504(3).

[62] See § 7–7 *infra*.

gests that a substantial discrepancy between the actual resale price of the collateral and what the court perceives as its fair market value (as evidenced by expert testimony, industry price guidebooks, and the like) will weigh heavily in the balance.[63] Section 9–507(2) goes on to provide that when a "recognized market" for the collateral exists, sale in the usual manner in that market, or sale elsewhere at the price current in such market, is commercially reasonable. Unfortunately, this provision will seldom benefit the secured party, since, to date, only stock exchanges and commodities markets have been regarded as "recognized markets." [64] Even in the absence of a "recognized market," however, a sale conducted in accordance with "the reasonable commercial practices among dealers in the type of property sold" is commercially reasonable.[65] And a secured party who wishes to ensure in advance that the circumstances under which he proposes to resell will be deemed commercially reasonable can obtain the approval of a court, creditors' committee, or representative of creditors.[66]

Are there situations in which "public" as opposed to "private" resale [67] is mandatory, or vice-versa? Section 9–504(3) gives the secured party his choice—but only within the bounds of "commercial reasonableness." When, for instance, the secured party knows of a buyer anxious to purchase an item of the sort in question or when the item is unique and no public market exists, a private sale may be the only commercially rea-

---

[63] This is hardly surprising, since the basic purpose of the "commercial reasonableness" requirement is to guard against unwarranted deficiency claims resulting from resale at an unfairly low price. It will be noted that the sale is particularly suspect when the buyer resells a short time later for a considerably higher price than he paid.

[64] Used automobiles and other durables have been held not to fall within the "recognized market" category.

[65] U.C.C. § 9–507(2).

[66] *Id.* A claim of "commercial unreasonableness" is still available, of course, when the secured party deviates from the approved course of conduct.

[67] On the distinction, see § 7–4 C (4) *infra.*

sonable alternative; whereas the reverse might be true for collateral (such as livestock) commonly sold at public auction. Clearly, in either type of sale, the secured party must make every reasonable effort to attract buyers of a type and number calculated to produce the greatest possible return. Public sales should be advertised in newspapers and trade journals well in advance of the resale with an accurate, sufficiently detailed description of the collateral and of the time, place, and terms of the resale.[68] In a private resale the secured party should contact a number of potential buyers rather than just one or two.

Timing of the resale is another important aspect of commercial reasonableness. On the one hand, the secured party should not resell hastily: Ample time should be taken to investigate the market,[69] to publicize the sale adequately, to refurbish the collateral,[70] and so on. On the other hand, a secured party who holds the collateral too long may incur liability for conversion or for damages under Section 9–507(1)[71] or may lose his right to a deficiency by having strict foreclosure forced upon him.[72]

(4) The Rights of Purchasers; the Secured Party's Right To Buy

In order to make foreclosure sales more attractive to buyers

---

[68] The requisites for public sale are further discussed *infra* § 7–4 C (4).

[69] Comment 6 to Section 9–504 indicates that it may be unwise to sell at a time when the market has collapsed. Likewise, it may be unreasonable to dump a large block of shares or large stock of inventory on the market at one time; that it, there may be a duty to sell in parcels rather than as a unit.

[70] Despite the seemingly permissive language in Section 9–504(1), some courts have found a *duty* to clean, repaint, repair, and so forth prior to disposition—at least when it is reasonably foreseeable that the cost of refurbishing will be outweighed by the enhanced resale value. The same may be true with respect to completing the manufacture of unfinished goods.

[71] See § 7–7 *infra*.

[72] See § 7–4 B *supra*. If the secured transaction involved a sale of goods, the secured-party seller may also lose his deficiency claim by overrunning the four-year statute of limitations in Section 2–725.

and thereby enhance the likelihood of high returns, Section 9–504(4) provides that a purchaser for value at resale cuts off the rights of the debtor and takes title free of any security interest or lien which is subordinate to the reselling secured party's interest. This holds true even when the secured party has violated the requirements of Part 5 [73]—provided the purchaser takes without collusion or knowledge of the violation and otherwise acts in good faith. Although the statutory language and comments suggest that purchasers at private sale may be held to a higher standard ("good faith") than purchasers at public sale ("not actively in bad faith"),[74] a good argument can be made that no such distinction should be drawn and that in neither case is there a duty to inquire into the circumstances of the sale.[75] It will be noted that the protection afforded purchasers in Section 9–504(4) extends only to *junior* claims; security interests or liens senior to the selling creditor's interest remain viable and can be asserted against the purchaser after resale.

The statement in Section 9–504(1) that resales are "subject to the Article on Sales" makes it clear that purchasers of goods at foreclosure sales may recover against the selling secured party for breach of warranty of title or of quality under the conditions prescribed in Article 2.[76]

---

[73] When, for instance, the secured party resells in a commercially unreasonable manner or fails to give the requisite notice to the debtor or to other creditors, the aggrieved party's remedy is against the secured party under Section 9–507(1), not against the purchaser.

[74] U.C.C. § 9–504, Comment 4.

[75] Imposition of a duty of inquiry would tend to frighten away prospective buyers, thereby thwarting the policy of facilitating disposition at the best possible price.

[76] *See* U.C.C. §§ 2–312 through 2–316. A claim for breach of implied warranty of merchantability under Section 2–314 will probably not lie against a bank or finance company (as opposed to a dealer), since these creditors are unlikely to qualify as "merchants" within the definition in Section 2–104(1) (that is, persons who regularly deal in goods of the kind in question).

The last sentence of Section 9–504(3) addresses the circumstances under which the secured party himself may purchase at the foreclosure sale. He may buy without restriction at a *public* sale but may purchase at a *private* sale only if the collateral is of a type that is (1) "customarily sold in a recognized market" or (2) "the subject of widely distributed standard price quotations." [77] The theory is that the competitive bidding at a public sale will discourage a buy-in at an unfarly low price, whereas no safeguards exist in a private sale unless there is an external standard against which to measure the price paid by the secured party. Since only commodities markets and securities exchanges may qualify as "recognized markets" and since it is uncertain how far the "standard price quotation" proviso extends beyond these narrow categories, the safest course for the secured party is to confine his purchases to public sales.

The restriction on purchasing at private sales raises the question of what qualifies as a "public sale." The sale should be by public auction with competitive bidding.[78] It should be advertised in one or more newspapers or trade journals or both, with an accurate description of the time (which should be convenient), the place (which should be accessible), and the terms of the sale. There should be a licensed auctioneer in charge, the collateral should be made available for inspection beforehand, and sale should be to the highest bidder. A secured party who purchases at a sale that does not satisfy these criteria runs the risk of incurring liability under Section 9–507(1).

(5) Rights and Duties Under a Guaranty or Repurchase Agreement or the Like

Assume that a dealer sells goods on secured credit to a customer and then assigns or sells the customer's installment con-

---

[77] In either instance the secured party is expected to purchase at the going price.

[78] See the reference to sale by auction in Comment 4 to Section 2–706, which section is cited in Comment 1 to Section 9–504, and see the reference to "bidders" in Section 9–504(4)(a).

tract ("chattel paper") to his own financer. If the latter is unable to collect from the customer, he may have a contractual right to compel the dealer to repurchase the chattel paper and pay the financer the amount owed by the customer.[79] In these cases, Section 9–504(5) provides that the repurchasing dealer acquires the rights and assumes the duties of a secured party under Part 5.[80] Thus the dealer would have the right to repossess the goods from the customer under Section 9–503, with the duty to do so without a breach of the peace; the right to retain the goods upon notification under Section 9–505, with the duty to dispose of them when required by that section; the right to resell under Section 9–504, with the duty to give notice thereunder; and so on. Section 9–504(5) also makes it clear that the repurchase transaction is not itself a "sale or other disposition," hence the financer would not be subject to the duties imposed by Section 9–504.

§ 7–5. REALIZING ON INTANGIBLE COLLATERAL—COLLECTION OR SALE

When a merchant who has sold to a customer on credit and then sold or assigned the resultant account, chattel paper, or instrument to a financer defaults on his obligation to the latter, the financer may, if he wishes, sell the intangible pursuant to Section 9–504, just as he would tangible collateral.[81] Since such sales are often at a substantial discount, however, the preferred method of realization is to collect from the customer (the "account debtor" on the account or chattel paper [82] or obligor on the instrument) under Section 9–502.[83] Regardless of whether

---

[79] On the right of recourse in chattel paper financing, see § 1–5 B (3) *supra*.

[80] The same is true of a guarantor or indorser who becomes liable to the secured party and receives a transfer of collateral.

[81] The sale must be "commercially reasonable" and otherwise satisfy the requirements of Section 9–504 discussed *supra* § 7–4 C.

[82] U.C.C. § 9–105(1)(a).

[83] Sale may be the more attractive alternative, however, when collection difficulties loom.

the security agreement contemplates an "indirect collection"/ "non-notification" arrangement (whereunder the merchant collects payments from the customer) or a "direct collection"/ "notification" arrangement (whereunder the financer notifies the customer to make payment directly to him)[84] before default, subsection (1) of Section 9–502 provides, in essence, that the secured party may institute the latter arrangement after default.[85] The subsection similarly permits the secured party to take over collection of "any proceeds to which he is entitled under Section 9–306"—including, for instance, receivables obtained by the merchant upon the sale of inventory financed as the original collateral.

Subsection (2) of Section 9–502 proceeds on the assumption that the parties to an outright sale—as distinguished from an assignment for security—of accounts or chattel paper normally intend (unless they provide otherwise in the security agreement) that the secured party have no recourse against the debtor for uncollectible items,[86] no right to recover a deficiency, and no duty to account for surplus.[87] In these cases neither the debtor nor his other creditors have any legitimate concern with whether the secured party makes diligent efforts to collect from the account debtor: Any losses are on the creditor's head. But when a right of recourse exists and the secured party can come

---

[84] On direct and indirect collection systems, see §§ 1–5 B (3) and 1–5 C (1)(a) *supra*.

[85] Subsection (1) also validates a clause in the security agreement permitting the secured party to switch from the former system to the latter even in the absence of default.

[86] Indeed, when the parties have not made it clear whether their transaction is a sale or security transfer, the prime indicator of the former is the absence of a right of recourse. For a discussion of the right of recourse in accounts and chattel paper financing arrangements, see §§ 1–5 C (1)(a) and 1–5 B (3), respectively, *supra*.

[87] In nonsale situations, on the other hand, Section 9–502(2) provides that the creditor has a duty to account to the debtor for surplus (a duty not waivable by the debtor, Section 9–501(3)(a)) and, unless otherwise agreed, a right to recover a deficiency.

back against the debtor for losses, Section 9–502(2) protects the latter (and other creditors) by imposing on the secured party a duty to collect in a commercially reasonable manner.[88]

§7–6. THE RIGHT TO REDEEM THE COLLATERAL

Section 9–506 permits the debtor or his other secured creditors to retrieve the collateral—that is, "redeem" it [89]—from the secured party by paying off the secured obligation [90] together with the secured party's post-default expenses.[91] The right to redeem continues only until the requirements for strict foreclosure under Section 9–505(2) have been satisfied [92] or the secured party has disposed (or contracted to dispose) of the collateral pursuant to Section 9–504,[93] and the right is waivable by a post-default agreement in writing.[94] It is partly to safeguard the redemption right (which enables the debtor or other creditors to protect themselves against the possibility of a poor re-

---

[88] As indicated in Comment 2 to Section 9–502, this means that the security holder may not simply "dump" the receivables—that is, sell them at a sacrifice price without making reasonable efforts to collect. It will be noted that the reasonable expenses of realization are deductible from the amount collected.

[89] The right to redeem extends to sureties and guarantors (Section 9–105 (1)(d)) as well as third-party owners of the collateral (Section 9–112(e)).

[90] Except when consumer credit legislation provides otherwise, if the security agreement contains an acceleration clause (as is usually the case), payment of delinquent installments will not suffice; the debt must be paid in full. On acceleration clauses, see § 7–2 *supra.*

[91] Included are "the expenses reasonably incurred by the secured party in retaking, holding, and preparing the collateral for disposition, in arranging for the sale, and to the extent provided in the agreement and not prohibited by law, his reasonable attorneys' fees and expenses."

[92] On the time when strict foreclosure is accomplished, see § 7–4 B *supra.* The right to redeem continues as long as notice of strict foreclosure has not been sent to a person entitled thereto.

[93] If the secured party has disposed of only part of the property, the remainder may be redeemed. U.C.C. § 9–506, Comment.

[94] A predefault waiver (for instance, in the security agreement) is ineffective. U.C.C. § 9–501(3)(d).

sale price) that Section 9–504(3) requires the secured party to give advance notice of resale. The right, however, is seldom exercised.

§ 7–7. REMEDIES FOR CREDITOR MISCONDUCT

A number of remedies are available to the debtor and other creditors for misconduct by the secured party in repossessing and realizing on collateral—misconduct that may, for example, take the form of repossession in the absence of an event of default, repossession involving a breach of the peace, retention of collateral in violation of Section 9–505, resale without proper notification or in a commercially unreasonable manner, or refusal to allow redemption. Some of the remedies are explicitly provided for in Section 9–507(1); others are not.

The first sentence of Section 9–507(1) allows the debtor (and, presumably, other creditors) to obtain prospective relief by way of judicial intervention when it can be shown that the secured party is violating or is about to violate his duties under Part 5. Under this provision a court might, for instance, enjoin a wrongful repossession or commercially unreasonable disposition or order the disposition to be carried out under specified terms and conditions or both. If an improper disposition or other violation of Part 5 has already occurred, the second sentence of Section 9–507(1) creates a right of recovery against the secured party for any loss caused thereby.[95] This right extends not only to the debtor but also to any other security holder who is entitled to notification under Section 9–504(3) or 9–505(2) or "whose security interest has been made known to the secured party prior to the disposition."[96] When, for instance, the secured party has resold the collateral in a "commercially un-

---

[95] Although it might be argued that the words "if disposition has occurred" prevent application of the second sentence to misconduct such as wrongful repossession or improper retention of the collateral, it is widely recognized that the provision applies to all violations of Part 5.

[96] The right also extends to sureties and guarantors (Section 9–105(1)(d)) and to third-party owners of the collateral (Section 9–112(d)).

reasonable" manner,[97] the normal measure of damages will be the difference between the price for which the collateral was sold and its fair market value or the price it would have brought at a properly conducted sale.

Since the amount recoverable for actual loss in small-ticket consumer transactions would often be insufficient to discourage creditor misconduct, the third sentence of Section 9–507(1) gives the consumer debtor his choice between actual damages under the second sentence and a minimum recovery for which no proof of loss is required, consisting of "the credit service charge plus ten per cent of the principal amount of the debt or the time price differential plus ten per cent of the cash price." [98] In other words, the consumer debtor can recover as the minimum the full amount of the finance charge ("credit service charge" or "time price differential") plus (1) 10 per cent of the price paid for the item when the creditor sold the item to the debtor,[99] or (2) 10 per cent of the amount of the loan when the creditor is a third-party lender.[100]

Courts in a number of jurisdictions have recognized various other remedies for creditor misconduct that are not mentioned in Section 9–507(1). For instance, repossession in violation of the "breach of the peace" limitation in Section 9–503 [101] may

---

[97] See § 7–4 C (3) *supra.*

[98] In some states, non-Code consumer credit legislation may permit recovery of a larger amount.

[99] Assume, for example, that the debtor pays $600 down on a $6,600 item and finances the remaining $6,000 over 24 months with monthly payments of $280 each. The amount of recovery would be $1,380, computed as follows: finance charge (24 × 280 = $6,720; $6,720 − $6,000 = $720) plus 10 per cent of the cash price (.10 × $6,600 = $660) equals $1,380. There is some uncertainty about whether the downpayment should be included as part of the "cash price"; if it were not so included in the foregoing computation, the amount of recovery would be $1,320.

[100] If one assumes the same facts set out in the preceding footnote except that the debtor borrowed the $6,000 from a third-party lender, the amount of recovery would again be $1,380. Here the downpayment would clearly not be included in the computation.

[101] See § 7–4 A (1) *supra.*

give rise to tort liability on grounds such as assault, battery, trespass, infliction of emotional suffering, invasion of privacy, or conversion; and particularly outrageous behavior may result in an award of punitive damages. An action in conversion may lie when the secured party has repossessed in the absence of an event of default [102] or retained the collateral in violation of Section 9–505.[103] And a few courts have forced strict foreclosure on a creditor for waiting too long to dispose of the collateral, although a strong argument can be made that this is actually a matter of improper disposition for which the appropriate remedy is recovery of damages under Section 9–507(1).

Another possible sanction not mentioned in Section 9–507(1) —the most controversial one—is denial of the secured party's right to recover a deficiency. Decisions on the availability of this remedy fall largely into two categories. According to one line of authority, a violation of Part 5 such as failure to give notice in advance of resale or disposition in a commercially unreasonable manner is grounds for absolute denial of a deficiency irrespective of the size of the deficiency or the amount of actual loss (if any) suffered by the debtor. To the extent that the deficiency exceeds the loss, this is a more severe sanction than recovery of damages under the second sentence of Section 9–507(1). Arguments advanced in support of this position are that Section 9–507(1) is not a comprehensive codification of remedies for creditor misconduct and that courts were not hesitant to disallow deficiency claims under the pre-Code Uniform Conditional Sales Act, which contained language similar to that found in Section 9–507(1). The other line of authority takes a more lenient view: upon a showing of creditor misconduct, a presumption arises that the value of the collateral equals the unpaid balance of the debt (that is, that no deficiency is recoverable), but the creditor is free to rebut the presumption by showing that a disposition in compliance with Part 5 would

---

[102] See § 7-2 *supra.*
[103] See § 7-4 B *supra.*

have realized less than the remaining balance of the debt. In other words, the secured party has the burden of proving that his deficiency claim exceeds the amount of loss caused by the misconduct. To the extent that the latter does not offset the former, the deficiency is still recoverable. The best argument in support of this approach is that it adequately compensates the debtor without unduly penalizing the creditor.

Table of Cases

Table of Statutes, Rules, and Regulations

Uniform Commercial Code

(The 1962 and 1972 codes are denoted by "(1962)" and "(1972)."
For an explanation, see § 1-1B.)

United States Code

Internal Revenue Code

Bankruptcy Reform Act of 1978

(92 Stat. 2549, 11 U.S.C.A. § 1 et seq.)

Bankruptcy Act of 1898

(ch. 541, 30 Stat. 544, 11 U.S.C.A. § 1 et seq.)

Code of Federal Regulations

Uniform Consumer Credit Code

Uniform Motor Vehicle Certificate of Title and Anti-Theft Act

(11 UNIFORM LAWS ANNOTATED 421 *et seq.* (1974))

Miscellaneous Acts

Index of Subjects